Sex, Society, and the Making of Pornography

Sex, Society, and the Making of Pornography

The Pornographic Object of Knowledge

JEFFREY ESCOFFIER

Rutgers University Press

New Brunswick, Camden, and Newark, New Jersey, and London

Library of Congress Cataloging-in-Publication Data

Names: Escoffier, Jeffrey, author.
Title: Sex, society, and the making of pornography: the pornographic object of knowledge /
    Jeffrey Escoffier.
Description: New Brunswick: Rutgers University Press, 2021. | Includes bibliographical
    references and index.
Identifiers: LCCN 2020019378 | ISBN 9781978820142 (paperback) | ISBN 9781978820159
    (hardcover) | ISBN 9781978820166 (epub) | ISBN 9781978820173 (mobi) | ISBN
    9781978820180 (pdf)
Subjects: LCSH: Sex customs—History. | Sex in motion pictures. | Pornography—History.
Classification: LCC HQ16 .E73 2021 | DDC 306.77/1—dc23
LC record available at https://lccn.loc.gov/2020019378

A British Cataloging-in-Publication record for this book is available from the British Library.

♾ The paper used in this publication meets the requirements of the American National
Standard for Information Sciences—Permanence of Paper for Printed Library Materials,
ANSI Z39.48-1992.

www.rutgersuniversitypress.org

Manufactured in the United States of America

In memory of
John Gagnon, mentor, intellectual comrade,
and above all friend

Contents

Sex, Society, and the Making of Pornography

Introduction

■■■■■■■■■■■■■■■■■■■■■■

Pornography is the royal road to the
cultural psyche (as for Freud, dreams
were the route to the unconscious).
—Laura Kipnis, *Bound and Gagged*

Even where they can be summed up in
a single sentence, phantasies are still
scripts (*scenarios*) of organized scenes
which are capable of dramatization—
usually in visual form. . . . It is not the
object that the subject imagines and aims
at, so to speak, but rather a *sequence* in
which the subject has his part to play and
in which permutations of roles and
attributions are possible.
—Jean Laplanche and Jean-Bertrand
  Pontalis, *The Language of
  Psychoanalysis*

An erection, penile or clitoral, is as heavy
with fantasies as a cod with roe. By
fantasies I mean meanings, scripts,
interpretations, myths, memories,
beliefs, melodramas, and built like a
playwright's plot, with exquisite care, no
matter how casual and spontaneous the
product appears. In this story—which

may take form in a daydream as one's
habitual method of operation for erotic
encounters, in styles of dress and other
adornments, in erotic object choice, and
in preference in pornography (in brief, in
any and all manifestations of erotic
desire) . . . *every detail counts.*
—Robert Stoller, *Observing the Erotic
Imagination*

In June 2017, *New York Magazine* published an article about Pornhub, a website that is the largest distributor of porn in the world. The author argued that Pornhub was "the Kinsey Report of our time" and that it "may have done more to expand the sexual dreamscape than Helen Gurley Brown, Masters and Johnson or Sigmund Freud." Such a claim implies that video pornography on the Internet is not only a hugely popular form of entertainment, but also a body of knowledge about sex that is both a form of sex education as well as a self-help guide.

Erotic visual representations have existed for hundreds, if not thousands, of years—from cave paintings to Greek vase paintings and murals in Pompeii, up to World War II pin-ups, Francis Bacon's paintings, and *Hustler* magazine. Up until the invention of photography, visual representations of sexuality were more fully mediated by fantasy and the human imagination. Photography introduced a realism certified by a degree of "automatism," based upon the chemical relationship between light and the film medium. And hardcore moving-image photography enabled the recording and presentation of live sexual encounters narratively organized by fantasy scenarios and accompanied with visible demonstrations of "real sex"—that is, "reality effects" such as erections, penetration, and ejaculations. The enhanced power of pornographic movies was due to its ability to blend fantasy and the "realism" of the photographic medium. Yet hardcore pornographic film media also produce misrepresentations of sex that demonstrate the indeterminacy of pornographic media. The indeterminacy reveals a gap between pornography as photographic representation of sex and the human experience of sex. The photographic representation of sex captures only the visible record of the physical activity of a sexual encounter; it isn't able to capture heart rates, feelings, or psychological self-representations. The indeterminacy of the representation of sex in pornographic movies raises many challenging questions about the medium. In *Hard Core: Power, Pleasure and the "Frenzy of the Visible,"* Linda Williams explores the generic and rhetorical conditions that underlie the photographic and filmic representability of sex. She shows that the medium's implicit "principle of maximum visibility" fails to provide an adequate representation of the female sexual experience—it is organized primarily around the visible display of male penetration, erections, and orgasms but is unable to visibly represent female climactic sexual pleasure.

Pornographic motion pictures exhibit other forms of indeterminacy. Gay pornographic movies also generate misrepresentations. They fail to consolidate and reinforce gay male sexual identity. The significant presence of "gay-for-pay" performers (heterosexual men) in gay pornography underscores the fundamental indeterminacy of video pornography. It situates homosexual desire within the masculine regime of desire irrespective of heterosexual or gay identities. Thus, the widespread employment of straight performers—estimates vary from 40 to 60 percent—in gay pornography intensifies the contradiction between homosexual desire as an expression of gay male identity and homosexual desire *without* identity, which confers legitimacy on homosexual behavior independent of gay identity.

The emergence of trans porn as a major genre reveals another form of indeterminacy. Trans porn challenges the stability of male heterosexual identity. In the porn industry, bisexual porn, in which some of the male participants have sex with women, is usually classified as a gay genre due to the presence of men having sex with one another, while trans porn is considered to be a "straight" genre because the sex is between women and men, even though the women may have penises and sometimes penetrate their male partners. Trans porn unsettles received ideas of the relation between gender and heterosexual sex and its representation in pornographic films and challenges straight male identity and the ways in which male heterosexuality is or is not a sexual orientation analogous to gay male identity.

The "sexual identity" of heterosexual males (in fact, of all performers) is unrepresentable in pornographic movies. Based on pornographic films, it is possible to argue that male heterosexuality is not strictly an "identity" but a default category that encompasses a wide range of sexual behavior that includes not only sex with trans women but also vaginal sex with trans men, strap-on videos in which heterosexual men get fucked by women, various kinds of bondage and discipline, as well as many other combinations, in which the "procreative model" of heterosexuality (the missionary position—male on top, female underneath) is only one script among many. Basically, it could be argued on the basis of its indeterminacy that male heterosexuality is an incoherent category.

The transition from softcore to hardcore pornography produced a dramatic break in the production of erotic cinema—both in how sex was portrayed on film and in the way the production of pornography was organized, who performed in it, and what other kinds of activities were associated with it. The defining characteristic of hardcore is "insertion"—oral, vaginal, or anal.

It required new performance conventions and new cinematic production requirements. In the production of softcore cinema many standard cinematic conventions of genre, performance, and narrative held sway; virtually everything changed in hardcore production. The feature-length softcore movies often resembled Hollywood features with the addition of some female nudity. The production of hardcore movies to some extent required the performance of "real sexual acts" that involved male erections, actual penetration, and ejaculation. The status of who performed in softcore versus hardcore pornography changed. In softcore, performers were actors; in hardcore, they were sex workers.

How is pornography a body of knowledge? Michel Foucault, in *The History of Sexuality: An Introduction*, argues that there have been two ways of organizing knowledge about sex. In ancient and Eastern civilizations knowledge about sex was codified as an *ars erotica*, based on practical experience to be passed down to the uninitiated. In Western Europe, a *scientia sexualis* emerged during the late nineteenth century, first as sexology and later by psychoanalysis, which has grown into the academic fields of gender and sexuality studies. But it has become obvious that moving-image pornography, combining as it does the photographic recording of live sexual conduct (and its scripts) with the innovative explorations of sexual perversity, constitutes an enormous archive of sexual fantasies. In the twentieth century, this pornographic archive became a mechanism of knowledge and power centering on sex, what Foucault would call a "strategic unity," that used sexual excitement as an instrument of psychological knowledge.[1] The knowledge accumulated in pornography is not a systematic body of knowledge but is instead an enormous catalog of loosely organized sexual fantasies and sexual scripts—like a cookbook in which every recipe must be tested, every pornographic scene is a test for feasibility of a particular perverse fantasy—where "every detail counts."

Thus the essays brought together in this volume are, to a large degree, about sex and what can be learned about it from pornographic representations. They explore two different aspects of pornography—both derived, in part, from the "ontological status of the photographic image." As Andre Bazin argued, the production of an image "by automatic means" (as opposed to media depending primarily on the human imagination and artistic skills) "has radically affected our psychology of the image." The photographic medium's "realism" (or illusion of) and its role in the creation of sexual fantasies in pornographic movies has conferred tremendous power on the medium.[2] One group of essays explores how moving-image photography captures the sexual behavior and eroticism of different historical periods and preserves it. Siegfried Kracauer, like Bazin, emphasized how photographic media capture what is literally in front of the camera—"things often taken for granted or not normally noticed" and how it can reveal to the viewer from another historical period differences in behavior or in cultural assumptions from the historical period in which the film was made.[3] The second group of essays is focused on the production of pornography and the employment of "reality effects"—that is, from, at one extreme, male erections, penetrations, and orgasms to the way that photographic media capture how light reflects off of skin, the delicate angles of necks, buttocks, legs, and so on. In that group of essays, I focus on the way the production process creates the necessary conditions for performers to enact credible sexual encounters on film.

Pornographic cinema emerged almost simultaneously with motion pictures themselves. Motion pictures were invented by Thomas Edison sometime around 1889. *Les Culs d'Or* ("Golden Asses"), probably the oldest hardcore movie known to exist, was made in France in 1908. The earliest extant American hardcore film is *A Free Ride* (also known as *The Grass Sandwich*), made sometime between 1919 and the mid-1920s (going by the model of the automobile used in it). The movie starts out with two women walking, somewhat wobbly, on a country road. A man driving by in a sedan convertible stops and offers them a ride. Giggling, they accept. When they enter the car, he immediately grabs their breasts and plays around a little, and then excuses himself to go off and pee. They hop out of the car and follow to watch him take out his penis and watch him urinate. They all go back to the car, but the women decide that they have to pee. In turn, he watches them and begins to play with his penis through his pants. Next he and one of the women go off into the bushes and start fucking. Soon the other woman joins them. All the characters are elaborately dressed (in the period's fashion), so the sex is somewhat obscured. One short segment shows one of the women performing oral sex on the man, but his penis is barely visible throughout the film. There is clearly penetration but no emphasis on either his erection or orgasm.

A Free Ride illustrates both aspects of the film medium's capacity to represent sex: (1) the historical differences between the sex shown in that period with the sex seen in today's pornography and (2) its reality effects in that period (the man's penis urinating and his obvious penetration of the women). The historical comparison is obvious—1920s vs. the present—but neither period's pornography should be taken as a literally accurate portrayal of sex in each period; the differences nonetheless capture historically different aspects of sex and attitudes toward it.

Sexual Scripts and the Production of Pornography

Human sexuality, whether it's a biological process or affected by the limitations of the human body, is shaped by social and historical forces. The narrative and behavioral requirements of sexual conduct are organized by sexual scripts.[4] Communities and other social groups offer some sort of education or training relevant to sexual conduct that reflects their values, dispositions, and expectations. The end product is a bundle of embodied social constructs of gender, race, and class that are then reproduced through an individual's values, preferences, and actions. This bundle consolidates different types of knowledge and dispositions, such as (1) repertoires of interactional skills, social protocols, and etiquette; (2) cultural narratives around families, learning, work and crafts, aging, and reproduction; (3) practical awareness of constraints, institutional boundaries, and relations of dominance and submission; (4) a repertoire of reasons, norms, and rules that govern everyday life; and (5) skills that involve strategic thinking or creative action. Sexual scripts draw on these embodied forms of knowledge and normative behavior.[5] Sexual arousal and the performance of sexual acts depend upon the meanings and cues of the social and cultural context—and they are incorporated into sexual scripts and help to make a sexual encounter into a relatively coherent performance.

Communities also pass on a small repertoire of sexual scripts that were constructed by earlier generations. These sexual scripts constitute a relatively stable genre of sexual scripts—most often organized around procreative sex. Sexual scripts are for the most part dialogues—between two or more participants, as well as fantasy partners. Individuals do not always literally follow a preexisting scripts, but they do coauthor them. Yet despite the dialogical and improvisational character of scripts, social milieus (whether of communities, subcultures, ethnicities, etc.) typically generate genres of sexual scripts consisting of a repertoire of scripts. Within each grouping is a certain degree of heterogeneity of sexual scripts that typically include short sequences of interactional dialogue, narrative frameworks, proverbs, and practical advice about consequences (such as commitment, pregnancy, sexually transmitted diseases, etc.).

Nevertheless, it is possible to identify broad, relatively simple genres of sexual scripts that group the heterogeneous scripts created by individuals or specific social groups that reflect personal fantasies, subcultural norms, and institutional contexts.

The scripts used in pornographic movies can also be organized into genres. They are basically fetish categories that draw on the spectator's "fetishized" expectations and establish ground rules for both producers and performers. Generic forms determine the narrative devices and the mise-en-scène that govern the sexual action. Over the course of more than fifty years, the pornographic film industry has developed a huge variety of sexual scripts and genres. New genres and new market niches emerged to cater to specialty interests—gay, BDSM, transsexual, MILF ("mothers I'd love to fuck"), and sexual fetishes of all kinds. New porn genres emerge or undergo changes due to historical shifts in attitudes toward certain types of sexualities. Nevertheless, sexual scripts are often quite flexible and plastic—as they must adapt to the interpersonal relations as determined by the participants' emotional or expressive needs, individual fantasies, economic status, or ethnic and racial characteristics. While each genre may be relatively stable, they may to some degree vary over time and reflect a period's cultural values and historical context, such as Freud's Vienna, Victorian London, 1970s New York City, or the San Fernando Valley in 1990. The scripts are not necessarily compulsory—though deviance from community, institutional, or religious norms may generate significant degrees of anxiety, guilt, and stigma.

The Pornographic Production Process

The making of pornographic films invokes "sexual scripts" in two distinctly different ways. On the one hand, there is the literal script or narrative action of the film itself. On the other hand, there are the sexual scripts of the participants: the director, various performers, and other participants in the process such as the script writer, the film editor, the lighting person, and even the marketing people. However, sexual scripts in pornographic movies operate on many different levels. To some degree, directors, editors, and performers are guided by their own daydreams, fantasies, and personal scripts. And there is also the fantasy script of the person who watches the video. The scripts in most porn movies or videos are more like storyboards, which may specify the setting (bedroom, gym, or outdoors) or costumes (lingerie, jock strap). They are fictitious aspects of scenarios of sexual fantasies. However, there are important nonfictional elements in pornographic movies—erections (even Viagra requires sexual attraction/stimulation) and orgasms. Thus, for the performers in a pornographic video production, sexual scripts (à la Gagnon and Simon) exist as a practical necessity in order to produce credible sexual performances.

The production process of pornography creates the social conditions that enable performers to engage in credible sexual performances. The producers (1) supply the social and physical space where these sexual activities can take place, (2) provide actors who expect to engage in sexual activities with one another, and (3) develop narratives of sexual activities that invoke culturally available sexual scripts that elicit and activate the sexual activities to be performed. Porn movie production organizes the space (both physical and social) where sex will take place. It is a social space dense with sexual cues. But the making of pornography necessarily requires drawing on the culture's generic sexual scenarios—the sex/gender scripts; racial, class, and ethnic stereotypes; the dynamics of domination and submission; and the reversals and transgressions of these codes. These culturally significant symbolic codes help to mobilize the actors' private desires and fantasy lives in the service of the video's sexual narrative. The production process is also a highly organized commercial space that supplies sex partners, symbolic resources and other erotic stimulants, and a video production technology that can produce coherent and credible sexual narratives and images.

Performing in cinematic pornography is a form of sex work and, like all sex work, requires the performance of sex acts according to the direction of the paying party. While porn actors, like other sex workers, may exclude certain activities from their repertoire, their sexual behavior is governed by the demands and constraints of the video production process. The repertoire of a performer's sex acts is very much a part of the actor's porn persona and depends upon the sexual scripts that exist in the culture at large, their own sexual fantasies, as well as those they can imagine in their everyday lives.

The making of a porn video requires not only the performance of real sexual acts but also the simulation of a coherent sexual "narrative." Real sex acts are usually performed, but the video representation of them is more coherent than the actual sexual activity recorded. The shooting of any sexual scene is made up of an apparently simple sex act photographed from several different perspectives. The performed act is interrupted many times to arrange shooting angles and lighting and to allow the male actors to "get wood" and regain their erections. For example, the camera man may crawl under actors fucking doggie style, then shoot them from above to show penetration, then from behind to catch yet another penetration shot of the hard penis going in and out. Then the "money shots" (shots of the male actors ejaculating) have to be choreographed often at the end of many hours of filming. The male actors may need help of various kinds to achieve orgasms: porno magazines, porn videos on monitors, a co-actors biting their nipples or kissing them to help them "get off." Thus a fifteen- to twenty-minute sexual scene may take six or seven hours to film. The short scene that the video viewer sees has been edited and patched together, with a soundtrack added, from the footage shot over many hours.

The video's director choreographs the sexual combinations and the action, working from a script that is more like a storyboard or a "treatment" than a script in the conventional sense. In most videos, casting the performers and teaming them up, planning their sequence of sex acts, and coaching them in their performances form the director's main job. Porn scripts frequently elaborate on or incorporate the culturally available sexual scenarios. The director fashions the sex scene by deploying material drawn from "cultural scenarios" (men dominate the object of desire, are active, etc.; men are sexual, but not emotional), from everyday interpersonal social dynamics, as well as from the actors' "intrapsychic" or personal identity scripts. The director shapes the video's script by exploiting and integrating these cultural resources.

Finding the Script: The Pornographic Object of Knowledge

While sexual excitement is a matter of a person's physiological state and relies to some degree on the stimulation of erogenous zones, fantasy plays a central role in producing sexual excitement. Psychoanalysts Robert Stoller, Jean Laplanche, and Jean-Bernard Pontalis postulated that frustrations, injuries, conflicts, and other interactions during infancy were encoded as perverse fantasies. Stoller, like Freud, believed that the dividing line between what might be normal and what might be perverse was difficult to identify. The perverse mechanisms that generated sexual excitement did not seem restricted to people who were clinically perverse. Stoller believed that "perversions" or "perverse fantasies" were part of the human condition—that, in fact, we are all "perverts." His research on sexual excitement, and on pornography, followed from his belief that "perversion is a fantasy put into action." Pornography packaged these perverse fantasies and distributed them to the public.

Stoller conceptualized that the infantile traumas that triggered sexual excitement were encoded as data (the perverse fantasies, the scripts, and the traumatic memories) resembling *microdots*—an early twentieth-century technological form of information storage:

> Everyone knows of the microdots of sexual excitement: a genteel clean woman in a quiet marriage of low erotic intensity is stabbed with excitement at the look and smell of a physically disreputable man of clearly lower class; a twelve-year-old boy puts on his sister's clothes, never before having cross-dressed, and has an instantaneous spontaneous orgasm, his first; a forty-year-old woman, well-experienced in sexual activity, is with a new man, who without warning gives her a slap on the buttocks, causing her to experience, simultaneously rage, humiliation, and fierce genital excitement; a man looks at a woman with a certain hairstyle and becomes nauseated; a philosopher (male or female) looks at an erect penis and starts to write a political tract; a woman looks across a room at an unknown man and decides she will marry him. The number of examples is endless.[6]

While erotic representations—stories, visual art, or movies—have portrayed some combination of both (1) objects of desire and (2) narratives of sexual action, Laplanche, Pontalis, and Stoller have argued that narratives are essential to the generation of sexual excitement.[7] Stoller believed that people used pornography to search for that bundle of "original erotic scripts" created by the traumas of infancy, struggles about gender identity, sexual frustration, and the perverse fantasies that begin to emerge as we approach puberty. Many of these scenarios are lost during childhood and cannot easily be found again. While the original script may not be immediately accessible, potentially it can be psychodynamically reconstituted by the development of "fantasmic" scenarios through substitution and displacement. Thus, pornography serves as a kind of vernacular epistemology of sexuality—the object of knowledge for the spectators of pornography is "the script" that provokes sexual excitement.[8]

The essays brought together in this book were written over a period of twenty years, and most of them deal with pornographic films made for the gay male audience, although much of what they have to say about gay porn films is equally relevant to other kinds of video pornography. Several discuss the role of heterosexual men as performers in gay and trans porn. And one deals with the labor process of the straight adult film industry and the industry's compensation practices where female performers are generally paid more per scene than male performers.

The essays in part I explore the historical context and significance of pornographic films for both heterosexual men (chapter 1) and gay men (chapter 2). But two essays also show how pornographic films can be seen as historical documents (chapters 3 and 4) and what they can tell us about gay male sexuality in the 1970s. Chapter 1 focuses on the potential impact of pornographic movies being shown in porn theaters during the 1970s. The availability of hardcore pornographic movies shown in porn theaters (the standard venue for exhibiting porn in that period) made many heterosexual men aware of other men's penises during heterosexual encounters—most men's fantasies about heterosexual sex probably did not include other men's penises. The availability of heterosexual porn movies, both in general and in public theaters, potentially helped to reconfigure the heterosexual male's sexual imaginary. In chapter 2 I review the emergence of gay pornographic films as a significant factor in gay men's lives and as a sector of the adult film industry. The transition from beefcake to hardcore was extremely important for gay men. The primary focus of beefcake publications had been on men as objects of desire, but hardcore films offered images, roles, and scripts that could serve as models for active sex rather than worship of ideal bodies. Thus, with the advent of gay hardcore movies, gay audiences were able to see gay men as active agents of homosexual desire.

Chapter 3 focuses on a group of porn filmmakers in New York City, whom I call "homo-realists" and who used cinema verité techniques to show porn in locations around the city where public sex of some kind was taking place. In chapter 4 I discuss the work of two of those filmmakers—Jack Deveau and Joe Gage—who made porn that explored some of the social aspects of gay male life at the time. Deveau was one of the first filmmakers in the 1970s to make gay films with hardcore sex scenes. In particular, he explored the impact of promiscuity—this was before the discovery of AIDS—on gay men's romantic relationships, on their neighbors and friends, and on their work lives. Gage made a trilogy of films widely considered to be masterpieces—*Kansas City Trucking Co.* (1976), *El Paso Wrecking Corp.* (1978) and *L.A. Tool and Die* (1979). Made in the same cinema verité style, these follow a number of men traveling across the across the country and engaging in various sexual adventures, mostly gay, some straight. None of these men think of themselves as gay, yet sex with other men is very important to them.

The essays in part II are centered on the production process of porn films—scripts, porn genres, performers, and their careers. A central focus is on the role that sexual scripts play in the making of pornographic films—drawing on John Gagnon and William Simon's work about the social aspects of sexual behavior, which bring together (1) everyday patterns of interaction, (2) society's cultural scenarios (norms, gender roles, power dynamics, etc.), and (3) the individual's erotic fantasies. Sexual scripts are necessary to produce credible pornographic scenes. Chapter 5 examines the way sexual scripts and film scripts interact in the production of video pornography. Chapter 6 focuses on the heterosexual men who are performers in gay porn movies (known as gay-for-pay) and how they utilize sexual scripts to successfully work in gay pornography. Chapter 7 looks at the straight side of the porn business to explore how the labor process of pornographic production is affected by the differences in compensation between women and men—women, on average, earning two or three times the amount that male performers earn per scene. Chapter 8 focuses on the typically short working life that performers experienced working in the gay porn film industry during the 1980s and 1990s and its relationship to other sex work opportunities as strippers (dancers) and escorts (prostitutes). Chapter 9 looks again at the heterosexual men who perform in trans porn and routinely engage in sex with trans women with penises and are frequently anally penetrated by trans female performers.

Sexual scripts are necessary at every stage of production and are the reason that people watch porn. There is a constant dialectic between the "realism" of photographic pornography and the indeterminacies of the medium—female pleasure and sexual identities of men (gay or straight) are unrepresentable. But the scripts, the fantasmic scenarios, in porn movies are what attract their audience to search for the one that works for them. Though moving-image pornography has its limits, its indeterminacies, the scripts are pornography's objects of knowledge.

Part I

Pornography and the History of Sexuality

■■■■■■■■■■■■■■■■■■■■■■

1

Pornography, Perversity, and Sexual Revolution

■■■■■■■■■■■■■■■■■■■■■

The first signs of the post–World War II "sexual revolution" appeared in the mid-sixties. In January 1964 *Time* magazine announced the arrival of a "second sexual revolution," signaled, in the magazine's view, by an increase in what it called "Spectator Sex"—representing a heightened degree of sexually explicitness in books, movies, and theater.[1]

Since then, what "sexual revolution" means, when it began (if it did), to whom it applied, and what changes it wrought have been highly contested subjects. Does it refer to large and dramatic shifts in sexual conduct? Or radical changes in sexual mores? Or did we only talk about it more? What historical and social processes underlie the grand narrative of the sexual revolution? What are the long-term consequences of changing the way that sex is regulated by social institutions? In order to take the term seriously as a historical phenomenon, it is necessary to examine its underlying assumptions—to identify a historical event as a sexual revolution one must satisfy certain criteria: there must be significant changes in sexual behavior, attitudes, and mores.[2]

The most influential theory of sexual revolution was articulated by Wilhelm Reich in *The Sexual Revolution*, his 1933 book on the fate of sexual reforms following the Russian Revolution. He had long argued that human suffering could not be alleviated solely by individual therapy but required social action—in fact, that sexual reforms were impossible without radical political action. Conversely, he also stressed that political revolution, including socialist revolution, was doomed to failure unless it was accompanied by the abolition of sexual repression.[3]

It would be difficult to overestimate the impact of Wilhelm Reich's thinking about sexuality in the decades following World War II.[4] The sexual revolution of the sixties was initiated by people who shared many of Reich's beliefs (whether or not they got them from him directly) about the detrimental impact of sexual repression. This perspective was reinforced by Alfred Kinsey's research—which also shared Reich's assumption about repression.

In 1976 Michel Foucault challenged Reich's theory, particularly its reliance on what he called its "repressive hypothesis." Foucault argued that sexual conduct was not shaped only by repressive mechanisms—as Freud, Wilhelm Reich, and others had claimed—but also by a process of discursive construction and social interaction. The constitution of sexuality was not an "essential" characteristic of human nature or gender but a social-historical construction.

In this chapter I examine the data we have about individual sexual behavior over time and offer a historical account of the roles played by the repressive regulation of sexuality and the emergence of a new discourse, that of pornographic films, that stimulated the production of new sexual scripts and what I call the perverse dynamic (or what Foucault called "the perverse implantation").[5]

The Long Sexual Revolution

Detailed, systematic, and continuous historical statistics about people's sexual behavior over time are almost nonexistent. Fragmentary data must be patched together from many different and imperfect sources. Until the beginning of the twentieth century, the only accessible information about patterns of heterosexual intercourse could be derived from demographic fertility data. But while those give us some sense that heterosexual intercourse took place periodically during certain stages of a woman's lifecycle, they tell us little directly about the age of first heterosexual coitus, the frequency of intercourse not resulting in the birth of a child, or other kinds of nonreproductive sexual activities. Nor do they tell us anything about the emotional meaning, physiological response, or cultural context of sex.

Demographic historian Daniel Scott Smith, for example, sought to determine the timing of the "first" American sexual revolution using data on premarital pregnancies (first births within nine months of marriage) to estimate patterns of premarital sexual intercourse between 1640 and 1966. Grouping his data into forty-year periods, he found a slow and steady rise in the number of such pregnancies up until the 1840 to 1880 period—increasing from 11.1 percent before 1701 to 25.1 percent in the period 1801–1840. There was a sharp drop in between 1841 and 1880, and then a large jump again after 1960. Comparing more recent data on premarital pregnancies (from the Current Population Surveys) and illegitimacy and some data from a number of early sex surveys (including Kinsey's), Smith found that the cohort of women who reached their twenties in the 1920s had engaged more frequently in premarital coitus than earlier birth cohorts or than those that came immediately afterward. Writing at the tail end (in 1978) of the "sexual revolution" of the 1960s and 1970s, Smith concluded, "The 'revolutionary' character of the sexual revolution can easily be overstated. The trend toward increasing nonmarital sexual intercourse has been going on for nearly a century from a level which was not fully restrictive."[6]

While some information like this can be gleaned from demographic statistics, since the early twentieth century, physicians, social activists, and other researchers have also collected some information from various surveys about sexual behavior.[7] Of course Kinsey is the most famous of the twentieth-century researchers to conduct such a survey. Earlier large-scale surveys, for example, were undertaken by Katharine Bement Davis in 1920 (on the sexual behavior of 2,200 upper-middle-class married and single women) and Lewis Terman in the 1930s (on the sexual adjustment of 1,133 married and 109 divorced couples).[8] Kinsey's survey is still one of the largest ever conducted—over 18,000 individuals were interviewed for the two books published in 1948 and 1953. From 1938 through the early 1950s, Kinsey and his colleagues collected an extensive body of information on the sexual behavior of men and women born between the 1890s through the mid-twenties.[9] In the subsequent years, the Institute of Sex Research at Indiana University, which Kinsey founded, and various offshoots sponsored a number of other surveys on a smaller scale. In 1970, the institute sponsored a fairly large survey on sexual morality that also collected some information on behavior.[10]

Most of our historical statistics on sexual behavior are derived from these and similar studies.[11] It is possible to group the retrospective responses of individuals into their birth cohorts. This allows us to estimate the prevalence of certain types of sexual behavior among age cohorts. The long-standing existence of the double standard makes changes in women's sexual activity a more sensitive indicator of any shift in behavior or norms. Reviewing data pulled together from a number of sources, Tom Smith found that rates of adolescent and premarital sexual activities among men and women increased for decades before and after the 1960s and 1970s (the decades usually constituting the "second" sexual revolution), but that rates among women grew more rapidly—from 12 percent of women born before 1910 to 62.9 percent born between 1965 and 1970. While these data indicate that increased rates of premarital activities are a secular trend, there was nonetheless a striking increase that took place between those who turned twenty in the 1950s and those who did so in the 1960s: jumping dramatically by more than twenty percentage points, from 40.9 to 62.9 percent.[12] In tandem with these changes, the age of first intercourse fell and the age at first marriage rose, thus indicating that young men and women had an increased period of time to engage in sexual activity before their first marriage than they had in the past.[13]

It is widely assumed that the sexual revolution implies a shift away from "monogamous" sexuality to a more open sexuality. The increased length of time that men and women were sexually active before their first marriage also suggests that they may have had more than one sex partner—most often a future spouse in their first marriage. The percentage of women ever married with two or more partners before their first marriage grew steadily from 3.3 percent for those born before 1910 to 25.8 percent for those turning twenty in the 1960s—with the largest increase occurring between those who reached twenty in the 1950s and those who did so in the 1960s. The male pattern was somewhat different: 49.2 percent of those born before 1910 had had two or more partners before their first marriage; for the cohorts born in the 1920s, 1930s, and 1940s, the percent of men with two or more partners remained relatively stable, reaching 70.1, 72.9, and 72.6 for each cohort, respectively.[14]

Homosexual conduct achieved new degrees of visibility and acceptance in the decades between 1960 and 1980.[15] Turner, Danella, and Rogers estimated rates of homosexual contact among men and women using the 1970 Kinsey survey (on which the Klassen et al. study was based) and a series of surveys conducted by the National Opinion Research Center from 1988 to 1990. Patterns of homosexual activity between women followed the secular trend exhibited by female premarital sexual activity—a steady rise in same-gender sexual contact from those born in the 1930s (who turned twenty in the 1950s) up through those in the 1960s birth cohort, who turned twenty during the 1980s. Male homosexual patterns display a modest cyclical pattern—but no dramatic changes over the course of the decades considered as the time frame for the sexual revolution.[16]

Many of these indicators show an increase in certain kinds of sexual activity in the generation that turned twenty during the 1960s. Other indicators of sexual conduct show comparable or even greater increases in the cohorts turning twenty in the 1970s. But do these indicators signify an increase sufficient to qualify as a sexual revolution? While these data reflect a secular trend that originated in the first decades of the twentieth century, they also show that the changes in the rates of sexual activity accelerated during the 1960s and 1970s.[17]

Albert Klassen and his colleagues, in their report on a Kinsey Institute–sponsored survey of sexual norms undertaken in 1970, found no indications "that such a revolution [had] occurred."[18] They found that Americans in 1970 showed few signs of increasingly liberal attitudes on sexual issues. Instead, they found that a majority of their respondents disapproved ("Always wrong") of homosexuality (with or without "love": 70.5–77.8 percent), prostitution (57.1 percent), extramarital sex (72.3 percent), as well as many forms of premarital sex (teenagers without love: 53.3–68 percent, adults—without love: 50.1–55.3 percent). Even masturbation, a near-universal behavior among males, was disapproved by 48 percent of males.[19] Klassen and his colleagues compared the results of the 1970 survey to a series of surveys undertaken between 1970 and 1978 that used the same questions. They concluded that "no matter how closely we examine our data, we can only reiterate that in 1970 most Americans did not report any change in their public moral evaluations of sexual behaviors" and that "American sexual norms have not profoundly changed throughout the 1970s, any more than they seem from our data to have done in previous decades."[20]

It is not unusual to find a gap between social norms and individual behavior, but what seems puzzling in the Klassen study is that during the same period (1970–1977) that he and his colleagues found no evidence of any change in professed sexual morality, public discussion of sexual issues grew dramatically. During the fifties, sixties, and seventies sex and sexuality and public discussion of it had come to occupy an increasingly significant place in American culture—in newspapers, books, movies, and theater; sex had entered the arena of public discourse in an unprecedented way.

Sexuality is socially constructed. Changes in sexual norms and behavior are much more likely to follow from broader changes in culture. In *Sexual Conduct* (1973) John Gagnon and William Simon showed how sex was shaped by its social context. Later Foucault elaborated on the cultural and historical implications of the social constructionist theory (as it later came to be called) of sexuality. His understanding of sex shared much with that developed by Gagnon and Simon. Like them, he argued that the self is socially constructed and that sexuality is shaped through the bodily coordination and symbolic interaction of social subjects. Foucault and his followers concentrated their analysis on the deployment of sexuality on a broad historical terrain, while Gagnon and Simon focused on the individual's scripting of sexual behavior through a three-way dialectic of cultural symbolic systems, an individual's fantasy life, and social interactional norms.[21] Trained in the Chicago sociological tradition, which had a long history of analyzing patterns of social interaction and how those patterns contributed to larger social institutions, they used the metaphor of a script to link everyday patterns of social interaction to larger cultural symbols and frameworks by seeing sexual conduct as a scripted activity—incorporating lines, cues, roles, cultural myths, and symbols to guide and shape sexual interactions.[22]

The very idea of sexual revolution implies that sexual behavior and norms can be modified by human action. And certainly the regulation of sexuality, whether by religion, morality, law, or psychiatry, is a social construction. The discourses and counterdiscourses governing sexuality are structured by a shifting, heterogeneous network of linked assertions, lacunae, and subversions that constitute normalized and heterodox speech. While the term "revolution" usually implies something that occurs rapidly and dramatically, the statistical evidence suggests that the sexual revolution of the 1960s and 1970s was the historical culmination of processes begun long before the two decades commonly ascribed. And those cumulative changes continued to produce significant changes in the decades that followed.[23] The sexual revolution of the late twentieth century more resembles the time frame of the industrial revolution, with its half-century transition from an agricultural society to one built on new technologies and industrial production. It was an immense and contradictory process stretching out over the life span of at least two generations.

Thus the sexual revolution of the sixties and seventies was less a revolution in sexual behavior than a cultural revolution in which the social framework within which sex took place was radically transformed—the everyday sexual scripts, the grand cultural narratives (of sex, gender, age, and race), and the scientific understanding of sex were all dramatically modified.

Obscenity and the Regulation of Sexual Discourse

The dramatic changes in the regulation of sexual expression and speech that emerged from the legal battles of the 1950s and 1960s were largely the result of dismantling the political and legal framework established by the federal Comstock Law of 1873. Passed at the instigation, among others, of Anthony Comstock, founder of the New York Society for the Suppression of Vice, the law stated

> that no obscene, lewd, or lascivious book, pamphlet, picture, paper, print or other publications of an indecent character, or any article or thing designed or intended for the prevention of conception or procuring of abortion, nor any article or thing intended or adapted for indecent or immoral use or nature, nor any written or printed card, circular, book, pamphlet, advertisement or notice of any kind giving information, directly or indirectly, where, or how, or of whom, or by what means either of the things before mentioned may be obtained or made, nor any letter upon the envelope of which, or postal-card upon which indecent or scurrilous epithets may be written or printed, shall be carried in the mail.[24]

The law had an enormous impact. It drove sexual speech into the private realm and excluded from public discourse discussion of the physiology of reproduction and the physical and social consequences of sexual behavior both inside and outside of marriage. Even advice about sexual reproduction, contraception, and abortion was prohibited. It promoted condemnation of sex outside of marriage, homosexuality, and other nonnormative sexualities. It prohibited the distribution of explicit representations of sex, whether for educational or prurient interests. It restrained the public use of vernacular sexual speech as either descriptive terms or expletives. It prohibited the sale and distribution of any publication or devices that might enhance sexual pleasure.[25] Within its legal framework the Postal Service, the courts, and local moral entrepreneurs (such as Comstock's New York Society for the Suppression of Vice) were able to mobilize moral and political capital in order to criminalize public discussion of sexual behavior or any activity that promoted unconventional sexual behavior or norms.[26]

It was only after World War II that the defense of obscenity cases invoked the First Amendment.[27] The first major case to do so was *Roth v. United States*, which was heard by the U.S. Supreme Court in April 1957. Samuel Roth had been arrested many times after 1928 for distributing works like D. H. Lawrence's *Lady Chatterley's Lover*, the Kama Sutra (the ancient Hindu sex manual that had been originally brought to the attention of Western readers by explorer Sir Richard Burton), a book of Aubrey Beardsley's erotic drawings, and many other lesser known but sexually "explicit" works. The main issue confronting the court was whether the Comstock Act of 1873, under which veteran pornographer Samuel Roth had recently been tried and convicted, was constitutional— and whether Roth's conviction was a violation of the First Amendment.[28]

Roth faced a twenty-six-count obscenity indictment in federal court, was found guilty, and was sentenced, at the age of sixty-two, to five years in a federal penitentiary and a substantial fine. His lawyer appealed the case, and it eventually made its way to the Supreme Court. Roth's lawyers argued that the controversial literature distributed by him was protected by the First Amendment. In contrast to many earlier cases, Roth's case involved no work with serious literary claims but primarily the promotion of cheap pornographic books, magazines, and sexually provocative drawings. The government's attorneys argued that "absolute freedom of speech was not what the founding fathers had in mind, at least where the interest in public morality was at stake."[29] The Supreme Court upheld Roth's conviction.

Justice William J. Brennan, who wrote the majority opinion in the Roth case, established a new definition of obscenity—a milestone itself—which went on to exercise a tremendous influence over legal issues of obscenity and pornography in subsequent decades. Brennan dismissed the Hicklin rule, the formal legal test for obscenity since 1868, which declared obscene any work that tended "to deprave and corrupt those whose minds were open to such immoral influences and into whose hands a publication of this sort may fall."[30] In his opinion, Brennan declared that any materials dealing with sex and sexuality could not be considered obscene unless "(a) the dominant theme of the material taken as a whole appeals to a prurient interest in sex; (b) the material is patently offensive because it affronts contemporary community standards relating to the description or representation of sexual matters; (c) the material is utterly without redeeming social value."[31] Brennan's opinion was, in fact, ambiguous. "Sex and obscenity," Brennan wrote, "are not synonymous. Obscene material is material that deals with sex in a manner appealing to the prurient interest. The portrayal of sex in art, literature and scientific works is not itself sufficient reason to deny material the constitutional protection of freedom of speech." He had upheld the distinction that many other judges had made since the 1920s that the exploration of sex in serious artistic, literary, and scientific works could not be found obscene, but he continued to maintain that prurient speech was not guaranteed protection by the First Amendment.[32]

In the wake of these decisions, publishers and booksellers had every reason to believe they could triumph over local censorship convictions—and they were proven right. The flow of books and publications dealing explicitly with sex and using sexually explicit language grew dramatically. Grove Press led the way with Lawrence's *Lady Chatterley's Lover* and Henry Miller's *Tropic of Cancer*, both the subject of important legal battles and court cases.

By the 1970s, newspapers with names like *Screw*, offering sexual information, personal ads, and sexually explicit photos and art, were available in news boxes on street corners in larger American cities. The legal victories often translated into phenomenal economic success for the publishers, filmmakers, and distributors of sexually explicit materials. Most of these materials were aimed at male audiences and sought to satisfy many traditional male sexual fantasies, thus contributing to the enormous success of magazines like Hugh Hefner's *Playboy*, Bob Guccione's *Penthouse*, and Larry Flynt's *Hustler*. Thus by the end of this process there were virtually no constraints on print publications. The issue was less clear-cut with regard to sexually explicit films.

The sexual revolution of the sixties and seventies would never have taken place were it not for the battles fought over obscenity and pornography during the late fifties by pornographers, stand-up comics, literary writers, and publishers. These prolonged debates and legal battles helped to create a public space in American culture for sexual speech, a space where it was permissible not only to discuss patterns of sexual behavior but also to portray sexuality honestly and bluntly in fiction, on the stage, and in movies—all of which would have helped to reconstitute sexual mores and contributed to the production of new sexual scripts in the decades since.[33] Freedom of sexual expression was the necessary condition for the later emergence of sexual liberation, identity politics, and social acceptance of sexual difference. Its realization relied upon an odd coalition between principled First Amendment activists, porn entrepreneurs, sex radicals, feminists, gay activists, and other sexual minorities. These battles initiated the broad cultural changes that became identified as the sexual revolution of the 1960s and 1970s.[34]

Sexual Representation and Erotic Cinema

Ironically, the creation of a market for pornographic films was the unintended result of a U.S. Supreme Court decision. The Court's decision in the 1948 *Paramount* case required the major Hollywood studios to divest themselves of their theater chains. Theaters were thus no longer routinely provided with films to run, and television had cut deeply into weekly ticket sales. Movie audiences shrank from 78.2 million ticket buyers per week right after World War II to 15.8 million by the end of the sixties—a drop of 80 percent. By the late sixties, movie theaters were often sparsely populated. Theater owners were desperate to bring customers back. But the Court's *Paramount* decision had also reduced the power of the Production Code that had established strict guidelines on permissible sexual themes and images—when the studios had controlled a vast major of American movie theaters, it was difficult to exhibit films that failed to pass the censors.

The legal guidelines defining obscenity in films changed continuously throughout the sixties. Between 1967 and 1969, the boundary between nudity and obscenity fluctuated constantly—both the degree of nudity and how sexually suggestive behavior could be. Softcore producers during the late sixties competed with one another to up the ante and routinely tested the legal limits. In the beginning it was considered pornographic to show pubic hair. Beginning in approximately 1967 short films shown in porn theaters, arcades, and peep shows showed women stripping and showing only their naked crotches (these short films were called "beaver" films). Soon the women spread their legs or labia to show better views (called "split beaver" films).[35] "Pickle and beaver" shots—the penis and the female crotch—soon followed. The porn loop went through a parallel process, from beaver to split beaver to pickle and beaver shots. The penis had to be soft—it could not be even slightly enlarged. No one was allowed to touch the penis.[36] By the middle of 1969 producers wanted "heavy, hard stuff."[37] Penetration was the last frontier; the defining characteristic of hardcore is insertion—oral, vaginal, or anal.

Hardcore emerged very quickly as a commercial imperative. Distributors and exhibiters clamored for movies showing explicit sexual acts to bring audiences back into their theaters.[38] The transition from softcore to hardcore produced a dramatic break in the production of pornographic films—both in how sex was portrayed on film and in how the production of pornography was organized, who performed it, and what other kinds of activities were associated with it. It required new conventions and new rhetorical devices. Whereas in the production of softcore cinema many standard cinematic conventions of genre, performance, and narrative held sway, virtually everything changed in hardcore production.[39] Feature-length nudie-cuties resembled Hollywood features with the addition of some female nudity. In softcore pornography the performers are actors, sex is simulated, and the production is more akin to traditional movie production; in hardcore porn the performers are sex workers and the production of hardcore scenes focuses on sexual performance and on genitalia—breasts, erections—and orgasms. And certain aspects of sexual performance, including erections, orgasms, and ejaculations, became central to the production process. The "cum shot," known also as "the money shot," emerged as the sign of the sex scene's narrative conclusion. Nevertheless, despite the many challenges, the switch from simple nudity to hardcore action took place almost seamlessly.[40]

The Cinematic Apparatus and the Perverse Dynamic

Pornography and pornographic films were an integral part of the sexual discourses that emerged during the sexual revolution of the 1960s and 1970s. Since then, pornography has become a significant current of mass culture and a dynamic market that grew from approximately $10 million in revenues in 1972 to over $8 billion in 1996.[41] It also opened up social space for the emergence of the "perverse dynamic."[42]

If the *Paramount* decision helped to create a market for softcore sexual films, growth in the number of theaters showing sexploitation movies—with their predominately male audiences—provided new opportunities for sexual activities in public.[43] The porn theater, part of the cinematic apparatus itself, had created the material circumstance that facilitated spontaneous live public sex. It became a complex form of sociosexual space, an erotic signifying system, and a stage for new fantasy scenarios.[44] While male audiences watched pornographic films in a state of arousal, the movies elicited images and fantasies that not only involved women but—in contrast to most heterosexual men's private sex lives—included male performers who engaged in various sex acts with female performers with varying degrees of prowess, endowment, and physical aptitude.[45]

Porn cultivates the desire for the perverse sexual object. It contributes to a reconfiguring of male heterosexual experience. While female prostitutes also worked in theaters showing softcore and hardcore heterosexual movies, such a charged context increased the likelihood that the men in the audience, whatever sort of film was being screened, might have sexual encounters with one another.[46] It was part of a pattern found over and over again in same-sex environments like public restrooms, jails, prisons, and military facilities.[47] In such a situation even a "straight" man in the audience may engage in mutual masturbation with another man or allow a man to suck his penis.[48]

The cinematic-architectural apparatus of the softcore porn theater had created a unique sort of space in which various kinds of sexual exchanges could take place—cinematic representation of sex (softcore and later hardcore) on the screen and real sexual activity in the audience.[49] In the late sixties, the live action in the audience often surpassed the erotic appeal of the relatively innocuous short beaver films and softcore narrative features. In the same light, French director Jacques Nolot's independent feature *Porn Theatre* (2003) offered an homage to the porn theater and the sexual diversity and solidarity that often emerged among the patrons of porn theaters from the 1960s through the early 1980s.

Pornography normalizes perversity. The men who regularly went out to the adult theaters saw thousands of hours of porn films and videos. In his memoir about his experience in New York's porn theaters, Samuel Delany described the audience's changing response to the sex portrayed in hardcore movies. The movies, he suggested,

> improved our vision of sex . . . making it friendlier, more relaxed, and more playful. . . . For the first year or two the theaters operated, the entire working-class audience would break out laughing at everything save male-superior fucking. (I mean, that's what sex is, isn't it?) At the fellatio, at the cunnilingus even more, and at the final kiss, among the groans and chuckles you'd always hear a couple of "Yuccchs" and "Uhgggs." By the seventies' end, though, only a few chuckles sounded out now—at the cunnilingus passages. And in the first year or two of the eighties, even those had stopped. . . . Indeed, I think, under pressure of those films, many guys simply found themselves changing what turned them on. And if one part or another didn't happen to be your thing, you still saw it enough times to realize that maybe you were the strange one.[50]

Pornography succeeded in the market because it articulated wish-fulfilling fantasies that resonated with its audience. But commercial success also fed the perverse dynamic: the constant push to identify new varieties of polymorphous possibilities—and at the same time offered strategies of symbolic containment. Pornography both harnesses those perverse desires and generates them. The shift to hardcore triggered the drive to seek out ever more unusual sexual fantasy content material—which would later become the central dynamic of the porn industry. Whether viewed as cultural expressions or as commercial products, growing out of a complex dynamic between the familiar and the new, the normal and the taboo, the ordinary and the perverse, the industry produced fantasies that represented ever more "perverse" sexual combinations in order to sustain erotic excitement among its jaded fans. Under the banner of sexual intercourse outside of the heteronormative marriage, pornography harnessed voyeurism and exhibitionism to portray sex with multiple partners, group sex, fellatio and cunnilingus, anal intercourse, lesbianism, male homosexuality, all kinds of sexual fetishisms, sex toys, BDSM, and other sexual practices. Thus, it promoted movement along a "continuum of perversions which underlies human sexuality," the historical dynamic of a polymorphic sexual economy that allows for the selection of diverse objects of desire.[51] Pornography played and has continued to play an ambiguous role in this process.

2

Beefcake to Hardcore

■■■■■■■■■■■■■■■■■■■■■■

Gay Pornography and
Sexual Revolution

> The cultural constraints under which we
> operate include not only visible political
> structures but also the fantasmatic
> processes by which we eroticize the
> real. . . . The economy of our sexual
> desires is a cultural achievement.
> —Leo Bersani, *Homos*

Hardcore pornography emerged as a significant current of popular culture in the 1970s. The first porn movie ever reviewed by *Variety* was Wakefield Poole's *Boys in the Sand* (1971), a sexually explicit gay film shot on Fire Island with a budget of four thousand dollars. Moviegoers, celebrities, and critics—gay and straight—flocked to see the film when it opened in mainstream theaters in New York, Los Angeles, and San Francisco. Within a year, *Deep Throat*, a heterosexual hardcore feature, also opened to rave reviews and a huge box office— exceeding that of many mainstream Hollywood features. It was quickly followed by *The Devil in Miss Jones* and *Behind the Green Door*. *Variety* reported that between June 1972 and June 1973, these three movies earned more—on a per-screen basis and in terms of gross revenues—than all but a handful of mainstream Hollywood releases. Thus was launched the era of "porn chic."[1]

Pornography was an integral part of the discourse that emerged during the sexual revolution of the 1960s and 1970s. Porn, however, played a more significant role in the life of gay men than among heterosexual men, not only because homosexuality has been a stigmatized form of behavior but also because historically there were so few homoerotic representations of any kind. Gay men become sexually active adults without any socialization in the social and sexual codes of the gay male subculture. Pornography contributes to the education of desire.[2] "For gay male culture," observes Thomas Yingling, "porn has historically served as a means to self-ratification through self-gratification."[3] This tendency was especially true during the late 1960s and early 1970s. But for young gay men of the last few generations, porn has provided knowledge of the body and of sexual narratives, and examples of gay sexuality and of sexuality within a masculine framework. Of course, it also has provided an extremely "thin" discourse, premised on an almost utopian lack of obstacles, encumbrances, and inhibitions. Moreover, in spite of its liberatory promise, it has conveyed stereotypes and other kinds of social misinformation. Porn emerged as part of a heterogeneous social framework that encompassed "many institutional structures, economics, modes of address and audiences"—including magazines, mail-order businesses and postal inspectors, movie theaters, public sex, vice squads, and the closet.[4] During the sexual revolution and since that time, porn has played a vital function in gay male life.

The transition from softcore to hardcore pornography represented a dramatic break in the production of pornographic films—both in how sex was portrayed on film and in the way the production of porn was organized, who performed in it, and what other kinds of activities were associated with it. It required new filmmaking conventions and new rhetorical devices.[5] As a rule, in softcore pornography the performers are actors, the sex is simulated, and filming is more akin to traditional movie production; in hardcore porn the performers are sex workers and the production of hardcore scenes focuses on embodied sexual functions—on genitalia, erections, and orgasms. To be credible the sexual encounters represented in hardcore require real erections and real orgasms—and those reality effects anchor the fantasy world that porn offers to its audience. Porn films serve as passports to worlds of sexual fantasy—enacted by real people with real bodies and, in the case of men, real erections and orgasms. The everyday obstacles to untrammeled sex are removed.[6] Fantasies are made more real because they are caught in motion and on film.[7]

For gay men, the Supreme Court's dismantling of the regulatory discourse set up and maintained since 1873 by the Comstock Law allowed for sexually explicit representations of homosexuality to move from private spaces inside the homes of gay men into public spaces on the screens and inside movie theaters. The transition from "beefcake," or softcore images, to sexually explicit hardcore porn films in the late 1960s was not only a change from one medium to another—from primarily still photography and drawings to a cinematic medium, from a static image to an action image—but a shift that entailed a modification in the representation of homosexual desire from a focus on men as the objects of desire to men as the active agents of homosexual desire.

Obscenity and Democracy

The sexual revolution of the 1960s and 1970s would never have taken place were it not for the battles fought over obscenity and pornography during the late 1950s by pornographers, stand-up comics, literary writers, and publishers.[8] Even though Samuel Roth, the plaintiff in the Supreme Court's *Roth v. United States* decision (1957), lost the case, Justice William Brennan's opinion altered the legal landscape. Over the next ten years, the Court decided several major obscenity cases, generally finding for greater freedoms of sexually oriented material.[9] Two of the cases reviewed by the Court dealt with issues that directly affected homosexuals. At the time, homosexual conduct was illegal in every state of the union, and no doubt many Americans considered the topic of homosexuality itself to be "obscene" or "pornographic." In 1954 the Los Angeles postmaster seized copies of *ONE*, a homophile civil rights publication, and banned it from the mail on the grounds that it was "obscene, lewd, lascivious and filthy." Lower courts upheld the postmaster's ban, but in 1958 the Supreme Court, citing *Roth*, reversed the lower courts' findings without issuing a written opinion.[10] The second case actually involved pornography. The U.S. Postal Service seized *MANual*, *Trim*, and *Grecian Guild Pictorial*, three "beefcake" magazines that carried photographs and illustrations of men scantily dressed in posing straps and bathing suits, all published by MANual Enterprises. The postmaster believed the magazines explicitly appealed to the prurient interests of homosexuals. MANual Enterprises sued the Postal Service. By 1962 the case had made its way to the Supreme Court, where the justices once again reversed the lower courts. The *MANual* decision contributed a new wrinkle—"patently offensive"—to the *Roth* test for obscenity: "These magazines cannot be deemed so offensive on their faces to affront current community standards of decency—a quality that we shall hereafter refer to as 'patently offensive' or 'indecency.' Lacking that quality, the magazines cannot be deemed legally 'obscene' and we need not consider the question of the proper 'audience' by which their 'prurient interest' appeal should be judged."[11] Although homosexual readers might find the pictures arousing, the Court concluded that as "dismally unpleasant, uncouth, and tawdry" as the images were, they "lacked patent offensiveness" and were thus not obscene.[12] In the wake of *Roth* and these other decisions, publishers and booksellers had increased reason to believe they could win their pleas against local censorship convictions; they were proven right.

At the end of this process, there was virtually no constraint on print publications. However, the issue was less clear-cut with regard to sexually explicit films. By the early 1970s, controversies no longer tended to focus on erotic nudity, four-letter words, or frank dialogue so much as on explicit content that often involved actual sex acts, often perverse ones. The ultimate irony of the *Roth* decision, and the later *Miller v. California* case (1973) in which the Supreme Court sought to establish a stricter test for obscenity, is that if some so-called prurient work (like the hardcore film *The Devil in Miss Jones*) could be shown to have some socially redeeming value (as the Supreme Court found in the prurient novel *Fanny Hill*) or some "serious literary, artistic, political or scientific value" (as Justice Burger stipulated in *Miller*), then that prurient work would have some constitutional protection. Thus many hardcore theatrical releases in the 1970s adopted some sort of high-concept, psychological angle or plot as an alibi against prosecution for obscenity. Eventually even the need for that stratagem evaporated.[13]

Beefcake

In September 1960, only a few years after the *Roth* decision, Newton Arvin—an eminent professor of literature at Smith College, political activist, and literary scholar who had written a National Book Award–winning book on Herman Melville and another on Nathaniel Hawthorne—was arrested in his home in Northampton, Massachusetts, for possessing a collection of "beefcake" magazines illustrated with seminude pictures of men. Among the magazines seized were *Grecian Guild Pictorial*, *Gym*, and *Physique Artistry*. Arvin's name had surfaced as the result of a recent postal investigation, and federal authorities had notified the local vice squad. Ned Spofford and Joel Dorius, two colleagues of Arvin's, were arrested at the same time. Local newspapers referred to the men as a "sex ring," and the *Boston Herald* published a story under the headline "Suspect's Diary Studied for Clues to Smut Traffic." The careers of all three men were destroyed in one way or another by the arrests. Arvin, who was forced into retirement and spent a year hospitalized for depression after a suicide attempt, died in 1963. Spofford and Dorius, both untenured faculty members at Smith, were fired.[14] Their convictions were overturned after the Supreme Court ruled in *MANual Enterprises, Inc. v. Day* (1962) that beefcake magazines could not be considered obscene.[15]

Gay life in the years before the Stonewall riots of 1969 was centered among small groups of friends and in bars; casual sex often occurred in public rest rooms, parks, and piers. Homosexuality was still considered a loathsome perversion by a majority of the population. Psychiatrists categorized it as a mental illness; every state in the union criminalized sex between men, and most states criminalized sex between women.[16] Pornographic materials—whether written or visual—were difficult to obtain, expensive, and even dangerous to possess. Homoerotic images—that is, photographs of nude men or drawings of erotic scenes—were available only through private networks or to "select mail-order customers." Such material was considered obscene and could not be sent through the mail, though in fact pornography had been distributed via the postal system even before the Civil War.[17] In such a context, gay male erotic culture emerged very slowly into the public light.[18]

Starting out as an underground phenomenon during the 1950s, small magazines with photographs of almost nude men were sold on newsstands in larger cities: New York, Chicago, Los Angeles, and so on. These "physique magazines" and the mail-order businesses based upon them became central to the development of the gay erotic imagination.[19] Photographs of nearly nude men were frequently published in health and bodybuilding magazines to serve as models of physical health and bodily development, not as objects of desire. The homosexually oriented physique magazines, however, aimed deliberately at an audience with a sexual interest. These magazines were not merely one aspect of a wider gay male culture, but as Valentine Hooven argues in his history of beefcake magazines, "they virtually were gay [male] culture."[20]

In 1948, the U.S. Postal Service launched one of its periodic campaigns to clean up the mail-order advertisements in men's magazines—clamping down on sales of suggestive cartoons, recordings of risqué night club acts, and novelty items as well as images of nude women and men. The Postal Service warned magazine publishers that if they did not exclude such advertising, they would not be able to use the mail. Although the photographs were technically not illegal, many magazines quickly banned all physique ads.[21] Bob Mizer, an amateur photographer living in Los Angeles, had frequently advertised in men's magazines and suggested to other photographers that they pool their mailing lists and issue their catalogs jointly. In 1950, while Mizer was experimenting with grouping the catalog pages together, it occurred to him to create a magazine; he called it *Physique Pictorial*. The publication featured photographs of young men wearing only posing straps, bathing suits, or loin cloths and almost no editorial content—except for long and deceptively chatty captions that frequently functioned as "editorials."[22]

By the mid-1950s there were more than a dozen small-scale (measuring five by eight inches) beefcake magazines—including *Apollo, Physique Pictorial, Male Nudist Review, Fizeek Art Quarterly, Grecian Guild Pictorial, Art and Physique, Trim, Tomorrow's Man, Male Pix, Vim, Adonis,* and *Young Adonis*— all publishing photographs and illustrations of attractive, almost nude young men, often posed in sexually suggestive situations. In their back pages, photographs of tanned and oiled bodybuilders were available by mail order.[23] Most publishers of beefcake were extremely cautious about identifying their readers as gay men, and by the 1960s nearly every major publisher or photographic studio had suffered legal persecution or harassment from the police—Bruce of Los Angeles and others had even gone to jail for periods of time, whereas *Playboy* had been publishing "cheesecake" images at least since the 1950s. If the Supreme Court's 1962 *MANual* decision helped to alleviate some of the legal repression, it did not completely stop harassment of beefcake photographers; as late as the mid-1960s, Mizer, who regularly referred the models represented by his studio (the Athletic Model Guild) to other photographers, was convicted of running a male prostitution business.

Despite the challenges, the beefcake magazines created a loose counterdiscourse to the homophobic discourses in American society at that time.[24] Christopher Nealon has argued that through their pictures, comments, and stories, the magazines suggested some sort of gay male solidarity, "an imagined community," that countered the pathological model of gender "inversion" ("a woman's soul in a male body") and that appealed to classical "Greek bodily and political ideals."[25] According to Thomas Waugh the total circulation of beefcake magazines during the late 1960s was over 750,000, probably the largest audience of gay male readers and consumers ever assembled up to that point in time.[26] They far exceeded the circulation of the more "political" homophile publications such as *ONE* and the *Mattachine Review*. "A minuscule magazine featuring a bunch of guys with their clothes off but not completely naked may not seem like much of a revolution in the history of sex," Hooven has argued, "but to the men who bought them, they were something new and daring. It took courage to purchase one of those little magazines in 1955."[27] That such was the case is illustrated by the experience of Arvin, Spofford, and Dorius. "The consumption of erotica was without question political," Waugh writes, "however furtive, however unconscious, however masturbatory, using pictures was an act of belonging to a community," and he notes that in the period before Stonewall, consuming erotic images was for gay men the "most important political activity of the postwar decades."[28]

Sex in the Cinema

A combination of industrial and social factors created a growing market for softcore sex films during the 1960s. The growth in the number of theaters showing sexploitation movies, with their predominately male audiences, also provided new opportunities for all-male sexual encounters.[29] Porn theaters had become a public space that facilitated sexual arousal because they provided their male audiences with an erotic mise-en-scène.[30] Male audiences watched pornographic films in a state of arousal, and the movies elicited images and fantasies that involved not only women but—in contrast to most heterosexual men's private sex lives—male performers who engaged in various sex acts with female performers with varying degrees of prowess, endowment, and sexual skill. Thus heterosexual male spectators found themselves in a state characterized by prolonged desire and an ambiguous relation to the objects of desire and fantasized events on the screen.[31] Although female prostitutes also worked in theaters showing softcore and hardcore heterosexual movies, such a charged context increased the likelihood that the men in the audience, whatever sort of film was being screened, might have sexual encounters with one another.[32] It was part of a pattern found over and over again in public restrooms, jails, prisons, military facilities, and other same-sex environments.[33] In such a situation even a "straight" man in the audience might engage in mutual masturbation with another man or allow a man to suck his penis.[34] The porn theater, part of the cinematic apparatus itself, had become a complex form of sociosexual space, an erotic signifying system and a stage for fantasy scenarios.[35]

The cinematic and architectural complex of the softcore porn theater had created a unique space in which various kinds of sexual exchanges could take place—cinematic representation of sex (softcore and later hardcore) on the screen and real sexual activity in the audience.[36] Brendan Gill described the space and the activities that went on in the theaters:

> For the homosexual, it is the accepted thing that the theatre is there to be cruised in; this is one of the advantages he has purchased with his expensive ticket of admission. Far from sitting slumped motionless in one's chair, one moves about at will, sizing up the possibilities. Often there will be found standing at the back of the theatre two or three young men, any of whom, for a fee, will accompany one to seats well down front and there practice upon one the same arts that are being practiced upon others on the screen. One is thus enabled to enjoy two very different sorts of sexual pleasures simultaneously.[37]

In the late 1960s, the live action in the audience often surpassed the erotic appeal of the relatively innocuous beefcake shorts and rather lugubrious softcore narrative features.

Starting in the late 1960s, the writer Samuel Delany went regularly to the porn theaters in the Times Square area. He cruised in them and frequently had sex with the men who attended them, despite the fact that the vast majority of the theaters showed straight porn and that most of the men there were also straight. Nevertheless, patrons, in large part because of the sexual activity that went on in the theaters, also developed a sense of community. In *Times Square Red, Times Square Blue*, Delany suggests that the encounters that took place in porn theaters encouraged the development of social relationships crossing lines of class, race, and sexual orientation and conveyed a sense of community.[38] The independent feature *Porn Theatre* (2003), by French director Jacques Nolot, offered an homage to the porn theater and the sexual diversity and solidarity that often emerged among its patrons from the 1960s through the early 1980s.

Only a few exploitation movies and nudie-cuties dealt with male homosexuality or gender deviance.[39] In fact, most porn filmmakers refused to make gay films, and the older generation of gay physique photographers—especially some of those who had made short eight- or sixteen-millimeter movies for their mail-order customers, such as Bob Mizer, Dick Fontaine, and Pat Rocco—were initially cautious about showing their work theatrically. Instead, homosexual themes were most commonly explored in avant-garde or experimental films by filmmakers such as Kenneth Anger, Jack Smith, and Andy Warhol, and these films were more likely to have theatrical showings in "art" venues.[40] Anger's short film *Fireworks* (1947) was one of the earliest films to touch on a homosexual topic. Inspired by the 1943 Zoot Suit Riots in Los Angeles, it portrayed a young man who, awaking from an erotic dream, goes out into the night in search of sexual adventure. The film is permeated with surrealistic sexual symbolism—statues under sheets representing erections and a Roman candle spewing white sparks from a sailor's crotch. Pervaded by homoeroticism, erotic images of male physiques, and violence, Anger's *Scorpio Rising* (1963) paid homage to the macho rites of a motorcycle gang, juxtaposing and intercutting images of fascism and delinquency, community and rebellion, motorcycle gangs and a Nazi rally, and ritual and violence, bringing together the sacred and the profane. The references to Nazism seem to point to the famed brutality of the Los Angeles Police Department—which terrorized Latinos and African Americans, as well as lesbians and gay men for so many years.[41]

Made for a mere three hundred dollars, Jack Smith's *Flaming Creatures* (1963) was another experimental film that touched on homosexual subject matter. The film is an abstract montage of the human body and its parts: penises (limp and erect), nipples, feet, and lips, a campy and bizarre tale of orgies, vampires, and transvestites. It created a sensation when it played in New York in 1963 and 1964. Intentionally shocking as were so many of the experimental films of the era, it was considered the most offensive of them all, generating a huge public outcry. When it was showed at the Gramercy Arts Theatre the following March, along with *Un chant d'amour* (1950), Jean Genet's portrayal of homoeroticism in prison, the police raided the theater, confiscated the print, and arrested the program's director for obscenity. Proclaiming the film as a milestone in the sexual revolution, critic and avant-garde film advocate Jonas Mekas wrote, "*Flaming Creatures* [was] . . . a manifesto of the New Sexual Freedom riders." In later years, the film inspired directors as different as Federico Fellini and John Waters.[42]

Warhol had directed or produced a number of the films that had touched on homosexual themes or subtexts, involved male nudity, or featured beefcake stars (Joe Dallesandro). Two of his early experimental films were included in the Park Theater film festival. Warhol shot *Blow Job* in the same year that Smith made *Flaming Creatures*. The title alone creates "pornographic" expectations.

The entire thirty-minute film focuses on the face of a handsome young man, a man who is getting his cock sucked. We never see who is giving the man the blow job. We don't know whether it is a man or a woman, whether a homosexual or heterosexual blow job—we can't even be sure that it is a "real" blow job, though it seems to be. It is a pure reaction shot. We see only the man's face, but we see him gaze into space, look down, drift off into an erotic reverie. We see him wince—with pain or pleasure, we don't know—then we see him relax; now and then he seems about to have an orgasm. Finally after a moment of apparent ecstasy, he lights a cigarette. We assume that he's had an orgasm.[43]

In 1966, after the success of his film *Chelsea Girls* in mainstream theaters, Warhol was contacted by the manager of the Hudson Theater on West Forty-Fourth Street, just off Times Square, for something that he would be able to show there. Warhol's collaborator, Paul Morrissey, suggested *My Hustler*. "They want to show something," Morrissey urged Warhol, "and the title will make them think it's a sex film like all the girl films being shown there." *My Hustler* opened there in July 1967 and grossed eighteen thousand dollars in its first week. The movie has a loose narrative, and unlike *Blow Job* it has sound. Set at Fire Island Pines, the film opens with a panoramic view of a beach. Far out toward the surf is someone, a speck on the sand until we move in closer, sitting in a beach chair. The camera zooms in on a handsome young man, a hustler named Paul America. On the soundtrack, we hear the voices of a man (Ed Hood) and two other people, another man and a woman arguing about the hustler whom they are both attracted to and whom they want to take for their own use. It is a movie about "sex" or at least as much about sex as movies of that period allowed—that is, no explicit sex—and more definitely about homosexual desire between men. The gossip magazine *Confidential* reported, "*My Hustler* has touched off the trend toward full homosexual realism in the movies. The reason according to the film critics, is that it is the first full length film to take a look at the lavender side of life without pointing a finger in disgust or disdain but concentrating instead on the way life really is in the limp-wristed world."[44] Considering that it has no sexually explicit scenes, *My Hustler* did surprisingly well in the Times Square arena.

The first theatrical screening of a complete program of gay softcore "erotic" films took place at the Park Theater in Los Angeles in June 1968, predating the Stonewall riots that sparked the gay liberation movement by a year; the film was not explicitly labeled as "gay."[45] Billed as "A Most Unusual Film Festival," it drew upon both experimental filmmakers and the local physique photographers and filmmakers such as Bob Mizer and Pat Rocco, for the first time showing their eight-millimeter short films theatrically. The program listed in the *Los Angeles Free Press* announced *Flaming Creatures*, *My Hustler*, and an Anger trilogy—all experimental films that alluded to sexual or homosexual themes in symbolic or coded ways. Other films billed for the series included gay softcore titles such as Rocco's *Love Is Blue*, *Nudist Boy Surfers*, *Boys Out to Ball*, and "Warhol's B-J (call theatre for title!)."[46] The narrative structure for gay softcore films had not yet evolved into a strict formula. The short films of Mizer and Rocco were quite different in that regard. Many of Mizer's films involved disrobing, wrestling, or fights; Rocco's tended to be love stories—with disrobing, kissing, and walking nude. None showed erections or penetration. Within the year, audiences in Los Angeles and other cities had grown tired of the sentimental and softcore short films made by the beefcake photographers.[47]

The first gay softcore feature film produced after the Park's film festival was Tom DeSimone's *The Collection*, released in 1970. Eschewing the sentimental style of Rocco's movies and the boisterous boyishness of Mizer's wrestling films, it told the story of a gay man who kidnaps young men and keeps them locked in cages for his sexual pleasure. Although there was nudity and simulated sex, there were no erections. However, the Los Angeles theater that showed it was raided by the police because of its S/M-styled subject matter.[48] The most ambitious gay softcore feature produced in this period was *Song of the Loon*, a romance between a white man and an Indian set in the wilderness of the American West. Made for seventy thousand dollars, it was released in 1970, just as hardcore movies started playing in San Francisco.

Gay softcore films had barely moved beyond frontal nudity and kissing. Very rapidly, by 1970, interest in softcore movies had begun to wane. Theater managers and exhibitors were clamoring for more explicit sexual action on the screens. None of the experimental art films had explicitly adopted homoerotic narratives, and the softcore features of DeSimone and other directors had merely sought to apply Hollywood formulas—especially sentimental or melodramatic ones—to homosexual content.

Going Hardcore, Representing Sex

By the middle of 1969 producers wanted "heavy, hard stuff."[49] The defining characteristic of hardcore porn is "insertion"—oral, vaginal, or anal—and penetration was the last frontier, signaling the shift from sexploitation into hardcore.[50] Once the transition to hardcore action took place, the production of sexually explicit pornographic films underwent a dramatic change. Whereas in the production of softcore cinema many standard cinematic conventions of genre, performance, and narrative held sway, virtually everything changed in hardcore production. Feature-length sexploitation resembled Hollywood films to some extent, with some female nudity thrown in. The move to hardcore required the development of new moviemaking techniques, but ones that had not yet developed or established the narrative conventions, iconographic formulas, or rhetorical strategies of a full-fledged genre.[51]

Hardcore emerged very quickly as a commercial imperative. Distributors and exhibiters clamored for movies showing explicit sexual acts to bring audiences back into their theaters. San Francisco was the first city where hardcore films were extensively played—by 1969 the city had twenty-five theaters offering hardcore movies.[52] New York soon followed, and estimates at the time placed the number of theaters nationally showing sex films between one and four hundred, in cities from Indianapolis to Dallas, Houston, and New York.[53]

In 1969, when the owner of a company that made softcore movies told his staff about the decision to move into hardcore porn, he asked anyone uncomfortable with his decision to leave immediately. He explained that he would stand by those who chose to remain and get them the best lawyers, but that if asked he would deny any knowledge of their activities. "And of course," one director noted, "we all knew that we'd have to go even further underground, because everything was getting busted."[54] At the time, hardcore producers not only operated outside the law; many conducted fly-by-night operations. "Stories are written on matchbook covers, and dialogue is made up by performers more noted for looks than talent," said an interviewee.[55] Having to perform "real" sex also changed who was willing to be cast in pornographic movies. Said one director of softcore films, "When you get into hardcore you are dealing with a different class of people. You can't get actors or actresses anymore, but pimps and whores."[56] In California it was illegal to pay performers to have sex. "You cannot make a hardcore film without violating the prostitution laws," Captain Jack Wilson of the LAPD told Kenneth Turan and Stephen Zito. "When you pay actors to engage in sex or oral copulation, you've violated the laws."[57] Sex films were no longer merely products made on the margins of the Hollywood film industry; they were outside both the law and the film industry.

The shift to hardcore necessitated creating a new production framework and conventions of performance that facilitated the enactment of real sexual activity, that is, with erections and orgasms. The director's role changed from directing actors in simulated sex scenes, with dialogue and some degree of character development, to directing and choreographing the performers through a series of sex acts that required encouraging and monitoring erections as well as eliciting and photographing successful "cum shots."[58] Producers had to establish the social and physical conditions for sexual performances: a bounded space where sexual performances are filmed, with a supply of sexual partners (via casting) who expect to perform sexual acts before a camera with other performers and some sort of production crew—at the very least a director and a cinematographer to articulate the mise-en-scène. And certain aspects of sexual performance—including erections, orgasms, or ejaculations—became central to the production process. The "cum shot," known also as the "money shot," emerged as the sign of the sex scene's narrative conclusion. Ultimately, it was up to the producer/director to establish the overarching visual and fantasy vocabulary of the movie—the erotic gestalt (the mise-en-scène) of the hardcore movie. In real-life sexual activities, personal "scripts" are usually improvised, to some degree, from the participants' personal fantasies, social roles, cultural codes, and symbols, in addition to the socially available interactional strategies, and are used to orchestrate a sexual encounter.[59] The mise-en-scène in hardcore organized the sexual performances and set the stage in order to create a credible fantasy world on film. Despite the many challenges, the switch from simple nudity to hardcore action took place almost seamlessly.[60]

For gay men, the transition from softcore beefcake to hardcore was extremely important. The primary focus of beefcake publications had been on men as objects of desire, not as agents of desire. Although there was an extensive underground business in sexually explicit drawings of men having sex with one another, the beefcake magazines were never able to publicly display it.[61] Over time, the magazines eventually began to show men interacting with one another—though not sexually. In images that were often coy and suggestive, the illustrations that were published in the magazines did imply (especially in the drawings and illustrations) that the men portrayed might have some potentially "erotic" interest in one another. In place of the "worship" of ideal bodies sponsored by beefcake publications, hardcore films offered images, roles, and "scripts" that could serve as models and legitimate active sex. Only with the advent of gay hardcore movies showing in public theaters were gay audiences able to see gay men as active agents of homosexual desire.

In 1969 and 1970, the challenge of making gay porn movies was, as it was for straight films, discovering the most effective way to represent sexual action. Straight hardcore sex fit easily into the existing narrative formulas; dealing with erections and getting cum shots were the new challenges. But gay hardcore sex posed unique obstacles to filmmakers: erections, anal penetration, and ejaculations (whose?) were seen as essential. Yet no standard sequence of sexual action had emerged. Who sucked or fucked whom, in what order, remained an open question. Initially the approach was purely quantitative: "Generally, I keep my actors to about six people," one director explained, "and that gives me three sex scenes and six cum-shots."[62]

Thus, determining the narrative significance of different sexual acts and recognizing the importance of shooting penetration shots, erections, and orgasms were of primary importance. For instance, fucking "doggie style" was impersonal; in some narrative contexts, face-to-face anal intercourse missionary position was considered more intimate. Riding a man's cock "cowboy style" was sometimes physically easier for maintaining an erection. Most of the conventions that we've come to expect in gay pornographic films—such as the sequence of sex acts from kissing to fellatio to anal sex, the close-ups of penetration shots and of performers' cum shots—were not yet in place. On top of everything else, production values were quite crude; locations, hair, clothing, the dialogue, and soundtrack resembled more closely a home movie than a professional theatrical feature.

One early gay hardcore film, *Desires of the Devil*, aptly illustrates the transitional phase of the new film genre.[63] Probably made sometime during 1971, it was directed by Sebastian Figg, a former actor who had appeared in softcore films (*Escape to Passion*, 1970) and who directed *The Specimen*, a straight hardcore feature, released a year later.[64] The movie has five scenes, but there is only one cum shot in the entire film. For example, in the first sex scene Jim Cassidy, the film's star, meets a man at a theater and is invited home for a drink. Eventually they go into the bedroom and undress. They embrace naked on the bed and the man sucks Cassidy's penis, but the camera does not focus on the fellatio. They shift position and the man lies on his back as Cassidy inserts his penis, but we never see the penis penetrating the man's ass. They fuck for a few minutes, separate, embrace, and fall asleep. The fucking looks faked; neither man has an orgasm. Cassidy wakes up and sneaks out after taking some cash from the man's wallet.

After Cassidy leaves the first man's apartment, he meets another man on the street and goes back to that man's apartment. They undress and quickly move from the man sucking Cassidy's cock to "sixty-nine," then to Cassidy fucking the man. There is no penetration in this scene either, but it is more convincing and looks as though there was real fucking. The man comes while he's being fucked, though again Cassidy doesn't himself reach an orgasm. The last three scenes have very little sexual action—only oral sex, no anal penetration and no orgasms. It's not clear why neither penetration nor the money shot was portrayed. Virtually none of the formulas used in later porn were in evidence. It is possible that the film was originally conceived as a softcore feature film and incorporated some explicit sex while in production during the period's hasty transition to hardcore. Perhaps the film's director and producer assumed that the story, the nudity, and the quasi-hardcore and simulated sex put it satisfactorily into the hardcore category. It may also reflect the fact that the conventions surrounding penetration, erections, and cum shots were not yet firmly established.

Once the transition to hardcore had taken place, theater managers set out to find hardcore material for their gay audiences, and a number started to produce hardcore films to show in their own theaters. Amateur filmmakers produced many of the early gay pornographic movies, and to some degree many of the films made in this period represented an expression of the filmmakers' own newly "liberated" homosexuality; this was especially true for many of the performers. Eventually after the gay movement gained momentum, numerous small companies were formed to explicitly produce gay male pornographic films and the gay porn "industry" began to take shape in San Francisco, Los Angeles, and New York.

Pornographic Realism and Sexual Emancipation

On a hot June night in 1969, police raided a bar in Greenwich Village. For once, instead of meekly lining up to file into a paddy wagon, the bar's patrons and the crowd that gathered outside fought the police, setting off five days of rioting. Drag queens, street hustlers, lesbians, and gay men—many politicized by the movement against the war in Vietnam—rioted and taunted the police, throwing bottles and rocks. The riots crystallized a broad grassroots mobilization across the country. The raided bar, known as the Stonewall Inn, became the central symbol of a gay and lesbian political movement that dramatically changed the public image of homosexuals. Ironically, in the same month, theaters in San Francisco screened the first hardcore pornographic films.[65]

A year later Broadway director and choreographer Wakefield Poole, his boyfriend, and two other friends decided to go the Park-Miller Theatre to see an all-male porn film. It turned out to be a disappointing evening and for Poole a somewhat jarring experience, not only because they had all begun to feel a new sense of self-respect and appreciation after the Stonewall riots but also because unlike the theaters that screened straight porn, the lights at the Park-Miller, which showed gay porn, were bright enough that the theater's customers could actually read. Indeed one patron, Poole reported, was reading the *New York Times*. There was no sex going anywhere in the audience, which routinely took place in the theaters showing straight porn, in part because at the Park-Miller the police repeatedly walked in and looked over the audience. A film called *Highway Hustler* was the main feature. It portrayed a young hitchhiker who is picked up and taken to motel where he was fucked while being held at knifepoint. Poole's companions reacted to the dreary unerotic plot by laughing or falling asleep. He and his friends had failed to find the film either arousing or romantic. Afterward, they wondered aloud whether it was possible to make a sexy porn film that wasn't degrading.

After his experience at the Park-Miller, Poole decided to make a "quality" porn movie. During a summer stay on Fire Island, he shot three sexually explicit scenes. Poole called his movie *Boys in the Sand*. The title both evokes the idyllic sexual playground that Fire Island had become and implicitly repudiates Mart Cowley's vision of campy and guilt-ridden gay men in his play *Boys in the Band*. It thus rejected gay male effeminacy as an erotically legitimate expression of gay male sexuality.

In *Boys in the Sand* each scene evokes some mythical or magical element: in the first scene a beautiful man rises from the sea like Botticelli's Venus. It is a scene deeply indebted to Poole's dance experience with the Ballets Russes; its Debussy soundtrack evokes Vaslav Nijinsky's famous ballet *Afternoon of a Faun*. (The ballet itself provoked a huge furor at the premier in 1912, when the faun—danced by Nijinsky himself—relieved his sexual frustration by lying on a nymph's scarf and rubbing against it seemingly to the point of orgasm.) In the second scene, a man responds to an ad in a gay newspaper for a magic pill to create a beautiful man. He tosses the pill into the pool and, like a genie from a magic lantern, a beautiful man emerges for a passionate sexual encounter. And in the third, a torrid sexual encounter is created in the imagination of two gay men as they openly cruise one another—one black, the other white—like the mythical homoerotic male couple of American literature: Melville's Ishmael and Queequeg in *Moby Dick*, or Mark Twain's Huck Finn and Jim.[66] In one fell swoop, Poole invoked the cultural archetypes underlying the American homoerotic imagination of the 1960s.

Boys in the Sand offered a new erotic template for the gay male erotic imagination. The tortured sublimated violence in the films of Kenneth Anger; the passive exhibitionism of Bob Mizer's physique photography; the flamboyant ode to androgyny in Jack Smith's *Flaming Creatures*; the blank eroticism of Andy Warhol's *Blow Job* or *My Hustler*; or the primitive homoerotic idolatry of Joe Dallesandro in Paul Morrissey's *Flesh* (1968) and *Trash* (1972)—all these were suddenly surpassed in Poole's three scenes.

By the end of 1972, four other feature-length gay hardcore movies were released in theaters in Los Angeles, San Francisco, and New York. Most of these films also played in New York at the Fifty-Fifth Street Playhouse, where many of Warhol's sexually themed movies had opened. Poole's *Boys in the Sand* opened there in December 1971 and was an immediate critical and financial success. It was followed by J. Brian's *Seven in a Barn* (1971), which was made in the Bay Area. In the following year, Fred Halsted's gritty sadomasochistic feature *LA Plays Itself* (1972) opened; then Jack Deveau's *Left-Handed* (1972), an urban tale of hustlers and betrayal set in New York City; and finally Jerry Douglas's *The Back Row* (1973), an almost documentary-like portrait of New York's raunchy post-gay-liberation sexual scene. Casey Donovan, who starred in two of these movies—*Boys in the Sand* and *The Back Row*—went on to become the first nationally recognized gay porn star. These five films launched the new wave of postliberation, gay, hardcore pornographic cinema.[67]

Two of the hardcore movies were made in New York during 1971–1972: *Left-Handed* (1972) and *The Back Row* (1973). Jack Deveau and his lover Robert Alvarez began making *Left-Handed* even before Poole's film had premiered. Encouraged by the actor Sal Mineo, Deveau and Alvarez were actively involved in both the city's avant-garde cultural scene and in the new gay sexual scene that had emerged in the 1960s. Deveau was an industrial designer, and Alvarez had worked for a number of years as a film editor on documentaries for

National Educational Television as well as a few "underground" films.[68] *Left-Handed* showed a cross-section of gay male life in Manhattan in the early seventies. The film told the story of an antique dealer, his hustler boyfriend, and their pot dealer—a typical story of the 1960s and early 1970s. The story recounts a gay man (the hustler) seducing a straight man (the pot dealer), with the gay man eventually topping the straight man. The straight man becomes emotionally involved and begins to explore homosexuality, even participating in a gay orgy. At that point the gay man loses interest in the sexually curious "straight" man.

In February 1972, within months of the premier of *Boys in the Sand*, Jerry Douglas, a young playwright and off-Broadway director known for directing nude plays (a somewhat unique theatrical specialty of the 1960s), was approached by a producer of television commercials to make a gay hardcore film. The producer asked Douglas to hire *Boys'* star, Casey Donovan, who was another old friend and had appeared in an off-Broadway play that Douglas had directed.[69] *The Back Row*, the movie that Douglas wrote and made, was a sexually explicit takeoff of *Midnight Cowboy*, the X-rated movie that recently won an Academy Award for Best Picture. Like that of *Midnight Cowboy*, *The Back Row*'s hero was a naïve young cowboy just off the bus from the West who takes a walk on the wild side of New York's gay sexual subculture. Following in the footsteps of *Boys in the Sand*, it too packed theaters.

Two films made in California, one in San Francisco and one in Los Angeles, defined two major strands of gay pornographic filmmaking. One was J. Brian's *Seven in a Barn*, made in 1971. It was shot almost entirely in a single setting, a straw-filled barn in which seven suntanned all-American young men, many of them blond, sit in a circle playing strip poker. The sexual action—ranging from a circle jerk to a round of oral and anal sex, a series of three-ways, some light bondage, and a dildo—established many of the conventions that gay pornography has continued to follow. "Brian's films," wrote Ted Underwood several years later, were "characterized, first and foremost, by the breathtaking golden boys. . . . All seem to be fresh, young, healthy, versatile, creatively kinky and apparently insatiable."[70] Brian originated a style of gay porn and a type of casting that eventually dominated the gay porn industry in the late 1970s and 1980s—the all-American young man in search of sexual fulfillment, suntanned and often blond. The film was often set outdoors, in idyllic surroundings that were increasingly exemplified as California. Throughout the 1970s numerous small companies—Jaguar, Brentwood, Colt, Falcon, and Catalina—set up shop in Los Angeles and San Francisco to make short films as well as feature-length movies set within the California fantasy.[71]

If J. Brian initiated the mythical California of golden boys and muscular outdoorsmen, in *LA Plays Itself* (1972), Fred Halsted propelled gay porn into a darker, noir-like Los Angeles. Clearly influenced by the films of Kenneth Anger,

Halsted had no connection to either the physique photographers or the early local porn production companies. Nevertheless, Halsted established elements of a homoerotic film genre and style that later gay adult filmmakers drew upon. *LA Plays Itself* opens with the camera moving quickly in the countryside outside Los Angeles. Zooming to wildflowers, rocks, and insects, it comes to rest on an idyllic sexual encounter in the Malibu mountains: two young men kiss, suck each other's cocks, and casually fuck. The second scene opens on a gritty street in a run-down neighborhood of Los Angeles. Fred Halsted himself drives through seedy side streets in Hollywood—lined with young men hustling, porn theaters, and shabby storefronts. On the sound track, a young man with a Texas drawl is reading a porno story. As we cruise the streets of Los Angeles, we overhear a conversation between two young men, one just arrived, the other coyly offering to show him around and warning the newcomer to avoid certain kinds of men. In the third scene, we look down at a young man standing at the foot of a long stairway. Halsted stands at the top, pale, shirtless, wearing only jeans and boots. For a moment, we are suddenly prowling with Halsted again among half-naked men standing in the shadows in Griffith Park. Then just as suddenly, we are back on the stairway again; Halsted pushes the young man into a bedroom and throws him on the bed. He ties up the young man, whips him, and finally puts his fist up the young man's ass.

Halsted had started working on the script for *LA Plays Itself* in 1969 and finished it shortly before its premiere in the spring of 1972. It was essentially the first installment of a trilogy of films summarizing what he called his "philosophy of sex." The second work of the trilogy, *The Sex Garage*, was shot over the course of six hours in December 1971. Then, after prolonged work on the script, he started shooting *Sextool*, the third installment, during the summer of 1974. Shot in high-contrast black-and-white, *Sex Garage*—unlike *LA Plays Itself*, which was shot in color—opens with a young woman giving a blow job to a garage mechanic, then a macho biker replaces her, but he seems more interested in fucking his motorcycle. He literally fucks the motorcycle's exhaust pipe. *Sex Garage* was confiscated by the NYPD purportedly for the latter scene.[72]

Halsted's films were booked as porn, but local critics reviewed them as contributions to experimental art film genres. There is also no clear sense of homosexual identity in Halsted's films. "I consider myself a pervert first and a homosexual second," he said.[73] Nor did he acknowledge the purely recreational aspect of sex. According to Halsted, sex violates the male characters' sense of self-possession in order to create an encounter with the sacred: "Coming is not the point. The point is revelation—the why."[74] Halsted's philosophy shared much with that of pornographer and philosopher Georges Bataille. Like the philosopher, Halsted believed that the erotic is transgressive and sacramental, that it is inherently violent, and that it involves acts of violation. Human beings, according to Bataille, are closed off from one another and cannot communicate because the bodies of others are closed off to them. In the erotic encounter those physical barriers are breached, if only briefly, through the other's bodily orifices. Although Halsted made only a handful of films, director Joe Gage—in *Kansas City Trucking Co.* (1976), *El Paso Wrecking Corp.* (1978), and *L.A. Tool and Die* (1979)—developed more thoroughly the ultramasculine style that Halsted initiated.

After *Boys in the Sand*, Fred Halsted's *LA Plays Itself* was the most successful gay porn movie of the time. Similarly, it was one of the first porn movies, not just gay porn movies, reviewed in mainstream newspapers. Both movies helped to define "porn chic" as a significant cultural moment in the early 1970s, and each was an example of an artistically serious hardcore film. Moreover, both films preceded *Deep Throat* as a pornographic film that played to general moviegoing audiences, though neither one was the first gay hardcore film playing in theaters. These films created the public perception that gay pornographic films represented a new more serious kind of commercial pornography compared to the softcore shorts or the Hollywood-style potboilers showing in theaters.

Pornography, Perversity, and History

Hardcore pornographic films are historical documents of sex and of the scripts, fantasies, bodies, and styles of sex.[75] They succeed in the market because they articulate or propose wish-fulfilling fantasies that resonate with their audience. Commercial success, however, also fed the perverse dynamic—the constant push to identify new varieties of polymorphous sexual possibilities—and at the same time generated strategies of symbolic containment.[76] Thus the transition from softcore porn to hardcore was also in part a shift from more euphemistic, somewhat idealized, versions of sexual desire and conduct to ones that were more realistic and perhaps more perverse, though not, of course, without the compensating idealizations of breasts, penises, and body types.

Gay porn films reinforced gay viewers' identities as gay men. That identification was enunciated through the pornography's dominant semantic and syntactical conventions: the "standard" narrative sequence (kissing, undressing, oral sex, rimming, anal intercourse) of sexual acts, a convincingly energetic performance, and, most important, the erections and visible orgasms that authenticate (and narratively end the erotic scene) the embodied forms of homosexual desire. Operating within the realism of porn and its "reality effects," the real erections and the real orgasms putatively "prove" to a gay male spectator that these "sexually desirable, masculine, and energetic performers" are really gay—thus seeming to affirm the gay male identity. Even when an individual movie deviated from these generic expectations, either through failure to provide a credible performance or by offering new or creative sexual variations, the film affirmed gay identity.

Ironically, the generic conventions that consolidated and reinforced the identity effects coexisted with representations of "straight" men engaging in homosexual acts. In this way gay porn reinforces the incongruity between male homosexual desire—traditionally stigmatized and abject—and the heterosexual dominance of the masculine regime of desire. It serves to situate homosexual desire within masculine territory irrespective of heterosexual or gay identities.[77] Thus, the widespread employment of straight performers in gay pornography intensifies the contradiction between gay male identity and homosexual desire without identity, which conferred legitimacy on homosexual behavior independent of gay identity.[78]

Gay hardcore pornography also helped to legitimate a reconfiguration of gay masculinity.[79] As gay men rejected the traditional idea that male homosexual desire implied the desire to be female, they turned to a traditionally masculine or working-class style of acting out sexually. Camp as an effeminized gay sensibility was out. The new style of gay man was macho and sexually provocative, and that style included denim pants, black combat boots, a tight T-shirt (if it was warm), covered by a plaid flannel shirt (if it was cooler). The rugged look of the Marlboro man was the iconic masculine model for the 1970s.[80]

Anal intercourse became the central act of gay male pornography. Rather than a strict dichotomy between the "trade"/masculine role and "queer"/effeminate role, or top and bottom (terms and a distinction not in use during the early 1970s), versatility represented the politically fashionable style of fucking. It promulgated a fantasy of sexual surrender to the intense pleasure of discharged sexual tension, and ultimately to the psychic shattering of the self through anal intercourse.[81] Pornographic film relies upon the real erections and the real orgasms (the reality effects of porn production) of sexual performers and is at the same time a fictional representation of sexual fantasies. The realism is central, if not always absolutely necessary, to the rhetorical effectiveness of porn cinema. "Ultimately, what viewers want to see is guys having sex, not actors pretending to have sex," one reviewer wrote.[82]

Freud classified all forms of nonreproductive sexual behavior—kissing, oral sex, homosexuality, and various fetishes—as perverse sexual desires. Moreover, he argued that perverse desires were incompatible with a stable social order; instead, he believed that perverse sexual desires must be transformed, through repression and sublimation, into forms of energy more compatible with "civilized society."[83] Pornography normalizes perversity.

Starting in the 1970s, the proliferation of pornography opened up social space for the emergence of the "perverse dynamic."[84] Under the banner of sexual intercourse outside of the heteronormative marriage, pornography harnessed voyeurism and exhibitionism to portray sex with multiple partners, group sex, fellatio and cunnilingus, anal intercourse, lesbianism, male homo-sexuality, all kinds of sexual fetishisms, sex toys, BDSM, and other sexual prac-tices. Porn both harnesses those perverse desires and generates them.

The shift to hardcore triggered the drive to seek out ever more unusual sexual fantasy content material. And the sexual fantasies supplied, whether viewed as cultural expressions or commercial products, grow out of a complex dynamic between the familiar and the new, the normal and the taboo, the ordinary and the perverse. In this pursuit, the industry has turned to fantasies that represent ever more "perverse" sexual combinations in order to sustain erotic excitement among its jaded fans. Thus the sexual revolution and its dis-courses of sexual liberation both emancipated those who were stigmatized for their sexuality and facilitated the social discipline of the newly emancipated identities.[85]

3

Sex in the Seventies

■■■■■■■■■■■■■■■■■■■■■■

Gay Porn Cinema as an
Archive for the History
of Sexuality

> Pornography . . . is profoundly and
> paradoxically social. But even more than
> that, it's acutely historical. It's an archive
> of data about our history as a culture and
> our own individual histories—our
> formations as selves. . . . Pornography is
> a space in the social imagination as well
> as a media form.
> —Laura Kipnis, *Bound and Gagged*

The forty years between 1960 and 2000 have been among the most tumultu-
ous decades in the history of gay male sexuality. For many gay men who came
out in the period after the Stonewall riots of 1969, the seventies were a golden
age of sexual freedom.[1] It was an era that not only opened up the possibility of
openly acknowledging one's homosexuality and fostering a sense of identity and
community, but also initiated a period of sexual experimentation.[2] The discovery of AIDS in 1981 changed all that.

The emerging epidemic provoked debate and conflict over what aspects of
the "gay lifestyle" might have contributed to the pattern of immune deficiency

among gay men. Many observers attributed the outbreak to sexual promiscu-ity, the frequent patronage of bathhouses and other public sex venues, and the general availability of sexual activity in the urban centers of San Francisco and New York.[3] The enormous body of epidemiological literature, social scientific research, and cultural studies as well as hundreds of memoirs and volumes of fiction documenting the sexual life of gay men before the emergence of the AIDS epidemic has identified patterns of sexual behavior, modes of sexual interaction, as well as the cultural norms and fantasies that shaped sexual con-duct before the emergence of the epidemic.[4] Pornographic films and video, I argue, should also be considered as documents in the history of gay male sexuality.[5]

The sexual revolution of the 1960s and 1970s, the emergence of the gay liberation movement in 1969, and the increased freedom of sexual expression society-wide, together with the massive migration and concentration of gay men during the 1970s in the urban centers of New York, Chicago, Los Angeles, and San Francisco, fundamentally altered, according to sociologist Martin Levine, the forms (both social and sexual) of gay men's lives.[6] The migration and increased visibility brought together a critical mass of gay men who would economically sustain the kinds of commercial leisure establishments (bars, bathhouses, sex clubs, porn theaters, vacation resorts, and dance clubs) that facilitated sexual expression and generated a thriving and permissive sexual subculture. Patrick Moore has argued that during the 1970s gay men adopted sex as a tool for radical change and developed "new models of sexual interaction." It was, he concluded, "an astonishing experiment in radically restructuring existing relationships, concepts of beauty and the use of sex as a revolutionary tool."[7] As a result gay men developed "a distinctive life in which the masculinized representation of beauty, sexual experimentation and drugs were central."[8] Moore likened gay men's use of "sex as the raw material for a social experiment" to experimental art. Among the artists, he included porn filmmaker Fred Halsted, impresario Bruce Mailman, owner of the famous disco club the Saint, and graphic artist and writer David Wojnarowicz. Moore also included the Mineshaft in New York and the Cat-acombs in San Francisco, sex clubs and bars where transgressive and experi-mental sex took place.[9]

Moore's thesis that gay men were engaged in radical sexual experimentation counters the negative view of the 1970s as a "shameful" episode that set the stage for the AIDS epidemic.[10] Philosopher and art critic Arthur Danto, in his book on the photographic achievement of Robert Mapplethorpe, adopted a position similar to Moore's.[11] Danto was deeply struck by the impact that participation in the gay male sexual subculture of the 1970s, which included sadomasoch-ism and group sex, had on Mapplethorpe:

It is the mark of fantasies that we return, obsessively and repetitively, to the same images and the same scenarios, over and over again. We do not for the most part live our fantasies out, and so they never evolve. But the form of life Mapplethorpe had entered had made of sex a public practice, and this enabled it to evolve in ways quite beyond the power of private fantasy to anticipate. Whatever one might think of it, sex was probably lived more creatively in those years when the barriers to its enactment had fallen than at any other time in history. It had become as public as a language.[12]

The arguments of Levine, Moore, and Danto were made within a historical context that implicitly assumed that whatever kind of sex took place before the 1970s was not as "experimental," "adventurous," or "creative" as that of the 1970s and, more explicitly, that after the 1970s gay men's sex was dramatically changed for the worse by HIV/AIDS.

Danto, however, goes somewhat further than either Levine or Moore and makes two interrelated claims. The first is about the psychosocial impact of what he calls "sex as a public practice," and the second is that "sex was . . . lived more creatively in those times [i.e., the 1970s] . . . than any other time in history." These are two steps of a rather complicated psychohistorical argument in which "sex as a public practice" provides the practical and pedagogic basis for "sex being lived creatively"—and thus during the 1970s lived "more creatively . . . than at any time in history." Danto presumes that "sex as a public practice" is a historically specific condition of the period, especially for gay men, between 1969 and 1981. While neither Levine nor Moore explicitly assigns causal force to "sex as a public practice," it is clear from their books that they recognized that during the seventies there was an enormous increase of uninhibited sexual expression among gay men.[13]

Sex as a public practice during the seventies is explicitly the topic of Joseph Lovett's 2006 documentary *Gay Sex in the 70s*.[14] The film explores the significance of promiscuous and casual sex in public in gay men's lives during the decade.[15] Focused on New York, *Gay Sex in the 70s* is constructed from the memory images of a dozen or so gay men who are survivors of the period—still alive in 2005 in the aftermath of the AIDS epidemic.[16] Somewhat hyperbolically, but in line with Danto's thesis, Lovett characterized the seventies as the "most libertine period that the Western world has ever seen since Rome." With still photos, artifacts, and film clips from the porn movies of Jack Deveau and Peter de Rome, Lovett evokes the atmosphere of the period between June 1969 and June 1981, from the Stonewall riots that initiated the gay liberation movement to the year that the disease later known as AIDS was first diagnosed— he offers extensive documentation of Danto's thesis on the importance of sex as a public practice. The film is both a celebration of the sexual freedom explored by the generation who had come of age in the era after Stonewall as well as a memorial to that same generation's devastating experience of the AIDS epidemic.

The wave of uninhibited and adventurous sexual expression during the 1970s, both by individuals and as a public practice, was also captured on film by a group of gay pornographic filmmakers based in New York. These filmmakers sought to document the underground sexual lifestyle that had emerged in the years before and immediately after the Stonewall riots of 1969. Like the Italian neorealist filmmakers working after World War II, the queer realist filmmakers of New York created a synthesis of a documentary-like view of the gay sexual subculture and the more psychopolitical themes of sexual liberation.[17] These men shot their early hardcore movies in the style of cinema verité—using naturalistic techniques that originated in documentary filmmaking, with its stylized cinematic devices of editing and camera work and deliberately staged setups to capture the rough and gritty feel of New York City. They were thus both pornographic movies as well as documentaries about the gay male sexual subculture.[18] Many of the films were produced by either Jack Deveau's Hand-in-Hand Productions or P.M. Productions, the production wing of New York's leading porn theater, the Park-Miller. Among them were films by Jerry Douglas (under the name of Doug Richards), Jack Deveau, Arch Brown, Peter de Rome, and Avery Willard (under the name Bruce King). Even Wakefield Poole's more fantasy-oriented film *Bijou* offered documentary-like slices of New York City life.

These films reveled in the sexual subculture that had emerged in the years immediately preceding Stonewall—amid the seedy, run-down, and unused industrial spaces that supplied so many opportunities for uninterrupted sexual activity with multiple and unknown partners. They all made a point to show the streets and the landmarks of the city's sexual landscape. Every one of these movies set sex scenes in public spaces of the city. Some, like Arch Brown's *Pier Pieces*, actually were shot on the piers along the Hudson River; both Jerry Douglas (*The Back Row*) and Jack Deveau (*A Night at the Adonis*) shot group sex scenes in porn theater restrooms; and three of the films were set in bathhouses (*Bijou*, *The Voyeur*, and *Muscle Bound*). Jerry Douglas's *The Back Row*, Peter de Rome's *Underground*, and Ian McGraw's *Subway* all had erotic scenes set in the subway system. Jack Deveau's last film, *Times Square Strip*, was shot at the Gaiety, a famous Times Square strip club. And all of them had sex scenes with three or more multiple partners and ostensible strangers. These films demonstrate that pornographic photographic media can make a unique contribution to the history of sexuality.

Sex, Historical Evidence, and Photographic Media

Historically, most of the physical evidence of sex disappears without a trace. Reproductive heterosexual sex leaves historical traces in the form of children, but that is only a small proportion of all heterosexual activity. Other historical traces show up in the form of demographic and epidemiological statistics such as birth rates or rates of sexually transmitted diseases. But these sources often convey little about the specificities of the sex itself, about either the sequence or character of sex acts, positions, and duration or the psychological and social meaning of particular sex acts. And apart from pornography— whether as prose, illustration, or photography—empirical documentation of homosexual sex is even scarcer.

While sex and sexuality are interrelated phenomena, we generally know much more about the history of sexuality than of sex. In an important essay, David Halperin posed the question, does sex have a history or is it only a natural fact? "Unlike sex," he countered, "sexuality is a cultural production."[19] Sexuality refers to broader orientations to sexual conduct, identities, and attitudes. Sex, however, has a specific meaning. It refers specifically to the corporeal practices of pleasure and desire that include various kinds of intercourse, but also including varieties of stimulation, penetration, and/or genital manipulation.

Though sex is indeed a physical act, it still has a history, a somewhat fraught one to be sure. Much of our historical knowledge about sex is either ambiguous or obscured by lies or half-truths or exists in the form of open secrets and complicated evasions.[20] In many historical periods (as well as in other cultures), it was covered over with shame or considered private.[21] As physical acts, acts of sexual intercourse may appear to share common corporeal mechanics, but as Carole Vance has argued, "Physically identical sexual acts may have varying social significance and subjective meaning depending on how they are defined and understood in different cultures and historical periods."[22]

Yet while many different kinds of historical sources enable us to understand the development of the cultural patterns that shape sexuality, we have much less evidence about the kind of sex that took place within many of those cultural frameworks.[23] Most of our historical information about sex and sexual practices is circumstantial, derived from marriage manuals, volumes of *ars erotica*, fiction, police reports, popular anthropology books on sexual curiosities, sexological research, and memoirs.[24] Pornographic drawings and writings may also offer some more explicit information.[25] Indeed, while sex is shaped by social norms and personal attitudes, it is scripted and enacted within different historical or cultural contexts—in some periods, certain acts may be proscribed and in others widely practiced.[26]

One needs only to contemplate the evidence of sex after the AIDS epidemic to the many accounts of sex before the epidemic to realize that sex indeed has a history.[27] In 1997, Larry Kramer, long a critic of the gay sexual scene of the 1970s, wrote that "you cannot fuck indiscriminately with multiple partners, who are also doing the same, without spreading disease, a disease that has for many years also carried death. Nature always extracts a price for sexual promiscuity."[28] Clearly Kramer's comment presumes a historical and sociological trajectory opposed to that of Moore or Danto. Nevertheless, at the time the AIDS epidemic appeared to be a crisis not only about gay male sexuality in general, but also about the kinds of sex that gay men in particular engaged in— fellatio, fisting, anal intercourse, casual sex with strangers and with multiple partners. For example, anal intercourse, one of the most efficient means of transmitting HIV, was, and still is, considered by many gay men to be one of the most valued aspects of their sexuality—for both the pleasure it yields, but also the complicated meanings it may have. As Joseph Sonnabend, a prominent AIDS physician, once argued, "The rectum is a sexual organ, and it deserves the respect a penis gets and a vagina gets. Anal intercourse has been the central activity for gay men and some women for all of history. . . . We have to recognize what is hazardous, but at the same time, we shouldn't undermine an act that's important to celebrate."[29]

AIDS changed the social context of sex, and many gay men clearly felt that sex in general, after the advent of AIDS, offered potentially less pleasure and more danger than before. "Sex is just a completely different thing now," porn star / director Al Parker exclaimed. "The entire time you're having sex you're thinking: 'I'm having sex with everybody this person ever had sex with. I wonder what he's done and where he's been and if he's positive or negative. I wonder if I'm giving him anything.' If you can keep a hard-on while all this is going on in your head, you're better than I am."[30]

Pornography has long played a special role in historical studies of sexual behavior and attitudes. Erotic drawings and paintings, pornographic fiction, ethnographic travel accounts, and sexually candid memoirs have served as sources for explicit accounts of sex in different historical periods.[31] For example, K. J. Dover's study of Greek homosexuality relies extensively on the portrayal of sexual interactions on Greek vase paintings, which show that "every point on a scale of intimacy is fully represented."[32] In *The Tears of Eros*, the culminating volume of Georges Bataille's lifelong study of eroticism, violence and death also drew upon visual representations of the erotic from Paleolithic cave paintings to the work of modern French painter Baltus.[33] Another prominent example is Steven Marcus's *The Other Victorians: A Study of Sexuality and Pornography in Mid-Nineteenth-Century England*. In addition to drawing on medical studies of gynecology and sexually transmitted diseases, Marcus also explored the extensive collection of pornography amassed by Henry Spence Ashbee, nineteenth-century pornographic novels, and the remarkable, eleven-volume anonymous sexual memoir *My Secret Life*.[34] In *Governing Pleasures:*

Pornography and Social Change in England, 1815–1914, Lisa Z. Sigel turned to pornography as a means to explore the "sexual imaginary" of nineteenth-century England. For her, pornography, of all varieties (writing, art, and photography), reflects sexuality like "a series of broken mirrors—that reflects, refracts and distorts a picture of sexuality" and shows a shift from the sexual representation as a political expression to one of consumer pleasures.[35] And Paul Deslandes has explored how erotic representations in gay porn magazines both reflected and validated the sexual lives of gay men during the seventies in Britain.[36]

However, photographic media with their indexical qualities offer a unique perspective.[37] It can show 'real' sexualized bodies and genitalia, both in dramatized sexual tableau (in still photographs) and performed in motion pictures. Because the photographic trace is recorded at a moment in time and then stored for future viewing, photographic images are automatically always historical representations.[38] In pioneering works, both Linda Williams and Thomas Waugh have drawn on photographic media to explore sexuality, its history, and its representations. In *Hard Core: Power, Pleasure and the "Frenzy of the Visible,"* Williams explores the generic and rhetorical conditions that underlie the photographic and filmic representability of sex.[39] And in *Hard to Imagine: Gay Male Eroticism in Photography and Film from Their Beginnings to Stonewall*, Waugh outlines a sweeping history of gay male sexuality in Europe and North America, drawing on both vernacular and art photography as well as early film. His work demonstrates the unique political role that photographic media—precisely because of their indexical character—have played to validate homoerotic sexual expression and the role it can have establishing community networks.[40] More recently, Tim Dean, in *Unlimited Intimacy: Reflections on the Subculture of Barebacking*, used contemporary condom-less pornographic videos as ethnographic evidence about the barebacking subculture among gay men.[41]

For the pioneering film theorist Siegfried Kracauer, the historical significance of film rests on its ability to "record and reveal physical reality," giving it the capacity to record things normally unnoticed, the fortuitous, the fragmentary, as well as the ephemeral phenomena of daily life, as an indexical archive.[42] But Kracauer also always stressed the double status of photographic media— as material objects that can be seen for their sensory surface (their indexicality, their realist images) and as symbolic representations that derive their power from the "evidential force" (as argued by both Roland Barthes and the historian of photography John Tagg) of the photographic media.[43]

In pornographic films, the line between fictional fantasies and cinematic realism is often blurred. Though they represent sexual fantasies, hardcore pornographic films depend upon what Roland Barthes called "reality effects" ("real" erections, "real" fucking, and "real" orgasms) to authenticate the sexual narratives that are their primary content. In that respect, they are somewhat like documentaries.[44] Softcore porn, lacking "real" erections, penetrative intercourse, and ejaculations, is but a pale simulation of sex. It is impossible to portray "actual" sex without actual sex in cinematic pornography. Only hardcore pornographic cinema has the capacity to preserve live acts of sex. This reliance on reality effects is what distinguishes pornographic films, videos, and live Internet scenes from all other genres of pornography. And together with the penetration, the gritty reality of skin, genitalia, and mucous membranes enhances the "realistic" representation of sex. Yet it is also an ambiguous medium, which is why Williams warns Tim Dean about using documentary-style bareback pornographic video as a form of ethnography. "Pornography on film, video or on the Internet," she cautions, "is always two contradictory things at once: documents of sexual acts and fantasies spun around knowing the pleasure or pain of those acts."[45] This warning is equally applicable to treating pornographic photographic media as straightforward historical documents. Pornographic film is a portal into a fantasy world, in which so many things are not "realistic" at all (the mechanical ease of sex, the lack of resistance, the readiness of all the participants to do anything), in addition to also appearing to be a document of "real sex."[46] And, in fact, the fantasies appear "more real" because they are "caught" on film, and thus confirm the material viability of those fantasies for viewers.[47]

Porn films record "sexual scripts"—that is, the scripts prevailing in a culture, among both the viewers and the filmmakers. But like any other historical documents, porn films must be critically examined. It is important to date them correctly, determine authorship, clarify their point of view, and authenticate them.[48] In addition, editing can affect the meaning of a film sequence or obscure some of the conditions that make it useful as historical evidence. But the challenge of using a pornographic film as a historical source in the history of sexuality is distinguishing the "fantasy script" from what the film may reveal about society's prevailing sexual scripts. And in fact, being able to distinguish them is itself historically valuable information. As Simon and Gagnon point out, the "cultural scenarios" and "interpersonal scripts" that shape sexual behavior utilize the symbols, norms, and social cues that are prevalent at the time of the film's production.[49] Though the fantasy may be widely held at the period when the porn film was produced, it is important to authenticate the fantasy and within it the realistic detail must be distinguished from genre's rhetorical conventions.[50] For example, the standard practice for the male to withdraw from his partner when he has an orgasm is a rhetorical convention of contemporary pornographic filmmaking; it is not necessarily a standard sexual practice.[51]

Most pornography before the introduction of photographic media incorporated a significant degree of fantasy through fictional exaggeration or artistic license: it often included descriptions of long penises, ample breasts, or complicated couplings. Still photographs give a "realistic," but static, view of attractive bodies. Cinematic pornography initiated a new phase in the historiography of sex and sexuality; it was only then that actual acts of sex could be recorded. The earliest pornographic films date back approximately one hundred years, to the early twentieth century. While those early films are not documentaries and were certainly not intended as documentaries but were meant to entertain and to stimulate arousal, they nevertheless are also historical documents of sexual behavior. But unlike the erotic drawings, paintings, phallic artifacts, and pornographic writing of the past, porn films have rarely been drawn upon as a source in the writing of the history of sexuality.

In pornographic films, the physical act of sex is embedded not only in grand cultural scenarios or the intrapsychic fantasies of the individual, but also in the interactional scripts of everyday life—the gestures, bodily rhythms, sexual comportments, and social interactions—basically, the social fabric of daily life as it was lived at the time. The films may be considered as historical evidence of the sociohistorical process within which they enable fantasies or take on sexual meaning and exercise an erotic effect. That effect ultimately depends upon the discursive system within which pornographic films are viewed. It is here, through Kracauer's "realism of the ephemeral," that pornographic films offer some "evidential force" about sex and its interactional and historical context.[52]

Sex as a Public Practice: Memory, Photography, and Film

Gay writers, historians, and sociologists have shown that public sexual activity flourished among men long before 1970s.[53] In a world where homosexual desire and conduct are stigmatized and criminalized, finding sexual partners was an important, though often a dangerous activity for gay men. Men who experience homosexual desire do not grow up within communities that recognize homosexuality and as a consequence are not socialized into cultural patterns "appropriate" for homosexual men. They grow up isolated in scattered families. Since homosexuality was a stigmatized and socially "invisible" form of sexual desire, it was also difficult to identify other men with similar desires. Cruising was the basic activity, the precondition for community among gay men, but successful cruising required decoding a complicated series of signs and at the same time the need to exploit the opportunity for anonymous and swift sexual encounters.[54] Over time, men in search of homosexual sex developed a network of places where they were able to manage the social and logistical contingencies of their stigmatized desires.[55] Many of these places were in fact public spaces—accessible to strangers or other members of local communities.[56] Sex in those public spaces became a common occurrence.[57]

After Stonewall, public sex became even more public—and by public sex, I mean sex that takes place in front others (in a group or in a public space) who are not necessarily in any sort of intimate relationship.[58] The men interviewed in *Gay Sex in the 70s* document that development. As they note, the new openness in cruising quickly turned into sex—in doorways, unused corners of subway stations, or alleyways. Cruising also led more directly to sex in "private" spaces. As Rodger MacFarlane explains, "I have been walking down Madison Avenue on the way to my office before work, eight-thirty in the morning, and seen a man on the street, exchanged [matchbook] covers and have sex during lunch in his office. . . . I have turned the corner at Christopher Street, smiled at somebody. He said, you got a minute; we went upstairs. Everybody I know has those kinds of stories from those days."[59] Photographer Tom Bianchi also recalls, "The subways were always a sexual opportunity, even when they were crowded. If you saw somebody that was sort of attractive on the subway . . . you could move in that direction and you might find yourself with a hard-on pressed against you. . . . Oh my God, we're both getting off at Sheridan Square . . . you've got somebody back at your apartment before your dinner date."[60] Gay men embraced the public places they cruised and where they had sex. And these places—the baths, the trucks, the piers—became landmarks of the gay male sexual subculture. This culture not only had its own folkways and myths but also helped to cultivate a new eroticized sense of self characterized by "a love of strangers," the allure of anonymity and adventure, and membership in a sexual community.[61] For some, participation in the sexual scene had political significance. A number of Lovett's subjects explained their participation in public sex in part as a reaction to the sexual repression that they had suffered growing up. Samuel Delany recalls, in his memoir, his astonishment upon seeing his first orgy at a bathhouse in 1963: "What the orgy at the baths pictured with frightening range and intensity, was a fact that flew in the face of that whole fifties image [of homosexuality]. . . . Whether male, female, working or middle class, the direct sense of political power comes from the apprehension of massed bodies. . . . But what this experience said was that there was a population—not of individual homosexuals . . . not of hundreds, not of thousands, but rather millions of gay men and that history had, actively and already, created for us whole galleries of institutions, good and bad, to accommodate our sex."[62] Participation in public sex (at a bathhouse, porn theater, or other locale) gave many gay men a chance to exchange sexual knowledge and learn new modes of feeling and thinking. It also allowed heteronormative pretenses to be dropped and separated sex from the distortions of closeted emotional dynamics. New York's raunchy sexual landscape generated a rich body of personal stories and in later years achieved a mythological status—as iconic references: "the trucks," "the piers," and "the tubs."

Public sex thrived in those parts of New York that were devastated by the city's industrial decline—the empty piers along the Hudson River, the converted loft spaces in SoHo, and the opening up of bars and sex clubs away from residential neighborhoods. A whole geography of sexual encounters was created. As the men in the film repeatedly confirm, plenty of gay male sex took place in public: out on the decaying Christopher Street piers, in the trucks parked under the elevated Westside Highway, in the Rambles in Central Park, in the showers at YMCAs, in the public toilets of department stores and libraries, and in the back rows of movie houses on Forty-Second Street. "You did not care," photographer Alvin Baltrop observed, "about the broken down, the danger, the dirty, the smell, the raunchiness. You cared about meeting someone and having sex."[63] The men interviewed in *Gay Sex in the 70s* provide an inventory of venues where gay sex took place in New York City during the 1970s.[64]

The piers were perhaps the most "operatic" of New York City's public sex venues during the seventies. They were more public than almost any other site—possibly more accessible to the public than many of the secluded groves in public parks where men had sex. Anyone could walk onto the piers at any time of day and there would be sex taking place. Not only were they grand stages for public sex, they also inspired and actually "showed" the work of painters and graphic artists like David Wojnarowicz, Gordon Matta-Clark, and Keith Haring. Photographers (such as Vito Acconci, Peter Hujar, Alvin Baltrop, and Arthur Tress) and writers (such as Andrew Holleran, Edmund White, and David Wojnarowicz) documented the activity at the piers.[65]

As the port of New York declined throughout the 1950s and the shipping industry had gradually abandoned piers along the elevated West Side Highway (a nearby section collapsed in 1973) near Greenwich Village, the docks and the buildings that had once served ferries, ocean liners, and cargo ships were empty and had begun to decay. Christopher Street, lined with bustling gay bars, was only a few blocks away. During daytime, gay men wandered down to the piers to sunbath, often nude, wearing only underwear or jock straps; during nighttime, men stalked each other inside the rotting structures. "There were thousands of people fucking in the dark" at the piers, Rodger MacFarlane recalled in *Gay Sex in the 70s*. "Every day of the week. No matter what the weather." But the piers were also dangerous. They were neither locked nor maintained nor inspected—and occasionally, in the dark, men fell through holes in the floor or rotting wood. The men lounging around the piers during the daytime periodically sighted floating corpses in the Hudson River near the piers.[66]

At the end of Christopher Street, under the elevated West Side Highway and near the piers, was where "the trucks" parked. After unloading their cargo, commercial trucks that brought produce and other goods to the city routinely parked under the elevated West Side Highway overnight, with the backs unlocked. Like the piers, every night the empty trucks were typically filled with hundreds and hundreds of men having sex in the dark. The stale smell of sex, sweat, and poppers emanated from the trucks. At one point, a street vendor parked a cart there selling food, soda, water, and even lubricant, but the trucks, like the piers, were also dangerous—pickpockets, police, and gay bashers occasionally raided them.

The porn theater also created a unique form of public space in which various kinds of sexual exchanges could take place—cinematic representation of sex (heterosexual or gay, softcore and later hardcore) on the screen and real sexual activity in the audience.[67] In the sixties, the live action in the audience often surpassed the erotic appeal of the relatively innocuous beefcake shorts and rather lugubrious softcore narrative features. Even later more explicit pornographic films often imitated situation comedies or amateurish melodramas. But pornography also celebrated gay male sexual activity, though, as Rodger MacFarlane observed in *Gay Sex in the 70s*, "Pornography couldn't compete with real life. . . . Anything that was in pornography you could have in abundance—on the street, any day, walk in any gym, more beautiful men, more dick, more available dick, right out the door into their apartment, the party starts in an hour, you can go in the backroom right now. It was like life was a pornographic film." That glaring disparity encouraged some porn directors to go out and shoot what was going on in public, on the streets, in the porn theater, at the bathhouse, and on the piers. Ironically, forty-five or fifty years later, pornography is a primary form of evidence that we have of the gay sex that actually took place in the 1970s.

In addition to the video clips (none of which include sexually explicit scenes) taken from homo-realist porn films, *Gay Sex in in the 70s* is also illustrated by many still photographs—of street scenes, gay pride marches, and people cruising and having sex on the piers, in the trucks, and at many other sites. In addition to still photos used in the film, photographers Alvin Baltrop and Tom Bianchi, both interviewees, have published books documenting the sexual scenes on the piers and Fire Island.[68] One of the other men interviewed, Barton Benes, was an artist who created small ceramic shards with the photographic headshots of men who died of AIDS. Believing that "you can tell a lot about a civilization through its artifacts," Benes frequently used photographic images in unusual forms (like the "shards") to commemorate the dead.[69] And while photographic images may ultimately lack the emotional resonance associated with the memory images of the living, photographs and even pornographic movies preserve some historical evidence of the quotidian sex lives of gay men in the seventies.[70]

New York's Homo-Realist Porn: Hardcore Pornography as Historical Document

During the 1970s, New York's crumbling urban infrastructure and industrial decay, high crime rates, heightened racial tensions, and proliferation of the effects of the sexual revolution—promiscuous sexuality, pornography, massage

Table 3.1
1970s New York Homo-Realist Porn Films

Title	Release date	Director
The Back Row	1972	Jerry Douglas (as Doug Richards)
Left-Handed	1972	Jack Deveau
Bijou	1972	Wakefield Poole
Underground	1973	Peter de Rome
Wanted: Billy the Kid	1975	Jack Deveau
Hot House	1977	Jack Deveau
The Voyeur	1978	Avery Willard (as Bruce King)
A Night at the Adonis	1978	Jack Deveau
Muscle Bound	1978	Arch Brown
Pier Groups	1979	Arch Brown
The Subway	1980	Ian McGraw
Times Square Strip	1982	Jack Deveau

parlors, nudity, and prostitution—represented for many people the "metaphor for . . . the last days of American civilization."[71] Amid the chaos, a new style of filmmaking emerged that reflected the urban realities of 1960s and 1970s New York.[72] The development of faster film, handheld sixteen-millimeter cameras, and lightweight quartz-iodine lamps inspired young documentary filmmakers like Richard Leacock and D. A. Pennebaker to shoot dramatic documentaries set in New York in the style of cinema verité, an outgrowth of postwar neo-realism, anthropological filmmaking, and the French nouvelle vague.[73] Filmmakers like John Cassavetes made improvisatory dramatic features in the same style. Cassavetes sought to capture the city with an apparent spontaneity that moved seamlessly from street and sidewalk into bars, jazz clubs, rehearsal halls, and tenements and showed the city in all its messy fullness: dilapidated storefronts, trash cans, and abandoned buildings.

Hardcore porn movies had only begun to appear in American theaters in June 1969, coincidently the same month that the Stonewall riots launched the gay liberation movement. Most of the gay hardcore movies shown in theaters were either cheaply made sixteen-millimeter shorts originally produced for private distribution or softcore features with extraneous sex scenes inter-jected.[74] Hardcore porn films represented a shift away from the idolization of the male as an object of homosexual desire (as in beefcake photos and films) to one that stressed gay men as active agents of homosexual desire.[75] Early in 1972, *Boys in the Sand* (directed by Wakefield Poole) opened at the Fifty-Fifth Street Playhouse (a mainstream movie theater) in Manhattan. Shot on Fire Island for a mere four thousand dollars, it set a series of explicit sex scenes within a loose thematic frame of fantasy at the popular gay resort—a beauti-ful man rising out of the sea and a beautiful man appearing after a magic pill was thrown into a pool. Only one of the scenes shows a sexual encounter resulting from strangers cruising, though that is shown to be taking place only in their fantasies. Yet it was a new type of hardcore porn film—affirmative and idealistic. It was a huge success and ran for many months, drawing both gay and straight audiences. This was before *Deep Throat* and other straight porn chic classics were released. But even before *Boys in the Sand*'s run at the Fifty-Fifth Street Playhouse was over, other local filmmakers began make other gay hardcore porn films.

One of the first films to be released after *Boys in the Sand* was Jerry Douglas's *The Back Row*—it opened at the Fifty-Fifth Street Playhouse, immediately after *Boys in the Sand* closed. It was also the first of what I call the homo-realist films.[76] Though it was not shot in the cinema verité style used by later homo-realist directors, it nevertheless resembled a travel documentary: a handsome gay man (Casey Donovan) cruises a new visitor arriving from Montana (George Payne) at the Port Authority Bus Terminal and basically takes him (leads him/follows him) on a tour of New York's gay sexual scene: playing cat and mouse on the subway, visiting a sex shop, and finally ending up at a porn theater near Forty-Second Street and an orgy in the theater's men's room.

The movie's preamble shows a meticulously choreographed scene between a young man and a sailor sitting in the back row of movie theater—they are gesturing, rubbing crotches, and shuffling their feet while moving toward each other. Eventually, they nod and open their flies, the young man goes down on the sailor's cock and eventually jerks him off.

Once Donovan and Payne cruise each other at the Port Authority, Donovan takes off and Payne basically follows him (in part because Payne is too timid to approach Donovan directly). Yet they constantly cruise each other—rubbing their crotches and opening their flies on the subway, carefully examining the sex toys at a sex shop. Eventually they go to the porn theater, where they cruise some more in the back of the theater, attempt to have sex in the men's room, get interrupted. Donovan then becomes engaged in a full-on three-way sex scene in the men's room. Payne watches. There is no spoken dialogue; all the communication is visual—gestural and positional signaling take place in every sex scene of the film. In his 1978 ethnography of public sex, sociologist Edward Delph called the world of homosexual public sex "the silent community," a social world that is without verbal exchanges or communications.[77] Silence was required by the public settings (such as toilets, parks, beaches, and movie theaters), primarily in order to avoid detection by nearby nonparticipants. In this silent world, whether or not sex takes places depends upon initiating a "series of significant communications, and [being] encouraged to continue the gestural conversation. Therefore the social world is transformed into a wide open arena of possible sexual encounters albeit a silent one."[78] Donovan and Payne move through this silent world until the very end of the movie, at which point they make friendly overtures, abandon the sexual stalking, and finally begin to have an energetic friendly conversation (as it were, offline).

Left-Handed was the other hardcore gay film released immediately after *Boys in the Sand*. Made by Jack Deveau, it was shot in the cinema verité style. In fact, Deveau was the primary creator of the homo-realist porn genre.[79] Like almost all of Deveau's films, *Left-Handed* was a heavily plotted film that tended toward melodrama. The film showed a cross-section of gay male life in Manhattan in the early seventies. The plot revolves around three young men: an antique dealer, his hustler boyfriend, and their pot dealer. The hustler seduces the straight man, but when the straight man becomes emotionally involved and begins to explore homosexuality (even going so far as to participate in a gay orgy) the hustler loses interest in him. While this film is not made in a strictly documentary mode, it does portray "a day in the life" of typical New York City gay men in 1972—for example, the hustler/boyfriend stops in a small local park on the way to meet his boyfriend to have sex in the restroom. The film is shot in the rough, spontaneous style of cinema verité.

Several homo-realist films had scenes in the New York subway system. In *The Back Row*, Jerry Douglas showed his two protagonists cruising each other and playing with their flies, while in Peter de Rome's *Underground* two men cruise and stalk each other in the subway, until they find an empty car where they covertly (as possible) engage in anal sex. In Ian McGraw's *The Subway*, the film's protagonist wanders throughout the subway system: cruising on platforms, in subway cars, and having sex in subway restrooms (the NYC subway system once had functioning bathrooms at every station), passageways (one is the passageway at the Canal Street Q, N, & R station), odd corners, or an abandoned section of a subway station.

Arch Brown's *Pier Groups* (1979) appears to be the only gay porn film that was set in or featured the piers. In some respects, it is the most documentary-like of all the homo-realist films. The setup is very simple. The film opens with two gay men waking up, engaging in oral sex, and masturbating. One of them then calls a fellow employee (who is in bed with his wife) and asks him to check out an abandoned pier to prepare submitting a bid for its demolition. While one of the gay men goes off to work, the straight employee puts on his hard hat and heads off to the piers. Before he leaves for work, the gay man's boyfriend gets a call from his job telling him to take the day off. So he heads down to the piers not too far behind the man in the hard hat. After that, we see the guy in the hard hat walk through the pier, taking notes, making structural notations, and passing by all kinds of sex (including a couple of scenes involving the boyfriend). The man in the hard hat looks on impassively and just keeps going on his rounds and doing his job. Though this movie has spoken dialogue at the beginning, there is almost no verbal communication. At the end, the hard hat goes back to his wife and the boyfriend back to his apartment. The hard hat's attitude illustrates the casual intersection of gay and straight men (and perhaps a degree of familiarity or even acceptance) in these "public" venues. One of the men in *Gay Sex in the 70s* observed a similar intersection. The piers were across the street from the meatpacking district, and at lunchtime the men from the meatpacking business would eat their lunch sitting along the sides of the pier and "watch the guys having sex. They would laugh or they would go over and join in."

Jack Deveau's *A Night at the Adonis* (1978) was made in the late seventies and is the culmination of the hybrid/Deveau style of homo-realism. It portrays the well-known porn theater as a community center where friends interact with a cross-section of sex hungry men, meeting up to have impersonal sex with friends, strangers, the theater's employees, or the regular characters who routinely stop by. Sex takes place throughout the Adonis, in the seats (in the balcony and the back rows), in the passageways, in the offices, behind the counters, and in the men's room, the site of a grand orgy. The sexual community at the Adonis contrasts sharply with "the silent community" that exists in *The Back Row*. Everyone here is talking. Released in 1978, it demonstrates the evolution away from the "silent community" of the pre-Stonewall era to what sociologist Etienne Meunier calls "collective intimacy" later in the seventies.[80] Some of the men at the Adonis are friends, others are regulars, and the man running the juice bar acts as the guide to a young "management trainee" (who got the gig through the "placement office at his college"). The juice bar manager explains the social protocols governing the sexual action that is taking place at the Adonis and characterizes each of the regulars by their cruising styles, pickup lines, or sexual proclivities. "In my experience," he explains, "men fall into three categories: One, 'got a match?' Two, 'what time is it?' And three, 'you live around here?'" People keep propositioning the young "management trainee" who turns everyone down because he has chosen to act professionally and is serious about learning the business, but the juice bar manager dismisses the trainee's reserve. "The only way to learn this business," he explains. "If you're not willing to play yourself, you shouldn't be running a playground." Thus *A Night at the Adonis* is almost a parable and shows the progressive development of a community that has emerged from the world of public sex.[81]

The homo-realist porn film hews to a fine line between documentary and fantasy; it attempts to integrate both sexual fantasy and the actual world. It is what film scholar Leo Braudy has called an "open" form of cinema in which "the world of the film is a momentary frame around an ongoing reality. The objects and the characters existed before the camera focused on them and they will exist after the film is over."[82] Thus homo-realism offered another kind of reality effect—one perfectly suited to the historical period immediately following the Stonewall riots. It both confirmed and celebrated an actually existing sexual culture.

Learning from Pornography

The homo-realist porn movies allow us to reconstruct the sexual scripts of public sex in the 1970s. They show how cruising, physical location, and sex itself contributed to a complex sexual geography of New York City. They identify the spaces where public sex took place during the 1970s—the bathhouses, porn theaters, and abandoned piers—and are almost nonexistent today, at least in the form that they once had. In addition, the decaying industrial city—with both its obscure and well-populated sexual spaces, is also gone or at least transformed. But they also illustrate how the physical environment created sexual opportunities, shaped the sexual action, and specified the sexual participants.[83] They show how sex roles, age, style, class, and ethnicity played out in the public spaces where gay men had sex during the 1970s.

The homo-realist films are important not only because they authenticate and amplify the memory images of men who were sexually active during the 1970s but for what the films show of the surface flux of gay men's sex lives in that period: their physical comportment, their self-presentation, and the interactional strategies of people unconscious of their situation, unaware of how their presence will shape history and thus unable to read the signs of their times.[84] Nor are these films purely ethnographic or documentary in style; most of them embed the sexual activities in fictive narrative contexts—the hick cowboy visiting New York, the gay man out cruising and having public sex while a lover is out of town, tensions in a relationship between a young kept man and his lover, a man coming out or even falling in love. They show cruising techniques, pickup lines, interactional styles, typical topics of conversation, and bodily comportment—with physical body types and hairstyles (two of the most noticeable markers of anachronisms in pornography made in different historical periods).

And most importantly, they reveal what appear to be trivial and uninteresting aspects of day-to-day behavior that are fraught with more significant implications. Many of these sorts of behavior play an important role in the reproduction of a community's culture. As Kracauer notes, "The inconspicuous surface-level expressions . . . by virtue of their unconscious nature, provide unmediated access to the fundamental substance of the state of things."[85]

These pornographic films portray and accentuate those very qualities that define the particular character of the sexual experiences and encounters of gay men in the decade between Stonewall and discovery of AIDS. In Simon and Gagnon's theory of sexual scripts, intrapsychic fantasies, cultural scenarios, and interpersonal (or interactional) scripts play an important role in the shaping of sexual conduct: they "specify appropriate sex objects, aims, and desirable qualities of self-other relations but also instruct in times, places, sequences of gesture and utterance and, among the most important, what the actor and his or her co-participants (real or imagined) are assumed to be feeling."[86] For the most part, at least in the twentieth century and in most Western cultures, homosexual sexual scripts have grown up outside the standard regulatory institutions of sexuality (primarily heterosexual dating and courtship or monogamous procreative marriage). Many homosexual sexual scripts were "situational" or "opportunistic" and were organized around master statuses such as gender roles (masculine, feminine), age, or class. Certain locations (such as restrooms, parks, porn theaters) could be characterized as "sexual opportunity structures."[87] The importance of specific locations (by offering sexual opportunities) among gay men grew out of the historical reliance on casual contact, cruising, and single-sex-segregated environments (public restrooms, bathhouses, porn theaters, prisons, etc.). Sociologist Edward Delph noted that such spaces attracted distinct clienteles: "The Canal Street subway toilet, for example, is heavily used by working-class people, of various ethnic groups, during the workweek. Upper east side IRT [now the 4 and 5 subway lines] subway toilets, reflecting the neighborhoods above the ground, tend to be rather homogeneous white, middle class and white collar. Gay bars located in the isolated extreme West Village beacon to 'western' and 'S-M' oriented identities. Subway toilets situated in West Village stations attract the same types. Those who find these categories of individuals of sexual interest will also be drawn to them."[88] In addition, these films embodied many of the period's sexual assumptions. Most of these films show their characters on the streets of the city and often also show a door or an entranceway from the street to either a public space where cruising and sexual encounter will take place or a private apartment where strangers will have sex. Thus public sex (or sex in general) is not only linked to real places but also embedded in the routine patterns of movement and familiar locations of everyday city life. An analysis of these homo-realist films reveals historically specific patterns of behavior and culturally generic traits:

1 Public cruising plays a prominent role, even in cases that lead to sex inside private interiors.
2 Sexual encounters in these films usually takes place between strangers.
3 Sex seems to be available in many "everyday" locations—subways, apartment building basements, abandoned industrial warehouses and piers that are visible from pedestrian passageways—as well as in porn theaters, bathhouses, and other "protected" spaces
4 Location often defines the encounter as a sexual situation, and sexual activity is usually initiated by some sort of sexual gesture—such as grabbing a crotch, feeling an ass, or kneeling to suck a cock.
5 Within that location all participants take responsibility for maintaining the "definition of the public setting as a sexual situation" through

supportive exchanges between participants or by initiating oral sex, etc.

6 Smoking marijuana or using poppers before or during a sexual encounter is almost ubiquitous.

Homo-realist porn films allow us to identify the underlying norms and conventions that guided public sex among gay men during the seventies. The presence of stigma, homophobia, and illegality constrained what Erving Goffman called "the interaction order" as it applied to gay men at the time. The "interpersonal scripts" identified by Gagnon and Simon drew upon the interaction order's "systems of enabling conventions, in the sense of ground rules for a game, the provisions of a traffic code or the rules of syntax of a language."[89] An impromptu sexual encounter in a public space, whether a subway, an abandoned pier, or a porn theater, consisted of focused face-to-face interactions that were sustained by maintaining cognitive and visual attention on fellow participants.[90] As Delph notes, "Individuals not only recognize, exchange, complement and reciprocally sustain the sexual claims of [other men], but through the subtle processes of significant gestural interests, identities, and roles without having to face the threat of painful rejection."[91] The films showed participants engaged in signaling fellow participants' entry and exit during a public encounter, initiating sex in the public setting, and the importance of reciprocal deference, especially through the reciprocity of sexual acts. Even the particular sex acts that took place were, to some extent, determined by the public space itself.[92] Oral sex was always central, while the anal sex was dependent on the physical setup: the missionary position was often logistically awkward, and anal sex while standing with fucking from behind the easiest. Of course, these actions were scripted and choreographed by the film's director or the performers, but they drew upon their unconscious assumptions of interpersonal scripts in the seventies. It would be possible to construct an ethnography of sexual encounters among gay men in the seventies using the homo-realist porn movies.[93] The films showed the interactional ground rules that governed public sex venues and that were necessary to establish a degree of trust among the participants, which, given the time period—with criminal sanctions and stigma against homosexuality, not to mention public sex—was itself quite remarkable. As such, they show "a plane of being, an engine of meaning, a world in itself."[94]

4

Porn's Historical
Unconscious
■■■■■■■■■■■■■■■■■■■■■■

Sex, Identity, and Everyday
Life in the Films of Jack
Deveau and Joe Gage

> Cinema is committed to communicate
> only by way of what is real.
> —Andre Bazin, *What Is Cinema? Vol. 1*

Porn is made within a historical and social context and is shaped by that context. In the 1970s, after two decades of debates about obscenity and pornography, the emergence of women's liberation in 1968, and the Stonewall riots for
gay liberation in 1969, the sexual revolution of the 1960s and 1970s was in full
swing. Softcore pornographic movies were shown in theaters across the country and had transitioned to hardcore in 1969. By the end of 1972, five feature-
length gay hardcore movies had been released in theaters in Los Angeles, San
Francisco, and New York. Wakefield Poole's *Boys in the Sand* opened in New
York in December 1971 and was an immediate critical and financial success
among both gay and straight audiences. It offered a new erotic template for the
gay male erotic imagination. The tortured sublimated violence in the surreal-
ist films of Kenneth Anger, the passive exhibitionism and campiness of Bob

Mizer's beefcake photography, the flamboyant ode to androgyny in Jack Smith's *Flaming Creatures*, and the blank eroticism of Andy Warhol's *Blow Job* or *My Hustler*—all examples of heavily coded and closeted homoeroticism—suddenly seemed outdated. The shift to hardcore was a milestone for gay men. The focus of beefcake publications had been on men as objects of desire, not homosexual men as agents of desire. Hardcore films, however, offered images, roles, and sexual scenarios that legitimated active sex in place of the worship of ideal bodies.[1]

Cinema Verité, Liberation, and Homo-Realism

During the 1970s, New York City was the frequent site of sex that took place in public—out on the decaying Christopher Street piers, in the trucks parked under the elevated Westside Highway, in the Rambles in Central Park, in the showers at YMCAs, in the public toilets of department stores and libraries, and in the back rows of movie houses on Forty-Second Street. These places were perceived as zones of "liberated" gay sexual culture.[2]

Heterosexual stag movies and theatrically screened softcore films made before 1969 rarely included homosexual scenes, and so when gay porn emerged, gay porn filmmakers initially developed scenarios that used plot devices drawn from situation comedies, TV melodramas, or idealized fantasy setups. However, the everyday reality of public sex in the city was more fantastic or more transgressive than many of the pornographic films. Responding to this, a small group of New York–based gay pornographic filmmakers—Jerry Douglas, Jack Deveau, and Joe Gage among them—sought to document the sexual culture that had emerged in the years before the Stonewall riots but which had become increasingly public afterward. These "homo-realists" developed a synthesis of documentary filmmaking with psychopolitical themes of sexual liberation.[3] They shot their movies in the style of cinema verité—using the naturalistic techniques that originated in documentary filmmaking and drawing on the style of editing and camera work that captured the raw and gritty feel of the city's sexual scene.[4]

The "pornographic realism" that emerged during this period offers a unique historical perspective on the daily realities of gay male sex lives during the 1970s and early 1980s. As film theorist Siegfried Kracauer proposed, the knowledge produced by motion-picture photography often resembles that produced by history—shot at one moment in time and stored for future viewing. Film captures, he argued, the "small random moments [that] constitute the dimension of everyday life, the matrix of all other modes of reality."[5] Pornographic films thus provided a record of many details of the typically unnoticed patterns of everyday life: the images of things so familiar, so habitual, and often so fleeting that filmmakers and contemporary spectators don't initially notice them. The homo-realist pornographic films of the 1970s captured knowledge of the patterns of gay life.

Like the neorealist movement among filmmakers that emerged in post–World War II Italy, these "homo-realist" filmmakers managed to combine a political perspective on sexual freedom and gay liberation with a form of erotic entertainment.[6] Among them were films by Jerry Douglas (under the name of Doug Richards), Jack Deveau, Arch Brown, Joe Gage (who shot films for P.M. Productions), Peter de Rome, and Avery Willard (under the name Bruce King). Many of the films were produced either by Jack Deveau's Hand-in-Hand Productions or by P.M. Productions, the production wing of New York's leading porn theater, the Park-Miller. These filmmakers made porn movies that explored the everyday lives of gay men during the first decade of gay liberation.

Everyday Life and Pornography

In everyday life, we maintain a sharp distinction between social reality and fantasy, but hardcore porn films combine sexual fantasy scenarios with a degree of realism that requires "real" sexual intercourse.[7] They portray a seemingly "real world" where the improbable and the desired take place—when, for instance, straight men drop their clothes without hesitation and have sex with other men in the locker room.

Many of the early gay porn movies portrayed sexual activity in idyllic or fantasy settings, primarily as a way of creating an imaginary world in which sex between men was free from the social, legal, and cultural obstacles that traditionally limited homosexual activity. Among the new wave of gay porn films in 1971 and 1972, Wakefield Poole's *Boys in the Sand* and *Bijou* were both fantasy features. For instance, Poole's *Boys in the Sand* was set on Fire Island, an idyllic vacation resort outside New York City, where a gay man sees a beautiful man arise from the sea or throw a magic pill into a backyard pool to produce a sexy man. Poole's second feature, *Bijou*, was also a fantasy film. Though set in a New York bathhouse, the sexual action was initiated by or set in fantasy contexts—that is, one removed from the course of everyday life.[8] For example, J. Brian's *Seven in a Barn* portrayed an orgy set in a barn in the California countryside. In these films, real sex was set in the context created by a fantasy scenario.[9]

Other early hardcore filmmakers developed films with melodramatic or comic plots like those used in Hollywood or television with explicit sexual action added somewhat arbitrarily, but Jack Deveau and Joe Gage made pornographic movies that engaged with the psychological challenges of a community emerging from a period of legal and social persecution. They created a unique strain of hardcore pornography that stands apart from the work of other hardcore filmmakers from the period.

Moreover, both Deveau and Gage shot their movies in the cinema verité style in order to record the sexual lifestyle that had begun to emerge during the sexual revolution—and after the Stonewall riots—of the late 1960s and 1970s, using naturalistic techniques that originated in documentary filmmaking to capture a rough and gritty feel. These films reveled in the sexual subculture that had emerged in the years immediately preceding Stonewall, amid the seedy, run-down, and unused industrial spaces that supplied so many opportunities for uninterrupted sexual activity with multiple and unknown partners. They all made a point to show the streets and the landmarks of the city's sexual landscape. But Deveau's movies also did something more. They explored the conflicts that gay men experienced during the 1970s between the vast field of sexual possibilities available and attempts to establish and maintain some sort of domestic life and other everyday activities.

Scenes from the Lives of Gay Men in the Golden Age of Promiscuity

Starting in 1971, Jack Deveau made a series of films that included sexually explicit (hardcore) scenes that explored the tensions and complications that arose between a new sense of sexual freedom that led to an increase in casual and impersonal sex and gay men's desire for intimacy and domestic relationships. In addition, he also went on to address the conflict between sexual availability and other aspects of a gay man's everyday life such as career, friendship, and community.

In the introduction to a catalog for a show of paintings and photographs portraying the domestic lives of lesbians and gay men, the show's curator, James Saslow, recounted an anecdote from his own life: "Before coming out to my father, I tested the waters by casually remarking that I'd met a gay couple who'd lived together for twenty years and had a nice relationship. 'People like that don't have relationships,' he sneered, 'they just have sex.' Before and after which, implicitly, they vanished into some limbo of suspended animation with no 'real life.'"[10]

Both Saslow and his father were partially correct—gay men did have long-term relationships that were meaningful, but many gay men, even ones in relationships, did have a lot of casual sex. The tension between the sexually exciting possibilities and the desire to create stable domestic relationships was explored by psychologist Charles Silverstein in *Man to Man: Gay Couples in America* (1981), written and published just before the advent of AIDS. One of the gay men interviewed by Silverstein summed up the situation that many gay men experienced during the 1970s:

> I have a lover, but we don't put any stress on fidelity. That's not the driving force in our life, but we don't lie to each other.
>
> Marriage is wonderful and warm and affectionate and all kinds of terrific things. One of the things it isn't is exciting, and I guess I just don't want to let go of that excitement. I've never articulated this before, but—I love the hunt. I love going out finding sex. I love cruising. I love going to the baths, cruising, prowling. . . . I'm not the most physically attractive man in the world; I'm not big and muscular. I'm twenty-five years older than most of the people, and I really like seducing and getting people to come home with me or doing it with me in the baths. I love sex itself, and I love to suck cock. I love to turn other men on because it turns me on, too.[11]

Silverstein found that the tension between the excitement of easy sex and desire to create a satisfactory domestic life with a long-term partner was a frequent source of conflict between gay male couples during that period.

Starting with his first film, *Left-Handed* (1972), and then in *Ballet Down the Highway* (1975), *Wanted: Billy the Kid*, (1976), *Hot House* (1977), *Dune Buddies* (1978), *A Night at the Adonis* (1978), *Fire Island Fever* (1979), and up until one of his last films, *The Boys from Riverside* (1981), Deveau's movies explored the lives of gay men in post-Stonewall New York.

Stonewall had legitimated, as many gay men at the time felt, "the promise of sex: free sex, better sex, lots of sex, sex without guilt, sex without repression, sex without harassment, sex at home and sex in the streets."[12] Though Deveau's films are porn films and include explicit sex, they also seriously explore the chaotic impact of the rampant sexual availability and above all the difficulties of forging a new sexual subculture that also made room for enduring romantic or domestic relationships and intimacy. Deveau's movies contain the DNA of their times.

Left-Handed, Deveau's first film, shows a cross-section of gay male life in Manhattan in the early seventies. A romantic melodrama, it focuses on an affair between a gay man (who happens to be a hustler) and a straight man (who happens to be a drug dealer)—an almost iconic story of the 1960s and the early seventies. Ray, the gay man, is challenged by a friend to seduce Bob, the straight man. Soon Ray and Bob embark on an affair, but as Bob becomes more emotionally involved and breaks up with his girlfriend, Ray loses interest in the sexually curious "straight" man. He declares that he is bored and wants something new. Thus *Left-Handed* introduces the theme that runs through much of Deveau's work—the challenges to establishing an intimate relationship in a period when sex has become easily available and less guilt-ridden.

Left-Handed also reflects the fluid boundary that existed between gay and sexual liberation in the early seventies. In the years immediately after Stonewall, the gay movement did not at first focus on the question of a gay identity, or even strictly on civil rights but on sexual liberation. Gay liberation, as Dennis Altman, one of its early theorists, noted, was "not only for those of us who are homosexuals, who are finding the courage and self-assurance to come out in public, but indeed . . . for everyone else." The early movement also emphasized "polymorphous perversity," the undifferentiated ability to take pleasure from all parts of the body.[13] Thus homosexual sex represented an expression of pleasure and love free from the social requirements of heterosexuality. *Left-Handed* acknowledges the sexual atmosphere of the period and includes a hardcore sex scene between Bob and his girlfriend, along with sex scenes in a tearoom and an antiques shop, several scenes between the gay man and his straight lover, and an orgy.

Deveau's films also address the tensions generated between promiscuous sex and other aspects of everyday life. *Ballet Down the Highway* (1975) is about a ballet dancer who has an affair with a straight truck driver. The affair interrupts his developing relationship with a fellow dancer, though they engage happily in a threesome with the truck driver. The film culminates in a dramatic scene in the dancer's apartment in which the straight man's straight friends discover the affair and go to the dancer's apartment to confront him, but all quite drunk, and instead of a confrontation, they all participate in an orgy. For the dancer, that is the end of the affair, and his new boyfriend, a fellow dancer, moves in. *Wanted: Billy the Kid* (1976) focuses again on a hustler, basically a struggling actor, who both earns his living and pays for essential needs such as his rent through prostitution. While sex seems to be freely available, most of it that Billy engages with is part of an economic exchange, and not as part of a personal relationship. In *Hot House* (1977), all the neighbors end up having sex with one another, despite various misunderstandings and minor abuses of hospitality. Thus, while most of the movies illustrate the conflict, they also show an acceptance of the situation.

Fire Island came to symbolize the wild promiscuity of the 1970s. Andrew Holleran's *Dancer from the Dance* and Larry Kramer's *Faggots* represent two opposed views on the centrality of the Fire Island experience. Holleran portrayed Fire Island as a sort of Paradise, though one with dark overtones, while Kramer ranted against what he saw as its devastating superficiality.[14] Deveau uses Fire Island to test his characters ability to resist the disruptions of sexual freedom. *Dune Buddies* (1978), unlike most of Deveau's other films, shows how one gay man refuses to accept the disruptions that promiscuous sex has had on his life. Set on Fire Island, it tells the story of a college professor who wants to get away from the sex that dominates his life in New York City on his summer vacation. "Career considerations aside," he explains, "I came to New York for the sex and that's exactly what I got. All the sex I wanted and more—in fact, too much! I got picked up on the way to work, on the way home from work and at work. It happened at the supermarket, the laundry. . . . It got so crazy, in fact, that I stopped enjoying it." When someone offers him a cheap rental for a month on Fire Island, he accepts hoping that he will have some peace and quiet. However, within his first twenty-four hours he has had so many uninvited sexual encounters—he cannot turn any of them down—that he decides to go back to the city and find another way to escape from the sex. He calls Fire Island paradise, but it's not what he needed. Deveau made another movie set on Fire Island to test another possibility. In *Fire Island Fever* (1979) a pair of lovers go to vacation on the island and decide to experiment by opening up their relationship. But they experience drug mishaps and fits of jealousy and thus decide to return to their previous status.

Deveau's most ambitious film to explore the ramifications of promiscuous sex was *A Night at the Adonis* (1978), set in the theater where most of his films were shown in New York and which was renowned for its untrammeled public sex. One former patron called it "a fuck palace."[15] The film was a tribute in part to the great role that porn theaters played in creating a sexual environment for gay men during the seventies and, in part, to Jerry Douglas's 1973 film *The Back Row*. *A Night at the Adonis* is considered to be one Deveau's best movies. Each of the film's characters ends up at the Adonis because some sexual or emotional disappointment leads him there as a distraction—for example, Jack Wrangler, goes to the Adonis when he fails to have sex with his boss, or like the "kept man" whose lover isn't spending enough time him. *A Night at the Adonis* is the most elaborate exploration of the tension between promiscuity and gay men's everyday lives.

Sex takes place throughout the Adonis, in the seats (in the balcony and the back rows) and passageways, in the offices, behind the counters, and in the men's room, the site of a grand orgy. Some of the men at the Adonis are friends, others are regulars, but everyone is there to have sex. People keep propositioning a young "management trainee" who turns everyone down because he has chosen to act professionally and is serious about learning the business, but the juice bar manager dismisses the trainee's reserve and admonishes him to acknowledge the sexual scene that exists at the Adonis: "The only way to learn this business," he explains. "If you're not willing to play yourself, you shouldn't be running a playground." Yet everyone ends up connected to the person with whom they started out wanting to have sex. In the world of the Adonis there are no boundaries that separate casual sex from everyday life.

The Boys from Riverside (1981), one of Deveau's last films, focuses on a couple celebrating their anniversary. They get into a fight before they start their dinner and both go off and end up having sex with various people—the doorman, the super's son, and so on. When they both return home, they find a messenger who was supposed to deliver an anniversary greeting having sex with the super's son. They make up and have sex.

Sex on the Road: Joe Gage's "Working Man's Trilogy"

The road movie as cinematic genre emerged after World War II and reflected both the advent of the automotive vehicle "as a fundamental expression of individuality" and the emergence of a mobile young suburban population looking for adventure.[16] It often showed the encounter between people from the cities and suburbs with people from the rural areas. The road movie also owed something to the documentary and was able to achieve a kind of intimacy through the cinema verité style. This combination of elements plus the exploration of male sexual desire were brought together by Joe Gage in his *Kansas City Trucking Co.* trilogy—*Kansas City Trucking Co.* (1976), *El Paso Wrecking Corp.* (1978) and *L.A. Tool and Die* (1979).

In 1975, Tim Kincaid, a TV commercial and film actor, shopped around a script for a gay hardcore road picture called *Highway Fantasies*. One person who saw it was a producer / theater owner who turned it down and remarked that he thought the title was "too soft." Eventually Kincaid, who adopted the name Joe Gage for his porn movies, and a friend raised the money to produce it themselves—and that movie became *Kansas City Trucking Co.* "I started off making it a journey," Gage said. "It was supposed to go from one place to another, and as I was writing, creating events that would illuminate character and would also be 'money events'—sexual episodes—I discovered that it was not only a journey, it was a journey of self-discovery."[17] Gage loved B-movies, Roger Corman horror movies, and biker movies like *The Wild One* (1950, starring Marlon Brando). "At the time, Wakefield [Poole] was bringing a very artistic, cultural sensibility" to the making of the gay hardcore movie, Gage recalled, "and I thought it would be great to have a sort of B-movie-Tom of Finland-Li'l Abner-balls-out-cartoon kind of moviemaking."[18]

Joe Gage's trilogy appeared as this transformation was under way. The emergence of gay identity as a political concept and as the focus of political organizing, however, took place in the large cities with large lesbian and gay communities. In the smaller cities and rural areas, the closet with all its ambiguities, contradictions, and evasions reigned supreme. And this was the world that Joe Gage took his camera into in order to portray the play of homosexual desire among men who lived outside the urban gay communities of New York, Los Angeles, and San Francisco. The trilogy can be seen as vivid documentary portrait of a submerged homoerotic masculine subculture among working-class men. It documents the ambivalence and reticence that was widespread among working-class and rural men during the late seventies. And the films include the women whose male partners explore their homosexual desires.

Kansas City Trucking Co. follows a trucker named Hank (played by Richard Locke) on a long haul to Los Angeles with a newly hired young man played by Steve Boyd who rides shotgun. Early porn star Jack Wrangler plays the dispatcher—he and Locke have a quickie before Locke goes on the road. Then Boyd, who at the beginning is dropped off by his girlfriend, has sexual fantasies about Wrangler as they drive to Los Angeles. Hank (Richard Locke) and his new sidekick jerk off together while on the road. Along the way, Locke and Boyd both fantasize about sex with men, experience flashbacks, or have sexual encounters along the way; and then at the end of the journey both join in an orgy at the truckers' bunkhouse in L.A.

Since *Kansas City Trucking Co.* did well with audiences and was financially successful, Gage decided to make a sequel, *El Paso Wrecking Corp.*, which launched almost exactly a year later. Again, it starred Richard Locke. Fred Halsted, the acclaimed director of *L.A. Plays Itself, Sex Garage,* and *Sex Tool,* shared equal billing with Locke. Even more than *Kansas City Trucking Co.*, *El Paso Wrecking Corp.* was the classic road movie / buddy film. When Locke and Halsted are fired from Kansas City Trucking, they get into a pickup truck and head to El Paso. Along the way, they stop at busy bars, public restrooms, and just on the side of the road to watch sex or to have it themselves.

Like all of the men in Gage's movies, they are neither gay nor straight, but both are equally up for any kind of sexual adventure. After Halsted has sex with a guy in the backroom of a bar while the guy's girlfriend watches, a homophobic patron picks a fight with them. Locke cautions Halsted, "You've got to learn to keep your hands to yourself."

> "Awh, shit I couldn't help it. Those two [the man and his girlfriend] were too much. Listen, Hank, no more guys. This time I mean it."

> "Yeah, I've heard that before." Locke replies, "Your dick gets you into more trouble than anyone I ever met."

The third picture, *L.A. Tool and Die*, was released a year after *El Paso Wrecking Corp.* Locke stars with Will Seagers, who plays Locke's love interest. Seagers is reluctant to commit himself to Locke and has a vivid memory of the death of an Army buddy in Vietnam whom he loved. But before he and Locke can get together, he must travel to L.A. for a job at L.A. Tool and Die. Locke agrees to meet him there. Locke almost misses his fateful get-together with Seagers when he gets caught up in an orgy in a restroom near where they are supposed to meet—but true to the spirit of the seventies, Seagers checks out the men's room and joins in himself. After their meeting Locke invites Seagers to live with him on the desert plot that he bought with his life savings. Unfortunately, when they go out to the plot of land, it is a big disappointment. They have decided to leave when they accidently discover water on the land—a figurative "money shot," it gushes like an ejaculating penis.

Each movie in the trilogy maps a different path of homosexual desire among men with no gay identity. In the first movie, Richard Locke, who stars in all three films, introduces a younger truck driver, who has a girlfriend, to the rigors of the road and the possibilities of homoerotic encounters. Though they masturbate together during the journey, neither has sex until the end, when both participate in a homosexual orgy. The second follows two friends who are familiar with each other's penchant for having sex with men. And they both have sex at numerous stops along the way. Each film reveals a greater awareness and openness about their homosexual desires. And though there is never any open acknowledgment of gay liberation or gay identity, *L.A. Tool and Die* implicitly assumes its existence.

Gage's three films had an enormous impact at the time, and all of the films are still in print and available. "Joe Gage's first three films," wrote Jerry Douglas in his assessment, ". . . celebrated the freedom of the sexual revolution that had spread across America during the years that they were being made. Today, in retrospect, the trio stand together as the definitive cinematic statement on the emergence of the macho homosexual whose sexual transiency and voracity influenced larger and larger numbers of gays—until the advent of AIDS."[19] Gage made a number of films after the trilogy—*Closet Set* (1980) and *Heatstroke* (1982) were among the most notable. *Heatstroke* almost seemed an extension of the trilogy. Richard Locke was again the star. Shot on location in Montana, it is set among a group of cowboys who head into town to raise hell over the weekend. "The results are primal America," writes Jerry Douglas, "a homoerotic wedding of Zane Grey and Tom of Finland."[20]

Gage also made a series of loops under the name of Mac Larson, for P.M. Productions, a local New York company. P.M. produced films, usually set in New York City and with low production values, for theatrical release at the Park-Miller Theatre. "We'd get the money on a Wednesday, start shooting on a Friday, start cutting on Sunday." Gage recalled, "We never shot for more than a day, a day and half. It's the kind of thing that you regret doing because you did it for the wrong reason—and that reason was money. And I regret them to this day." Gage considered most of the films he did for P.M. to be "pretty seedy."[21] He retired from making gay adult films in 1986, but eventually returned to porn filmmaking in 2001.

The world that Joe Gage created in his films was a twilight zone between the closet and being open about one's homosexual desire. The ambivalence and the reticence about sexual identity resonated with a great many men in the late seventies and early eighties. Gage himself inhabited that twilight zone. He had never identified as a gay man. In the eighties, he married and raised two sons with his wife. Unlike some of the characters in his films, Gage abstained from having sex with men after he married. "I was one hundred percent faithful to my wife," he explained, "during my years as a full-time husband."[22] Nor has Gage ever portrayed or identified anyone in his films as gay—"they're never 'straight' though," he told *Butt* magazine, "that's the point. People constantly say, 'Oh here's another Joe Gage movie, he's going to have straight guys going gay or straight guys having sex.' But no, that's not it at all. My stuff is always about guys who get up in the morning, go to work, do their job and then see what happens."[23]

Sex, Gender, and the Structure of Feelings, 1976–1979

Jack Deveau's and Joe Gage's films show us the "structure of feelings" that shaped gay male sex in the 1970s after Stonewall.[24] Conceptions of gender are fundamental to all kinds of pornography—heterosexual, bisexual, lesbian, trans, or gay. And as a form of popular culture, pornography draws on the central myths of our culture—the role of the sexes, the meaning of pleasure, the play of gender, and the power of sex. By drawing on both the documentary and fantasy aspects of porn, Deveau's and Gage's films allow us to articulate a historical interpretation of homosexuality during a period in which both homosexuality and masculinity were redefined.

Jack Deveau explored the promiscuity and casual sex of the era as a problem that posed complications for the everyday life of gay men. He noted the conflict between the pleasures and joys of casual sex and the emotional limitations—he portrayed it, in part, as a comic problem. While Joe Gage's films focus less on promiscuity and the dilemmas of gay life in the gay urban centers, his movies, as Jerry Douglas points out, focus on men's unrestrained sexual initiation into pansexuality. His films are rife with women, sexual women whose men (while not explicitly bisexual) are or become firm believers in the sixties adage: "If it feels good, do it."[25] But for Gage, sex was always more significant than identity. "I think it's so confining," he recently told Frank Rodriguez, "so diminishing to say, 'I am a gay man.'"[26]

Made in a documentary (cinema verité) style, the worlds that Gage created resembled closely "a fantasy-world of uncomplicated and exaggerated male sexuality." Like Tom of Finland, Gage "created a whole type of men, square-jawed, thick-lipped, with powerful muscular bodies, packed jutting asses and huge cocks. . . . [He] was always rendering explicit the sexuality of certain male stereotypes—lumberjacks, cowboys, hitch-hikers."[27] More than most gay male pornography, Gage's films are preoccupied by the meaning of and playing out of masculine codes of behavior. They reflect the transition from the unacknowledged homoeroticism of the era before Stonewall to new styles of masculinity among gay men. Camp as an effeminized gay sensibility was out. The new style of gay man was both macho and sexually provocative; and that style included denim pants, black combat boots, a tight T-shirt (if it was warm), covered by a plaid flannel shirt (if it was cooler). The rugged look of the Marlboro man was the iconic masculine model for the seventies.[28]

Yet in both Deveau's and Gage's worlds, "The best homosexual sex is anonymous, impersonal, promiscuous and public." They helped to develop a "New York" tradition in gay erotic filmmaking that also included Jerry Douglas and Arch Brown. Often shot in a documentary style, it was darker, raunchier, and often more macho than the style created by Matt Sterling, John Travis, or Falcon on the West Coast.[29] Gay hardcore pornography made in the 1970s by Deveau, Gage, and other directors helped to legitimate a reconfiguration of gay masculinity.[30] As gay men rejected the traditional idea that male homosexual desire implied the desire to be female, they turned to a traditionally masculine or working-class style of acting out sexually.

These new styles reflected the generational backgrounds of their producers in the early 1980s.[31] It is difficult to look back at the promiscuity of the 1970s or for that matter at the casual and unprotected sex so visibly portrayed in early porn films without reflecting on its relation to the AIDS epidemic. Deveau treated the promiscuity and casual sex of the era as a problem that posed complications for the everyday lives of gay men. He noted the conflict between the pleasures and joys of casual sex and the emotional limitations—he portrayed it, in part, as a comic problem. For Gage, unconstrained masculine sexuality poses a problem only for heterosexual relationships. When the early porn filmmakers made these films, no one had any idea that HIV existed or that it was circulating among gay men at the time.

Part II

Producing Sex: Sexual Scripts, Work, and the Making of Pornography

▪▪▪▪▪▪▪▪▪▪▪▪▪▪▪▪▪▪▪▪▪▪▪

5

Scripting the Sex

■ ■

Fantasy, Narrative, and Sexual Scripts in Pornographic Films

In Billy Wilder's great film *Sunset Boulevard*, the writer-hero played by William Holden complains that most people don't realize that someone "writes a picture; they think the actors make it up as they go along." If that seems like something of an exaggeration for movies, it is probably exactly what most viewers of pornography believe about the sexual action in triple-x films. It strikes many viewers as somewhat unlikely that anyone actually plots the sex in a porn movie, directs or choreographs it—no doubt, most of those who watch porn videos believe that all any porn scene requires is two hot performers going at one another. In fact, the ability of pornographic films to create credible sexual fantasy worlds depends upon scripts and scripted performances both figuratively and literally.

What role do the sexual scripts that shape everyday sexual conduct play in the production of these commercial sexual fantasies? What role do overarching narratives and stories play in the construction of sexual fantasies? John Gagnon identified two stages in the transformation of fantasies into everyday sexual scripts. The first stage consists of a mélange of "erotic mental fragments," images and emotions that are subsequently encoded in a second stage into the "organized cognitive scripts" that guide an individual's sexual conduct.[1] The production of porn movies requires these two stages to take place simultaneously—the movies activate the fragments and emotions of sexual fantasies and require for their completion the pragmatic use of the cognitive scripts formulated by performers, directors, and script writers in order to realize both the sexual performances and the filmed version of the fantasies. However, these sexual performances and scenes of sexual action are often embedded in larger narrative structures and film genres. What role do these overarching narratives play in the shaping of sexual action that is portrayed?

In this essay I examine the interplay between the everyday sexual scripts of the sort employed by individuals in their sex lives and the film scripts (which can exist either as completely written scripts or as loosely sketched outlines) used in the production of porn movies. I discuss how the sexual fantasy worlds created in porn films draws upon the everyday sexual scripts of performers, scriptwriters, and directors. One of the things that link adult film scripts to the sexual scripts of everyday sexual conduct is the significance in pornographic movies of erections and orgasms to a realistic and credible representation of sexual behavior. It requires the male performer, in particular, to activate his own sexual fantasy scripts in order to achieve an orgasm that can be visibly displayed (the money shot).[2] These reality effects (erections and orgasms) make performing in pornographic films something more than only acting as though one was being sexual (though there is a great deal of that in adult movies). While the argument I make in this essay relies upon an analysis of gay male pornography, much of it applies to straight pornography as well—in fact, the reality aspects of male performance and the signifying role of erections and orgasms are important in both gay and straight porn.

Scripts in Gagnon and Simon's theoretical perspective are a metaphor for understanding how people conduct themselves within social life. In order for people to engage successfully in any aspect of social life, something resembling scripting must take place on at least three distinct levels: cultural scenarios, interpersonal scripts, and intrapsychic scripts. Cultural scenarios guide an individual's behavior as a participant of collective social life—providing prescriptions for various social, gender, or occupational roles, class and racial identities, sexual beliefs, popular cultural ideals and symbols, and broad social values and norms. Interpersonal scripts are those improvised by social participants to guide everyday patterns of interactions. These scripts are suggested by each individual's presentation of self and focused interactional strategies and draw upon cultural scenarios for normative and symbolic materials. Fantasies, desires, expectations, and ambitions are articulated through an individual's intrapsychic scripts. In these scripts the private world of wishes and desires is linked to social meanings and actions.

Thus, in Gagnon and Simon's view, everyday sexual scripts incorporate informal guidelines, rules, and social norms governing sexual conduct. These scripts bring together both symbolic and nonverbal elements in an organized and time-bound sequence of conduct. Such scripts take into account the participants, their personal and social qualities, their implied motives, and various behavioral cues. "Scripts" help organize a sequence of verbal and nonverbal activities that produce sexual experiences for its participants.

Porn movies, like all movies, involve scripts, camera movement, composition, editing, sound recording, and music. These elements shape the sexual fantasy materials for the film's viewers. For the most part, these elements are coordinated by the film's director. Though the performers, the film's editor, and even other members of the production team help to shape the sexual action of a film, the final product is refracted through the sexual scripts and fantasy materials of the director. Ironically, porn movies exemplify, even more than conventional (non-porn) feature films, the significance of the director and mise-en-scène—the central tenets of *Cahiers du Cinéma*'s classic auteur theory.[3]

The sexual action in porn movies is often explicitly scripted. It is scripted in a number of different ways—sometimes the sex to be performed is actually described in a written script with dialogue and nonsexual action, and at other times the sex is implied by the setting and casting or directed by the director in person. Video scripts take different forms, but they are all examples of a more general category of scripted behavior—the sexual scripts that John Gagnon and William Simon have explored both jointly and individually, in a series of publications since 1972.[4] Thus to explore the connection between everyday sexual scripts and porn film scripts requires an exploration of the social production of sexual fantasies.

The Laws of Desire: Fantasy, Sexual Scripts, and Performance

The pornographic film creates a fantasy world—which for many people is usually constructed from fragments of narratives, from loose sets of related situations or full-fledged stories—in which a utopian sexuality exists without the everyday encumbrances of social convention, endurance, or availability. The cinematic realization of a sexual fantasy world as envisioned by the script writer or director—and as a fantasy, it consists almost always of some sort of story or at the very minimum implies a story/script. Whether or not the fantasy world that is created succeeds or fails with its viewers depends upon whether or not the film's actors (with the help of editing or special effects) give credible sexual performances.

Sexual performers must rely on their ability to activate and use their own sexual scripts—the cultural scenarios, social interactional, and, of course, especially their intrapsychic scripts—to perform in the sexual scenes. In particular, male performers must achieve erections, engage in sexual activities that produce and show erections, and ultimately achieve an orgasm—the "money shot," the result that performers need to produce in order to be paid, but also the filmed act that makes a sexual scene credible—and marketable.[5] Sexual scripts are necessary to the performers in order to successfully create the fantasy world of a hardcore movie.

The effectiveness of video pornography depends upon the viewer's belief that the sex is plausibly "real" in some way; a pornographic film or video is both a documentary and a fantasy, of successful arousal and orgasm as enacted by the performers. The viewer's sexual arousal requires a suspension of belief in pornography's fictional character. A "documentary illusion" exists in the photographic pornographic genres, which promises to enact certain sexual fantasies and certify them through the "authenticity" of erections (although some significance may be lost with the increased use of Viagra and other drugs) and orgasms.[6] The psychological as well as the ideological power of pornography is achieved through this certification of sexual fantasy by its "documented" sexual conclusions—visibly displayed orgasms.[7]

The successful production of fantasy is primarily dependent not on the physical desirability per se of the performer, but on the performance and the setting of the performance together—that is, the mise-en-scène: the physical setup (the set), decor, costumes, props, lighting, positions of the camera, and movements and actions of performers themselves. Arousal, according to Elizabeth Cowie, "is stimulated by the scenario of presentation, by the *mise-en-scene* and the implied narrative."[8] Pornography, like fantasy, follows the laws of desire— it is created by the construction of an imaginary script elaborated from our wishes, frustrations, pleasures, denials, conflicts, daydreams, and memories of past events, erotic and nonerotic—and is never solely stimulated by an "object of desire" itself, but by an entire setting, scene, or narrative that the spectator can imaginatively enter. The successful sexual performance in a fantasy or in a porn movie protects the spectator's excitement from being ruined by anxiety, guilt, or boredom and allows adult movie producers to simulate reality without the risks that we all face in real-life situations—unless, of course, we have power to manipulate reality, especially real people. It is the fantasy scenario that stimulates a subject's desire; it is not the fulfillment or satisfaction of the desire. "Through fantasy," Slavoj Žižek has pointed out, "we learn how to desire. Desire is not something given in advance, but something that has to be constructed— and it is precisely the role of fantasy to give coordinates of the subject's desire, to specify the object, to locate the position the subject assumes in it."[9] And for many people, erotic excitement is heightened when the fantasy's outcome is uncertain—when it includes an element of risk, danger, mystery, or transgression.[10]

The virtual porn script—as the blueprint for a cinematic fantasy world— consists of a number of identifiable components: the setup, that is, the physical setting (locker room, kitchen, barracks, bedroom) or the situation (the loss of a diary, runaway boyfriend) that frames the physical and social space necessary to realize the fantasy; the objects of desire (the desirable bodies of performers); idealized sexual action in which the physical or social obstacles (performance anxieties, physical exhaustion, satiation) to unrestrained sexual activity are eliminated; reality effects (real erections and/or orgasms) that authenticate the sexual fantasy.

For most spectators of porn, masturbation is the primary activity that accompanies watching an adult movie and helps to establish both the pace and timing of a sexual scene and its narrative of sexual action—kissing, oral action, anal action of various kinds, penetration, and finally orgasm. "Pornography's narrative form, in each of its many genres," Andrew Ross has noted, "is closely tailored to the demands of its traditional male market, broadly based around the activity of masturbation."[11] Masturbatory fantasies also frequently suggest a scene's implied narrative. For instance, a scene's setup may imply a narrative that activates certain fantasies. Jerry Douglas observes that

the set-up has its roots in a masturbatory—in the director's masturbatory fantasy, that he assumes is shared by his viewers. I remember quite vividly, one of the first men I ever interviewed in this industry was Matt Sterling. We talked about one of his most famous loops, which is "Mr. Egan and the Paperboy." It's legend; it's one of the landmark loops. . . . I said, "Where did the idea for this come from?" And he said, "Oh, I don't know. I just always thought that every time my paperboy came around to collect for the weekly subscription, I always thought, 'What if this turned into a sex scene?' And I'm sure I'm not the only one who's ever thought that."[12]

Though we construct our fantasies as a loose narrative, we rarely retell our fantasies as narratives, as Andrew Ross points out: "The plot of realist films is often recounted to others in the same way as we reconstruct dreams out loud to friends, but pornography is like fantasies in this respect: no one would dream of recounting the narrative form of either. Pornography, for the most part, provides a stimulus, base, or foundation for individual fantasies to be built upon and elaborated. It merely provides the conditions—stock, generic, eroticizable components such as poses, clothing, and sounds—under which the pleasure of fantasizing, a pleasure unto itself, can be pursued."[13] The narrative dimension of a porn film does not necessarily have to be presented as a story, but a story must be implied in order to set up and activate the fantasy scenario. Thus in porn, the narrative—whether explicit or implied—motivates the setup and establishes cues and other signs for the activation of desire.

The spectator's fantasy video script is elaborated through an intrapsychic dialectic that oscillates between desire and identification—the movement between the arousal stimulated by the setup and for the desirable objects (the active role) and imagined substitution of oneself in place of the objects of desire (the passive role). It is the continued imagining of an unattained but possible sexual satisfaction that nurtures desire. The pleasure of sexual fantasy and pornography is sought for itself, not as a means to physical sexual gratification.

The spectator's fantasy script is created as he (or in some cases she) watches the porn video by fast-forwarding through the boring parts, pausing on the exciting moment, or running the favorite scene in slow motion in order to savor the action. The spectator uses the remote control to edit the commercial sexual fantasy into one that is more immediately arousing.

Thus, in porn films sexual scripts operate on many different levels—most importantly, each of the participants' conduct on the set is guided by their own scripts. In addition, the film itself is the product of a formal (or not so formal) film script, but it also shaped by the director's sexual choreography (and direction of the performers) of the sexual action implied or explicitly included in the script, by each performer's enactment of the sexual action (in the film script as choreographed by the director) and the scripts dictated by their own sexual fantasies, and last but not least by the film's editor who with or without the director assembles the final print of the film.

The Production Frame: Making a Pornographic Film

The porn production frame organizes the sexual activities of the performers hired to appear in a pornographic movie.[14] Within the production frame, performers are supplied with two other kinds of sexual scripts. One is the script per se, which may be a fully written text with instructions about the sexual activity to be filmed or merely an outline that the director uses as the basis for choreographing the sexual activities of the performers. The second production script is the mise-en-scène, the overall visual style of the production and the sexual activity that is to take place before the camera.[15] Ultimately, the mise-en-scène establishes the overarching visual/fantasy vocabulary of the movie—the erotic gestalt of the porn movie.

The porn film production framework also contributes to the scripted behavior in several other significant ways. It establishes the social and physical conditions for sexual performances to be filmed: it creates a bounded space that is defined as a set (creating access to a setting where certain type of sexual activities are expected to take place) where sexual performances will be filmed, it supplies sexual partners (via casting) who expect to perform sexual acts before a camera with other performers, and it employs a production crew—the producer, director, cinematographer, lighting expert, makeup person, editor, and composer—who will help to produce (direct, film, edit, supply music, and prepare the performers) the final product.[16]

And like any other form of sexual conduct, pornographic film performances rely upon scripting capabilities of individual performers, directors, and film editors to create a cinematographically convincing fantasy world through its construction of credible sexual performances. Video scripts and vernacular sexual scripts function somewhat differently. Video scripts and their mise-en-scène organize sexual performances and set the stage in order to create a credible fantasy world on film, whereas in real-life sexual activities scripts are usually improvised, to some degree, from the participants' personal fantasies, social roles, cultural codes, and symbols, in addition to the socially available interactional strategies and are used to orchestrate a sexual encounter.

Many porn scripts are mere outlines—a sheet of paper with the situational premise, cast, and sequence of action. The screenplay may include detailed descriptions of the sex to be performed (as do those of Jerry Douglas), but it may also leave the choreographing of the sex to the director, who is sometimes also the author of the screenplay (for example, Wash West). The movie's screenplay sets the stage, introduces characters, provides dialogue, and sketches the sex scenes. But the written—or sometimes unwritten—script draws upon the scriptwriter's and/or the director's personal fantasies (what Gagnon and Simon have called intrapsychic scripts) and extensively upon cultural symbols, roles, and social types (cultural scenarios)—as well as the interactional skills and private fantasies of the performers (the performer's repertoire of sexual scripts).

Casting can also play a significant role in the shaping of a film's story line and sexual action. Thus every adult film's script draws on the socially available sexual scripts that Gagnon and Simon have delineated—the specific roles, norms, and symbols embodied in the cultural scenarios; the interpersonal scripts that include the social cues, norms, and interpersonal strategies that guide everyday patterns of interaction and that draw on the screenwriter's and/or director's intrapsychic fantasies, desires, and sexual preferences.

The market for which a porn film is made also affects the film's script and the various behavioral/social scripts used by the director and the performers to produce credible sexual performances. If the intended audience is heterosexual male, heterosexual couples, gay, or other more specialized sexual preferences, such as those for trans women, bondage, or wrestling videos, then the film script, cultural scenarios, and interactional scripts will differ significantly. And of course the performers intrapsychic scripts may also differ depending on the type of movie in which they are performing.

Performers not only draw on their personal sexual scripts in order to provide credible sexual performances but also adopt personas (which are also porn industry career scripts) that shape both characterization and sexual repertoire—and affect the performer's realization of the film's script and have an impact on the performances of fellow performers.[17] Very rarely are the sexual activities recorded in a commercial pornographic video ever wholly spontaneous. They are written by scriptwriters or verbally coached by directors and, in conjunction with the director's choreography, partly improvised by the performers.

When I first began to interview the people who work in the gay porn industry, Michael Lucas, who has worked as a performer and currently directs porn videos for his own company based in New York City, asked if I had ever thought of writing porn scripts. Though I hadn't thought of doing so before, over the next week I wrote four or five with a friend. Though none of them was ever produced, it was a useful lesson about which elements go into developing a porn script. Lucas gave me a very strict formula that has been almost universally acknowledged as the correct one—and an important aspect of the production frame. The script must consist of four or five scenes, eight or nine performers, and roughly equal numbers of tops and bottoms, and only two of the performers could appear in more than one scene. Lastly for Lucas, the video must be set in New York City and reflect the ethnic mix of the city. Such generic formulas are important components of the production frame—in part, they are economic constraints. The scripts that my friend and I wrote told archetypical New York stories (a white-collar crime investigation, tourists and taxi cab drivers, and an immigrant's arrival in the city) and presented characters based on locale (tourism, Wall Street, Washington Heights), occupation (NYPD detectives), and ethnic social types (Dominican baseball players, South Asian taxi cab drivers). These scripts were concepts more than literal scripts; my coauthor and I described the sexual action but didn't write any dialogue. In the end, Lucas decided not to use any of them because he found it more convenient to develop scripts with particular performers in mind.

This story illustrates that writing a script for a porn video is not, in itself, sufficient to generate a credible fantasy world. As Lucas suggested, casting is an important part of developing a porn script, and as I have found in my research, so is direction. But though particular performers lend a script some unique individual personality, physical desirability, and sexual energy, the formulaic framework incorporates many fairly abstract elements of local knowledge, social and sexual roles, and cultural beliefs to set the stage for the re-creation of a sexual fantasy (the writer's). One young director, Doug Jeffries, discovered this as well:

> I'm so overbooked I thought, "Let me get rid of this scriptwriting and let me direct somebody else's script." But I can't do it. First I all, I need to live with my script, and secondly, whoever is writing the script doesn't know the performers. I've always had one or two stars in mind who are the central. As Scott Masters from Studio 2000 said to me, when you write these scripts you're not writing for actors, you're writing for the personality of the person you're casting. There's a performer named Cade Devlin, who's streety and boyish. When he works for

Falcon and Studio 2000, they always tell him to tone it down. In the movie I did with him, *Looking for Trouble*, I let him be wild, wear jewelry and be a street boy and that's what he was. He was amazing in that movie.[18]

But ultimately, the realization of that fantasy will require the director's choreography and the actors' sexual performances and draw on their own intrapsychic scripts in order to produce a credible sexual scene.

This suggests the primacy of mise-en-scène as the coordinating script of porn production. The explicit porn script and the personal sexual scripts of all porn productions' participants are "keyed," to use Goffman's term from *Frame Analysis*, by the mise-en-scène. Keying takes place when a set of conventions and rules by which a given activity, in this case sexual activity, which is meaningful in terms of everyone's daily framework of sexual conduct, is transformed into a pornographic performance and representation, that is, something patterned on everyday sexual activity but seen by both participants and in this case viewers as something else.[19]

The textbook definition of mise-en-scène is "the contents of the frame and the way they are organized," which includes lighting, costumes, decor, props, the set, as well as actors and their staging; it is everything that the viewers see and the way they are invited to see it).[20] The importance of mise-en-scène implies the overwhelming significance of the director as the "auteur" of the porn movie. It is the director who choreographs the sexual action, who casts the performers who costar with other, who coaches the performers before and during a sex scene, who selects and then steers the videographer, who approves the wardrobes, hairstyles, and makeup of the performers, who selects the set, and who by such means evokes the basic fantasy scenario.

Can Sex Tell the Story? Narrative and Sexual Action

Narrative has a special place in the thinking about pornographic movies. To the degree that all scripts involve a sequence of related events, they are narratives. Most early pornographic films consisted of short sexual episodes unrelated to one another—called "loops" because they were often run as looped shorts in a video player set up in small booths at adult bookstores. In loops, the sexual action provides the narrative—from the initial oral action through various other forms of sexual play (rimming, cunnilingus, bondage, sex toys, anal play) to the concluding intercourse (vaginal/anal) and the money shots (i.e., male ejaculations). However, with the emergence of feature-length productions, the short sexual episodes are ever more likely to be organized into an overarching narrative or storyline.

Plot-oriented feature-length porn films first emerged as a significant category of adult films in the 1970s. In *Miller v. California* (1973), the U.S. Supreme

Court declared that a work was obscene if it was "utterly" without redeeming social worth and lacked "serious" literary, artistic, political, or scientific value. In the wake of *Miller v. California*, plot offered the adult industry a basis for legally defending sexually explicit film productions by allowing the industry to claim that its films—like *Deep Throat*, *Behind the Green*, and *The Devil in Miss Jones*, all strongly narrative porn movies—had some redeeming social worth and "serious" literary or artistic value.[21] Plot also serves as an alibi for those spectators who felt that plot makes porn more intellectually acceptable.[22]

For a long time, the review section of *Adult Video News* (*AVN*), the porn industry's trade journal, explicitly distinguished in its review section between "plot-oriented features," based on a traditional three-act script that relies upon acting and dialog, and "all-sex productions," which have no overarching plot structure. The latter films (successors to the earlier era's loops) are also known as "wall-to-wall" productions and by definition consist of a series of sex scenes that may or may not include a connecting device.[23] There are, of course, many specialty genres—such as those devoted to S/M, girl-girl, fat or foot fetishes, but the vast majority of porn films produced for the general audience are in these two broad categories.

There is a long-standing debate about the compatibility of narrative and sexual action in film.[24] Many viewers of adult videos consider a strong narrative to be a distraction and unnecessary—something to fast-forward through. Others find that a strong narrative enhances and heightens the sexual excitement. Some critics consider narrative and explicit sexual action essentially incompatible. *New York Times* columnist Frank Rich has argued that sex acts bring a narrative to a halt—"like the musical numbers in a 1930s musical."[25]

Cultural theorist Slavoj Žižek also contends that explicit sexual action interrupts the narrative. For example, during the unfolding of a love story, "instead of the sublime Thing, we are stuck with a vulgar groaning and fornication."[26] Without reference to any pornographic films, he concludes that "congruence between the film narrative (the unfolding of the story) and the immediate display of the sexual act, is structurally impossible."[27] Žižek concludes that what he calls "the fantasy ideal of pornographers" to preserve the "impossible harmony" between narration and explicit sexual action is unattainable; explicit sexual action, to the degree that it involves erections, penetrations, and orgasms that appear to be "real" sex, throws the spectator off-balance and makes it impossible to believe in the fictional reality of the overarching narrative.[28]

The primary weakness of Rich and Žižek's argument is their failure to examine or discuss a pornographic film. Their argument relies on arbitrarily and hypothetically inserting an explicit sexual scene in the narrative of a commercial romantic film that is not a sexual story. But pornographic narratives are not "love stories"; they usually are stories about sex, sexual adventure, or, as in much gay porn, sexual identity—in which case the portrayal of sexually explicit action is not necessarily inappropriate. These narratives often explore interplay between sex and the dynamics of power through social roles and stereotypes (for example, gender, age, body type, sex role) and cultural mythologies (religion, sports, masculinity/femininity)—often stories of sexual acceptance, transgression, and a utopian freedom from the encumbrances of everyday life to engage in sexual activity.

In *Hard Core*, Linda Williams, appealing, like Frank Rich, to the example of musicals, came to the opposite conclusion: "The episodic narratives typical of the genre are not simply frivolous pretexts for the display of song and dance; rather narrative permits the staging of song and dance spectacles as events themselves within the larger structures afforded by the storyline. Narrative informs number, and number, in turn, informs narrative. Part of the pleasure . . . resides in the tension between these different discursive registers, each seeking to establish its own equilibrium."[29] In Williams's view a narrative porn film's sexual scenes function in several different ways: as regular moments of pleasure (to viewers and/or to the film's characters), as representations of sexual conflicts (among the characters), and as resolutions of those conflicts. She argues that "the episodic structure of the hardcore narrative is . . . more than a flimsy excuse for sexual numbers: it is part and parcel of the way the genre goes about resolving the often contradictory desires of its characters."[30]

Director Wash West, discussing the possible function of plot in porn movies, has noted, "Most people think that plot is the story, but it is also what the audience wants to happen." In his movie *Naked Highway*, the central characters, played by Jim Buck and Joey Violence, "don't have sex until you've been with them for an hour or so . . . during which they've been having sex with other people. So it builds up anticipation with the audience. So often porn will have no suspense because the people meet and five seconds later they're dropping their pants. There's no anticipation."[31]

Narrative and sexual action are thus not necessarily contradictory aspects of adult filmmaking. Gay porn filmmaker Jerry Douglas, who wrote a musical based on Arthur Schnitzler's play *La Ronde*, a series of sexual vignettes analogous to pornographic loops, realized that sexual action and narrative could be integrated:

It came to me in a blinding flash very early on, and I just can't imagine why more people didn't see it. It seems to me absolutely transparently obvious. Just in one example: after Rodgers and Hammerstein's *Oklahoma*, the whole idea was to integrate the musical numbers into the fabric of the story.

And in an adult film, I usually know where my sex scenes are going to fall, and then I have to build the libretto or the webbing or whatever you want to call it, around them. If I do it right, the sex scenes will do what a good number in a musical comedy does: it will reveal character, it will push the plot forward, and it will enrich the theme.

How does one go about achieving this, aside from the number of people in any given scene or the location? The answer to me was always, that we fuck for different reasons. We fuck to pleasure ourselves, we fuck to pleasure our partners, we fuck to hurt our partners, we fuck to hurt ourselves, we fuck to show off. There are any number of reasons why we have sex.

What has always interested me was that this is one of the most primal impulses of the human animal. Art, in the history of the Judeo-Christian ethic, has always faded to black just at the time it gets interesting. So, I always try to make each sex scene push the story forward and reveal the state of mind of the characters at any given moment.[32]

Many of Douglas's films exemplify this approach of situating the sexual action in the context of a story. In her essay on Douglas's *More of a Man* (1989) Mandy Merck also examines this question. The film tells the story of a young man struggling against the Catholic Church's prohibitions of his homosexual desires and portrays the furtive and sometimes degrading ways he gives in to them. Eventually with the counsel of a drag queen (played by noted porn director Chi Chi LaRue) whom he meets at a local bar, he achieves sexual self-acceptance and has a liberating sexual experience with an activist during the annual gay pride parade. Merck found that Douglas had successfully managed "to reconcile porn with cinematic narrative" and concluded, in sharp contrast to Rich and Žižek, that it was "remarkably easy to fuse sex with story."[33]

While most writers on porn have commented on the place of narrative in porn movies (and its converse, the place of explicit sex in film narratives), the discussion has largely focused on the compatibility between explicit sexual action and narrative. Does explicit sexual action disrupt a narrative? Can a scene of explicit hardcore action move the story forward? However, there is another debate that takes place primarily among the viewers of adult movies—whether or not a narrative in a hardcore movie enhances or detracts from the fantasy potential of a sexual scene.

What impact does narrative have on the spectator's "fantasy scripts"? For the most part, viewers watch pornography to become aroused and masturbate. An individual's relation to plot in pornography may differ according to their situation—as performer, spectator, or author. Performer Gus Maddox recently told an interviewer that "personally I like porn with no plot—that's what I like to watch, but because I'm an actor/writer, it's more fun for me to make porn with a plot."[34] Does narrative impinge on the fantasy potential of a sexually explicit scene? While both narrative frameworks and realistic social contexts are potential sources of fantasy material, they strongly frame the fantasy potential

of the explicit sexual scene. Many viewers, however, reject the narrative's framing effect on the sexual scene. Narratives foreclose viewers' ability to engage
with certain fantasies that might otherwise be suggested by the sexual action—
without the narrative context, that same scene would enable different fantasies. Thus, a hardcore film consisting only of sexual scenes, without any narrative,
offers a fantasy potential that is different from one with a story.

Sex, Genre, and Cultural Scenarios

Narrative porn movies often appeal to preexisting film and cultural genres, like
popular movies, TV shows, novels, or sports events, and by adapting them for
a pornographic movie production they invoke the underlying sexual implications of the genre. Adopting generic conventions also helps to organize an adult
film's narrative components such as characters, setting, plot, and even visual
techniques without requiring in-depth character development or a complex
story line. Most importantly, by adapting or parodying conventional genres,
porn filmmakers appeal to society's cultural beliefs encoded in typical story-
lines, popular social types, and cultural mythologies.[35]

Gagnon and Simon argue that individuals in their everyday sexual conduct
draw upon society's cultural scenarios—romantic narratives, the coming-out
process, stories of success, tales of emotional development—for practical clues
to performing social roles, interpreting cultural stereotypes (of gender, age, or
race), and identifying typical patterns of behavior.[36] As they put it, "The most
basic sources of sociogenic influence are the cultural scenarios that deal explicitly with the sexual or those that can implicitly be put to sexual uses. Such cultural scenarios not only specify appropriate objects, aims, and desirable
qualities of self-other relations, but also instruct in times, places, sequences of
gesture and utterance and, among the most important, what the actor and his
or her co-participants (real and imagined) are assumed to be feeling."[37] By
adapting preexisting film genres and narrative styles adult films can incorporate influential cultural scenarios to frame the fantasies stimulated by the sexual action.

Jerry Douglas is one of the leading proponents of the narrative approach in
adult movie making. A graduate of the Yale School of Drama, he is a playwright
and directed a number of off-Broadway nude productions in the late sixties and
early seventies. His first film, *The Back Row* (1973), was one of the first porn
movies that aspired to and in fact achieved professional quality. It offers a vivid
portrait of the gay sexual culture in New York City in the early 1970s that
emerged and flourished in the wake of the Stonewall riots and gay liberation.
It had a loose picaresque story of a young visitor from out west (something of
a takeoff on the popular John Schlesinger film *Midnight Cowboy*) accidentally
encountering and then exploring the somewhat raunchy gay sexual scene in a

porn movie theater. Douglas made only two more movies before quitting in frustration over control of film rights, money, and bookings with unscrupulous theater owners and distributors.

After 1989, when Douglas returned to making porn movies, he brought a new perspective from his work in musical theater—in particular the example of Rodgers and Hammerstein, who revolutionized the American musical by using the musical number to move the plot along, with the libretto weaving the songs into the narrative. In Douglas's view of porn narratives, sex tells the story—the sex as performed is an aspect of a character's development, reveals the film's underlying themes, and moves the plot along. Nearly all of Douglas's later movies involve a thoroughly worked out script, often as long as sixty pages—even the sex is scripted and is integral to the plot and character development. Thus the porn movies of Douglas's later career are feature-length productions in which the sex is embedded in a larger story. Douglas frequently quotes his good friend, Stan Ward, a fellow porn scriptwriter and former *AVN* editor—"Sex always takes place in context."

Flesh and Blood (1996), considered by many to be Douglas's best movie, is a porn film noir and is more specifically a tribute to Alfred Hitchcock; it operates fully within the generic conventions of film noir. While film noir, as a genre of film production, flourished in the 1940s and 1950s, it became a particularly influential cultural category in the last quarter of the twentieth century—eventually serving as a kind of popular mythology. In film noir sexual desire, paranoia, and murder are central elements of film narratives. As film scholar Foster Hirsch noted, "Noir posits an unstable world, in which terror lurks in wait just beneath a deceptively placid reality. . . . In noir no one is safe from himself or from others—and those others include spouses, siblings, neighbors, best friends."[38] In particular, sex is rarely represented in a romantic context, but one in which sexual desire is driven by obsession and provokes criminal acts. "The noir psychopath," writes Hirsch, "is bedeviled, pursued by ghosts from the past, and is often fatally self-divided. Sometimes the . . . motif is presented in a literal way . . . as stories about good and bad twins."[39]

In *Flesh and Blood*, Douglas exploits many of these motifs and conventions. The film tells the story of Derrick, played by Kurt Young, investigating the murder of his identical-twin brother Erik (also played by Young). Derrick, who mentions that he is engaged to be married soon after his arrival, discovers that his brother left behind a series of betrayed sexual partners, both male and female—his brother's cruel treatment of his partners is revealed through a series of sexually explicit flashbacks. Initially each character is a suspect. Each declares their love of Eric and tells Derrick the story of their sexual relationship with Eric in a self-serving way. But the flashbacks reveal the false notes, delusions, and lies in their stories as well as Eric's unscrupulous manipulation of his partners through seduction, misrepresentation, and lies.

Thus the sexual action of each scene reveals the psychological character of the person who relates the scene and shows us how in each case the narrator's own delusions about Eric's sexuality or about themselves allowed Eric to manipulate them sexually. His sex with Kenny, the young man who claims to be Eric's boyfriend, is not reciprocal—Kenny bottomed for Eric, Eric did not bottom for Kenny—which suggests that Kenny's love was not reciprocated by Eric. The flashback demonstrates that Kenny's vulnerability lies in his romantic naïveté. The bisexual three-way that Marilyn, who claims to be Eric's fiancé, gives as proof of her and Eric's sexual openness and of their trust to one another instead reveals her self-delusion; Eric only has sex with the man. Eric's sexual manipulation of a young man who insists that he is straight shows that the young man is also self-deluded—about his sexual desires. Each of Eric's suitors fantasizes about Derrick as a possible replacement for the murdered brother—another degree of their self-delusion. When the supposedly murdered Erik suddenly comes out of hiding, Derrick must engage in sex with his brother in order to solve the mystery. But like the others, Derrick succumbs to Eric's ruthless domination because he too is self-deluded—about his own sexual desires and about his brother's thirst to destroy. Derrick has risked everything, but he fails.

Few porn films are predicated on the relentless exploration of the characters' delusions about sexual relationships, their sexual desires or identities, or a narrative that begins with and ends in murder. The title, *Flesh and Blood*, alludes both to family ties and to the mythology of film noir—invoking the claustrophobia of forbidden sexualities, incest, and secrecy. Through the positioning of the camera as a spectator within the internal space of the scene, the dark angular lighting, and the claustrophobic set, Douglas's mise-en-scène replicates the visual style and mood of the traditional noir film. Within the film's narrative, the explicit sexual action contributes to development of the film's characters, revealing their illusions and in some sense illustrating the danger of deluding oneself about sexuality—so commonly the topic of traditional film noir.

One extremely common device among porn script writers and directors is to adapt or parody a mainstream movie, television show, or even book—*The Rear Factor, Drill Bill, Volume 1*, or *The Bachelor*. Sometimes this goes no further than the title—in which the porn title makes a sexually explicit joke on the original title (All World Studio's *Dawson's Crack* after the WB series *Dawson's Creek*), but in most cases it can involve a full-fledged erotic adaptation of the original.

One recent example, among gay porn videos, is Wash West's *The Hole* (2002), which is a porn parody of the popular horror movie *The Ring* (2002)—the tale of an urban legend about a videotape filled with nightmarish images, which is followed by a phone call predicting the viewer's death in exactly seven days. The title of *The Hole*, of course, plays on the significance of anal eroticism among gay men. West's movie follows a group of jocks who see a videotape of obscure images while staying at a run-down motor lodge. In this case, the videotape is followed by a phone call warning that the viewer will turn gay in exactly seven days. Thus, the overall concept of the movie plays on the masculinity of athletes and ambivalent erotic appeal of straight jocks to many gay men. There is an added irony on a meta-cinematic level as well; all but two of the main sexual performers in this very popular gay porn film identify themselves as heterosexual (this fact is discussed in reviews in local gay newspapers or on the many discussion boards and forums devoted to gay porn). There is no doubt that many viewers of *The Hole* will assume that merely performing in this video "predicts" that some of the film's heterosexual performers may eventually become gay. On some level, *The Hole* remains a horror movie for those "straight" homophobic viewers who believe that merely seeing a gay porn movie will help make them gay.

Within this comic framework is a coming-out story in which the ultimate outcome, though a surprise to the characters, is in every case a positive one. A local reporter (played by Tag Eriksson) investigates reports of these sexual transformations by interviewing the jocks affected and going so far as to view the tape himself. Does he view the tape to investigate the story or to initiate his own transition to a gay identity? It's not clear—nor is his ambivalence completely resolved by the fantasy he has based on a still photograph/video scene of noted straight porn actress T. J. Hart in a scene with man—the images of both Hart and the man flash before him as he has an orgasm.

This account of *The Hole* gives a sense of the overall concept of the movie and the cultural scenarios invoked in the movie: the coming-out narrative, the supposedly counterintuitive idea of gay athletes and masculine homosexuals, the nonsensical nature of urban legends and their superstitious appeal. But while these cultural notions influence our ideas of sexual identity and affect our fantasies, they are not by themselves erotic or pornographic. It is the sexual performances within the film's mise-en-scène that stimulate erotic arousal—abetted to some degree by the extra-filmic awareness of spectators that most of the leading performers in the film are straight. Thus, the film provides the fantasy (outside either the story or the film's scenic presentation) of "actually" straight athletes performing homosexual acts—and within the film's story, turning gay. The sexual scenes implicitly allude to these outside conditions—all the straight actors but one perform as tops (as penetrators in anal intercourse). The one "straight" actor who performs as a bottom is widely rumored to be "really" gay.

What is the script in these two porn movies? Certainly, the literal script of each movie probably will not strictly coincide with the fantasy script of every spectator. Yet the director certainly envisions a fantasy script of some sort—presumably his own. The mise-en-scène of each film invokes the laws of desire—those fantasies elaborated willy-nilly from our wishes, denials, delights, clashes, daydreams, and memories, both erotic and nonerotic, in order to establish a scene that will arouse the viewer. It is in some ways a hit-or-miss operation—explaining, in part, the routine complaints from viewers of the tedium and repetition of pornographic movies. And, of course, it is not possible to say what role, if any, the literal script or the fantasy script played in the performer's ability to produce a credible sexual performance.

Coaching the Libido

Directing a porn film requires a sophisticated sexual imagination and strong sense of the mise-en-scène of sexual encounters. Despite the centrality of porn stars—as the performers are often referred to—and the significance of casting both for the film's mise-en-scène and the marketing, the director plays the most important role in the production of pornographic movies. Mise-en-scène involves coordinating all the elements of a film in order to create a credible fantasy world—coordinating the sexual scripts, both literal and figurative, of performers and other members of the production team, the positioning and movements of the camera, the framing of the sexual action, as well as the editing and sound mixing in postproduction. For the most part, these elements are coordinated by the film's director. And these elements provide the raw material for the fantasy scripts that the spectator fashions from his viewing of the movie—by scene selection, fast-forwarding, slow motion, and replaying.

One of the contemporary masters of gay porn is Chi Chi LaRue. Far and away the most prolific director in the history of gay porn, he has also become, since the late 1980s, one of the leading directors of straight porn—being the preferred director of such leading female performers as Jenna Jameson and Tera Patrick. He is widely considered the best and most original director of sex scenes in gay porn today.

LaRue is the preeminent director of all-sex porn videos—and he is especially well known for his orgy scenes. Group sex, particularly with a large group, is very difficult to choreograph. All-sex movies and orgies often have no discernible narrative structure, other than that they start with oral sex and kissing, move on to rimming and fucking, and culminate in the money shots. However, the sexual activities are usually cumulative—the sucking, kissing, and rimming are added step-by-step. Only orgasms bring the sexual narrative to a conclusion.

Everyday sexual scripts, the erotic fantasy fragments, and the implied narratives of setups are the raw materials of LaRue's mise-en-scène. "I don't write stage directions on my scripts," LaRue told me, "only the dialogue. All the sex, all the movement comes out of my head. Sitting right there. . . . I'm a sex director."[40] The performers' responses to LaRue's improvisatory style are also important: "I have to give some credit to the performers . . . I was doing an oral scene and the [performers] came up to me and said, '[W]e want to fuck, we don't want this [scene] to be just oral.' It was going to be this little, tiny oral movie, and it blew up into this big, giant movie that turned out not just to be oral."[41] LaRue's improvisational style extends even to the preparation for future movies—visits to the hardware store can yield material for his next film: "I love water sports, so I do as much dirty water sports as I can get away with. . . . I'll go to a hardware store and look at anything weird that's used for gardening or hosing off the driveway and I'll think, "Oh that'll look great up a butt!" and I'll buy and use it in a movie.[42]

Another aspect notable about LaRue is his directing style. He shouts out instructions ("Go down on him!"), encouragement ("Yeah, that's fucking hot! . . . Harder, harder . . .") and exclamations (That's hot!") as he coaches the performers step-by-step through the sexual scene. He literally supplies the sexual script to the performers, the videographer, and the film crew and at the same time establishes his own sexual script as a framework. While some performers are uncomfortable with his approach, most find LaRue's method valuable. Usually the biggest problems created by this approach occur in postproduction when the sound editor must go through and meticulously strip LaRue's voice from the recorded soundtrack. The immense irony here is, of course, that LaRue voice will be erased from the audio recording, but the film is nonetheless an expression of his voice as a director, as a coach of sex.

Directing an all-sex movie requires a different approach from directing a narrative porn feature; it is much more like filming a sports events, as Jerry Douglas points out: "You can never story board a fuck scene. The best metaphor I've ever heard is that it's like photographing a football game. You try to cover it from as many angles as you can and don't have the slightest idea of how it's going to turn out. But your eye had damned well better be on the ball, or in this case, the balls."[43] Nevertheless wall-to-wall sex movies require considerable planning and advanced preparation. These preparations are utilized through the mise-en-scène in order to achieve the spectator's potential fantasy script that will arouse them and encourage their orgasm.

All the elements of the all-sex video must be coordinated. One of LaRue's biggest commercial successes was the *Link* series of movies (1997–1999) made for All Worlds Studios. They were shot in a San Francisco leather bar, and the performers were dressed in leather, harnesses, chaps, and black denim. The sexual action took place in dark dimly lit rooms, in slings, through glory holes, and in an enclosed area of chain-link fencing; there was fisting, a beer enema, and mild water sports. Many of the group sex scenes were performed by muscular, hairy men. The set, the costumes, the casting, and the lighting created an atmosphere of rough sex, of underground and hidden places, and of uninhibited sex. LaRue himself characterized the *Link* movies, despite their darkness and sexual intensity, as "leatherette movies because they're not heavy leather, even though they are total sex pig movies."[44]

One of LaRue's more recent movies, *Bolt* (2004), was initially thought of as another *Link*, but he took it in a completely different direction by making it bright and "clean" ("not the sex, the sex is dirty") rather than dark and dingy by using silvers, chromes, and Lucite.[45] In conjunction with *Bolt*, LaRue's company introduced a large industrial-style metallic bolt as a dildo—used throughout the movie. *Bolt*, like *Link*, is also a "total sex pig movie," though with a different sort of casting—younger men and more men with blonde hair, wearing torn white jockey shorts and tank tops rather than leather. Consequently, it conveys a very different erotic atmosphere and mood than the *Link* movies.

While narrative hardcore movies invoke cultural scenarios and symbols by developing the context within which the sexual action places, the setup and the implied narrative suggested by the setup are central to the all-sex video. Many all-sex videos are essentially four or five loops with a theme. The setup scene is always set in some highly charged symbolic and erotic milieu such as a gym, barracks, dungeon, alley, or warehouse and suggests an implied narrative that the spectator's fantasy will elaborate on. The director's mise-en-scène exploits the erotic and symbolic significance of the setup. Thus, for example, the widely held belief that the sports world is a rampant arena of homoeroticism implies a (fantasy) sexual encounter in the locker room or the gym.[46] The erotic charge of such implied narratives is enhanced by the uniforms, typical physiques, and props of various sports. The military environment exercises a similar erotic fascination for the gay male spectator—sometimes it is established by the mere presence of someone who is a Marine or a sailor (thus the appeal of Dirk Yates's Private Amateur Collection); other times an implied narrative is created by set design to look like a barracks or a scene of military-like disciple.[47]

Postscripts: A Gathering of Thoughts

The sexual scripts of everyday life and those that operate within the context of pornographic production are closely related. Everyday sexual scripts are elaborated by the person engaging in sex through an interplay of their interactive and intrapsychic scripts and the society's cultural scenarios. In the pornographic film, like everyday sexual encounters, a "dialectic of scripts" is operating, but in this case they resemble palimpsests—layers of fantasies, interactive cues, and cultural narratives overlying the deeper layers of the participant's personal fantasies, scripts, and beliefs about social roles. The porn production dynamic starts out from the director's personal sexual scripts and imagination (often embodied by the director/scriptwriter's script) and is enunciated by the mise-en-scène.[48]

The male performers' sexual scripts enable them to achieve the erections and orgasms that are central to the genre's expectations—the visible, physiological effects that authenticate the sexual performances that take place within the director's overarching script and direction. Ultimately, the director's mise-en-scène integrates the film's visual vocabulary, the implicit or explicit narrative, and the film's sexual action. Veteran performer Rod Barry, discussing the role of the director from the performer's perspective, proposed this formulation: "Having an eye for the B-roll [i.e., the setup, dialogue, etc.] and sex. How to tie it all together and make people believe that what happened should have happened, based upon the characters built-up from the B-roll—that's my hypothesis."[49] The utopian aspect of pornography has to do with realizing fantasies without the usual social and physical limitations that commonly inhibit sexual activity. Nevertheless, Barry's perspective reflects the genre's underlying sexual-psychological realism.

The porn production frame transforms (or "keys," as Goffman terms the process) those daily sexual fantasies into material that enables performers and the production crew to record credible sexual performances. The participants in the production of porn movies all, to some degree, organize their behavior on the set—whether they are performers engaging in sex or part of the production crew lighting, filming, or directing sex—on the basis of their own sexual scripts, but in the production of a pornographic movies the imagined fantasy script (of the spectator), which is the desired end result of the production process, is framed by the director's mise-en-scène.

Porn movies attempt to create fantasies that will arouse the spectator and encourage them to engage in masturbation and to produce an orgasm. The director provides, through the mise-en-scène, materials for the spectator's fantasy script—which the spectator themselves create via the remote control device—fast-forwarding, slow motion, pause and replay, and so on—basically the viewer's techniques of editing via juxtaposition and montage. Pornography is a form of discourse in which sexual acts and fantasies are explicitly examined, tested, and represented in order to be watched, thought about, and engaged with.

6

Gay-for-Pay

■■■■■■■■■■■■■■■■■■■■■■■

Straight Men and the Making
of Gay Pornography

"Situational homosexuality" is not a widely used term anymore in contemporary sociological discussions of sexuality. For many, the term has a slight anachronistic aspect—like "latent homosexuality," it suggests the 1950s. The term was originally used during the late 1940s and early 1950s to distinguish between the occurrence of homosexual behavior in social settings and institutions that were predominately same-sex—such as prisons, barracks, naval vessels, and boarding schools—and the homosexual "identity" of those who might be considered "real" homosexuals.[1] The model of sexual behavior underlying the concept of situational homosexuality is the adaptation, in socially or physically segregated circumstances, of members of a same-sex population to the absence of those of the opposite sex by entering into sexual relations with members of the same sex.

As the term "situational homosexuality" was used in the 1940s and 1950s, such sexual relations were assumed to be temporary. But this conceptualization also implied certain sociological and sexual assumptions. It assumed that such temporary patterns of homosexual behavior were due primarily to physical isolation. It also implied that sexual energy exerted a constant pressure on the individual in same-sex settings and that without their preferred heterosexual outlet they would be willing to engage in homosexual activities—during the 1940s and 1950s, use of the term "situational homosexuality" implied a core hetero/sexual self. This "hydraulic" model of sexuality was first articulated by Freud in his *Three Essays on the Theory of Sexuality*: "The libido behaves like a stream whose main bed has become blocked. It proceeds to fill up collateral channels which may hitherto have been empty.... The fact is that we must put sexual repression as an internal factor alongside such external factors as limitation of freedom, inaccessibility of a normal sexual object, the dangers of the normal sex act, etc. which bring about perversions in persons who might otherwise have remained normal."[2] Thus, it was a sexuality *faux de mieu*—not chosen, but only makeshift.

Recently, Regina Kunzel has suggested a conceptual reexamination of situational homosexuality that preserves both the original notion of homosexual behavior as specific to a social setting and its distinction from the homosexual role or identity—but it replaces the Freudian "energistic" model (and the 1940s–1950s notion of a core hetero/sexual self) with a more fully social constructionist account of homosexuality. Such a reconceptualization of "situational homosexuality" allows her to examine the historical and social changes in the constitution of homosexualities in prison settings. But Kunzel's suggestion also opens up the possibilities of examining other forms of homosexual behavior that cannot be explained by contemporary notions of gay identity. Among some of the forms of male homosexuality that fall outside the identitarian framework are men who identify primarily as heterosexual but who have casual or opportunistic sex with men, those who are sex workers or prisoners, and/or those who belong to same-sex cohorts of immigrants. Recently, research on HIV prevention strategies has focused on several populations of men who do not identify as homosexual but who may, nevertheless, engage in sex with other men under certain circumstances. Resuscitating "situational homosexuality" as an analytical term can help us identify social environments that enable high-risk behavior.[3]

While there are distinct differences between these categories of homosexual behavior engaged in by men who do not identify as gay, there are also ways in which these social patterns overlap and blend into one another. In some sense, they are all species of situational homosexuality—that is, sexual behavior strongly conditioned by situational constraints whether physical (prisons and jails, ships at sea, barracks, men's restrooms), economic (porn actors, hustlers, homeless youth), cultural (immigrants), or social-structural (married men, adolescents).[4]

Situational homosexualities emerge when heterosexually identified individuals encounter institutional settings that permit or reward homosexual behavior. Simon and Gagnon's theory of sexual scripts allows us to understand situational sexualities as the result of interplays among stereotyped social cues, prescribed role-playing, enabling social conditions, and the converging intra-psychic motivations of participating individuals.[5] Both the norms that regulate sexual behavior and the enabling social conditions that elicit and permit homosexual conduct from heterosexually oriented participants can be activated using sexual scripts that circulate throughout the culture. Cues and social roles are embedded in culturally available scenarios, while the enabling conditions are often those material circumstances (prisons, barracks, economic need, drug use, or porn studio) that limit or exclude the supply of potential heterosexual sex partners.[6] In contrast to its use in the 1940s and 1950s, I distinguish situational sexuality from sexual behavior as governed by the individual's sexual identity, which, over the course of their life, is constantly forged, reinforced, interrupted, and reconfigured within and through culture and history.

In many cases, sexual scripts are situationally specific. The "situation," in part, emerges from the characteristics (gender, race, age) of the potential population of sex partners that constrain or normalize a sexual repertoire not normally chosen by the situated individual. Albert Reiss's classic essay "The Social Integration of Queers and Peers" explored a form of homosexual prostitution that took place between young men ("peers") who did not "define themselves either as hustlers or as homosexuals" and homosexual men ("queers") who performed fellatio upon them.[7] Reiss found that certain norms governed the sexual transactions that occurred between the young and homosexuals, the most important that it be undertaken "solely as a way of making money: sexual gratification cannot be actively sought as a goal in the relationship." Another was that the transaction between them "must be limited to mouth-genital fellation. No other sexual acts are tolerated." Reiss also found that the young men defined someone as homosexual "not on the basis of homosexual behavior, but on the basis of participation in the homosexual role, the 'queer' role."

In this chapter I examine the homosexual activities of a group of men whose primary sexual identities are not gay yet who regularly perform in gay pornographic videos. These men are widely known in the porn industry and among spectators as "gay-for-pay," the implication being that they would not engage in homosexual conduct were they not paid to do so. Of course there are many explanations for such behavior. I argue that this group of men exemplifies "situational homosexuality." There is no irrefutable evidence establishing these men as really straight or actually gay but in denial. However, all sexual conduct in the video porn industry is to one degree or another an example of situational sexuality inasmuch as the performers are often required to engage in sexual acts for monetary compensation that they would not otherwise choose to perform and with partners for whom they feel no desire.

The Gay Porn Industry: Identity, Politics, and Markets

Since the late 1960s, the pornography industry in the United States has grown rapidly. While there is little reliable information about its size or annual revenues, experts estimate that the "adult entertainment" industry—which includes XXX videos and DVDs, Internet porn, cable and satellite porn, peep shows, phone sex, live sex acts, sex toys, and porn magazines—takes in somewhere between eight and ten billion dollars per year. That is comparable to Hollywood's annual domestic ticket sales and the annual revenues of professional sports. Again, while there are no reliable estimates, the gay market represents a significant portion of this amount—probably from 10 to 25 percent.[8]

Until the early 1970s male homosexual pornography was produced and distributed under black-market conditions. The first commercial male pornographic films were probably made in the late 1960s, but they were few in number.[9] Only after the gay movement had gained momentum were companies formed explicitly to produce gay male pornography. The production and distribution of commercial gay pornography took off between 1970 and 1985. Initially, gay pornographic movies were made by amateur filmmakers, and to some degree many of the films made in this period represented an expression of the filmmaker's own newly "liberated" homosexuality—this was especially true for many of the performers. This development also reflected the liberating effect of the sexual revolution: during the same period, straight erotic films, such as *I Am Curious (Yellow)*, *Deep Throat*, *The Devil in Miss Jones*, and *Last Tango in Paris*, often played in mainstream movie houses. Wakefield Poole's gay *Boys in the Sand* opened in 1971 followed shortly by Jerry Douglas's *Back Row* (1972), and like straight erotic movies, both films played in mainstream movie houses.

After 1985, production of gay pornography entered a new period in which video technology and extensive ownership of VCRs lowered its cost and made pornography more accessible. It became inexpensive and easy to rent. The new technology also enabled pornography to be viewed privately and at home. The AIDS crisis reinforced the privatized experience, some viewers turning to video porn out of fear of engaging in homosexual activities.

Moreover, starting in the mid-1980s, the gay market developed into a lucrative and dynamic growth sector for many industries, supplying specialty consumer goods to satisfy the aesthetic, social, and sexual preferences of homosexuals. The commercial development of gay male pornography also benefited greatly from the growth of the gay market and urban gay communities by supplying erotic images to a growing number of self-accepting gay men. This demand helped shape the business in a number of ways: the standards of physical attractiveness, the repertoire of sexual acts, the production values, and the narrative conventions closely reflected the prevailing attitudes of gay male consumers.[10]

In the early days of gay commercial pornography, it was difficult to recruit performers because homosexual behavior was still highly stigmatized and production was illicit. The performers were frequently recruited by the filmmakers (who were primarily gay) from among friends, casual sexual partners, and boyfriends. There was no preexisting network or agents to recruit performers for gay pornographic films. One early filmmaker, Barry Knight, described how "central casting in those days was The Gold Cup restaurant on the corner of Hollywood Boulevard and Las Palmos [in L.A.]. Whenever they needed an actor, or an actor didn't show up, they'd go down to 'central casting.'"[11]

Today, the gay pornography industry has a highly developed infrastructure of production companies, distribution networks, and technical services as well as agents and scouts for performers. If the first phase (1970–1985) in the development of commercial gay pornography attracted primarily gay men as performers, the second phase (post-1985) began to attract performers who did not identify as gay or homosexual. One contributing factor is that male performers were better paid in the gay pornography industry than in the straight side of the business. Given the heterosexual focus of straight pornography and the primarily male audience, the industry's female performers are better paid than most of their male counterparts. The prolific director Chi Chi LaRue estimates the number of straight men in gay pornographic videos to be 60 percent. I suspect that this is on the high side or may merely reflect her selection of performers for her own work. By the mid-1980s there was active recruiting of performers by scouts, photographers, and others who work in the gay segment of the industry.

The Spectator of Gay Pornography: Documentary Illusion and Identity Effects

Pornography probably has a more significant role in the life of gay men than it does among comparable groups of heterosexual men. Gay men often turn to gay pornography for cultural and sexual validation. As film critic Richard Dyer has noted, gay pornography contributes to the education of desire—it provides knowledge of the body and of sexual narratives and examples of gay sexuality and of sexuality within a masculine framework. Since most gay men have become adults without having been socialized in the social and sexual codes of their communities, pornography can contribute to that as well.[12]

The pleasure and sexual excitement that viewers of porn experience depend, to some degree, on the patterns of social and sexual interactions (i.e., the narratives, cues, and symbols) that circulate in the larger culture.[13] The gay spectator's psychological response to the fictive world of pornography and sexual fantasy—the symbolic conditions of sexual arousal—and the everyday life of social roles, values, and social structures is mediated by the ideological and social developments of the gay community; not only do psychosocial elements predominate in the organization of the pornographic materials, but both the immediate social context and wider social environment also influence the sexual response to pornography. Gagnon and Simon, in their analysis of pornography, show that an individual's fantasy life and their capacity for sexual arousal are significantly influenced by cultural context and historical situation.[14] For example, in gay porn condoms are widely used (for many years they have appeared in almost all videos) for anal intercourse, in sharp contrast to their virtual absence in heterosexual pornography. However, some gay men find that they are not aroused by the sexual action in movies produced in the "pre-condom" era, before the discovery of AIDS—in this way the ideological and social context clearly influences the potential for sexual excitement.

In the case of video pornography, its effectiveness stems from its ability to satisfy the viewer's expectation that the sex is plausibly "real" in some way—a pornographic film or video is a "document" of sexual pleasure, successful arousal, and orgasm. The viewer's sexual arousal presumes the suspension of disbelief in pornography's fictional character. A "documentary illusion" exists in the photographic pornographic genres, which promise to enact certain sexual fantasies and certify them through the "authenticity" of erections (although some significance may be lost with the increased use of Viagra and other drugs) and orgasms. The psychological as well as the ideological power of pornography is achieved through this certification of sexual fantasy by its "documented" sexual conclusions—visibly displayed orgasms.[15]

Viewers' responses and reviews of porn videos often minimize the genre's ambiguous expectations between fantasy/fiction and real sex. The sexual acts portrayed must seem genuinely exciting to the performers in order to arouse the viewer (they must be realistically credible), while also representing fantasies that invoke the culture's sexual scenarios. Reviewers sometimes will stress the "realness." "Ultimately what viewers want to see," one reviewer writes, "is guys having sex, not actors pretending to have sex. A few times there were some moans and some 'Oh, yeah, fuck me!' that sounded like typical porno soundtrack, but other than that this all seemed very authentic."[16]

Gay pornography is a cultural form through which its spectators accrue significant libidinal and symbolic investments.[17] It has also played a role in the construction of a gay male viewer's sexual identity. Post-Stonewall "gay" pornography is a legitimating representation of the sexuality of gay men.[18] Pornography's identity effects are enunciated through the genre's dominant semantic and syntactical conventions: the "standard" narrative sequence (kissing, oral sex, rimming, anal intercourse) of sexual acts, a convincingly energetic performance, and, most importantly, the erections and visible orgasms that authenticate (and narratively close the scene) the embodied forms of homosexual desire. Operating within the "documentary illusion," the erections and the orgasms putatively "prove" to a gay male spectator that these "sexually desirable, masculine, and energetic performers" are really gay—thus affirming the gay male identity. An individual video may often deviate from these generic expectations, either through failure to provide a credible performance or by offering new or creative sexual variations.

In addition to its identity effects, gay male porn also has a somewhat paradoxical "hetero/masculinist effect," in which the generic conventions that consolidate and reinforce gay male identity coexist with frequent representations of "straight" men engaging in homosexual acts. In this way gay porn reinforces the incongruity between male homosexual desire—stigmatized, abject—and the heterosexual dominance of the masculine regime of desire. It serves to situate homosexual desire within masculine territory irrespective of heterosexual or gay identities.[19] Thus, the widespread employment of straight performers in gay pornography intensifies the contradiction between gay male identity and homosexuality without identity, conferring legitimacy on homosexual behavior independent of gay identity.

The creation of a market for gay pornography relies upon the cultural and economic significance of gay identities, and not—however widespread it may be among males—homosexual desire.[20] Its expansion into other identity markets continues to reflect a significant trend in the gay pornography business, hence the growing number of videos targeting various demographic or sexual audiences—Latinos, black men, and other gay men of color, the leather, S/M and bear subcultures, and all sorts of sexual specialties like spanking, uniforms, and other fetishisms.[21]

The central ambivalence between identity and behavior in gay male porn frames the reactions of spectators to—along with their libidinal investments in—porn "stars."[22] The gay men who buy or rent and view a video expect the sexual pleasure portrayed to be "authentic" enough to produce an orgasm. For the most part, the orgasm affirms the sexual act leading up to it and contributes to the viewer's own sexual arousal.[23] But if the performer isn't gay, then the potential "meaning" of the orgasm is ambiguous. It can mean that orgasm is "acted" (or dramatically fabricated in some sense—"It's really only a heterosexual orgasm!"), or it can mean that even a straight man experienced an orgasm from sex with a man—this is one of the central ambiguities of gay porn.[24] It potentially undermines the viewer's willingness to suspend disbelief in the fictional aspect of the porn video. Thus, while every pornographic movie made for a gay male market manifestly performs at least two tasks—to sexually stimulate its viewers and, in some way, to affirm their sexual identity—it may also perform a third and more contradictory task: to provide evidence of homosexuality without identity.[25] It may do so either narratively, through the inclusion of scenes portraying straight men having credible sex with gay men, or by employing "known" heterosexual (gay-for-pay) performers to credibly represent gay male sexuality.

The Theory of Sexual Scripts

John Gagnon and William Simon, in their 1973 classic *Sexual Conduct* and in a series of theoretical refinements published in the 1980s, elaborated the view that sexual conduct requires learning and that physical acts of sex become possible only because they are embedded in social "scripts." Gagnon and Simon introduced a thoroughgoing conception of sexual behavior as a learned process, one that is possible not because of instinctual drives or physiological requirements, but because it is embedded in complex social scripts that are specific to particular locations in culture and history. Their approach stressed the significance of individual agency and cultural symbols in the conduct of our sexual activities. "Undeniably," they wrote, "what we conventionally describe as sexual behavior is rooted in biological capacities and processes, but no more than other forms of behavior . . . the sexual area may be precisely that realm wherein the superordinate position of the sociocultural over the biological level is most complete."[26] No previous theorists of sexuality had interpreted sexual behavior as so completely social. They redefined sexuality from being the combined product of biological drives and social repression into an arena of creative social initiative and symbolic action. Gayle Rubin, feminist theorist and anthropologist, proclaimed that Gagnon and Simon "virtually reinvented sex research as social science."[27] Gagnon and Simon sought to replace biological or psychoanalytic theories of sexual behavior with a social theory of sexual scripts. They argue that individuals utilize their interactional skills, fantasy materials, and cultural myths to develop scripts (with cues and appropriate dialogue) as a means for organizing their sexual behavior.[28]

Sexual arousal and the performance of sexual acts frequently depend upon the meanings and cues of the social and cultural context. In fact, human sexual behavior is organized by structured expectations and prescribed interactions that are coded like scripts. The theory of sexual scripts as formulated by Gagnon and Simon provides a useful analytical framework for exploring the dynamics of sexual performance in pornographic production. Scripts are metaphors for the narrative and behavioral requirements for the production of everyday social life. In their theory of sexual scripting, Gagnon and Simon suggest that these "scripts," with cues and appropriate dialogue, which are constantly changing and reflect different cultural groups, circulate in societies as generic guidelines for organizing social behavior. They distinguish three distinct levels of scripting: cultural scenarios provide instruction on the narrative requirements of broad social roles; interpersonal scripts are institutionalized patterns in everyday social interaction; and intrapsychic scripts are those that individuals use in their internal dialogue with cultural and social behavioral expectations.[29] For example, interpersonal scripts help individuals to organize their self-representations and those of others to initiate and engage in sexual activity, while the intrapsychic scripts organize the images and desires that elicit and sustain individuals' sexual desire. Cultural scenarios frame the interpersonal and intrapsychic scripts in the context of cultural symbols and broad social roles (such as race, gender, or class).[30]

Thus the making of pornography, like other forms of sex work, relies upon the learned sexual responses of its participants—much of the sexual behavior shown in pornography is a display of situational sexuality. However, unlike other forms of sex work, gay pornography as a representational genre, which often implicitly reflects as well as affirms an identitarian agenda, is explicitly marketed to self-identified gay men. However, the gay male pornography industry routinely recruits men who do not identify as gay or homosexual to perform in gay videos. In addition, non-gay-identified men frequently have used their work in gay pornography to launch lucrative careers as escorts. Nevertheless, the fact that industry gossip about sexual orientations circulates constantly demonstrates how important these issues are to the industry's operation as well as to the audience's response (for examples of this kind of fan discourse, see the forums at www.atkol.com). In gay pornographic videos, the ability of actors who are self-defined and otherwise behaviorally heterosexual to perform homosexual acts, maintain erections (both while penetrating and while being penetrated), and have orgasms provides the opportunity to explore the construction of situational homosexuality on the gay pornography set.

One distinctive characteristic of video pornography is that it is a dramatic fabrication of sexual activity that also requires demonstrations of "authentic" sexual signs, that is, erections and orgasms. The dramatic fabrication is achieved not only by the performers enacting sexual scenes but also by elaborate editing and montage of the filmed sexual acts themselves. Usually the filming of a sexual scene requires many takes, stops, and starts and requires the performers to regain their erections. The maintenance and refreshing of erections—"wood" in the industry vernacular—is a constant preoccupation of video pornographers.

The gay pornography business, through its employment of men who are heterosexual or who do not self-consciously identify as gay, provides straight actors with social conditions that enable situationally specific sexually behavior. The pornography industry supplies (1) the social and physical space where these sexual activities can take place, (2) other actors who expect to engage in sexual activities with one another, and (3) narratives of sexual activities that invoke the culturally available sexual scripts that elicit and activate the filmed sexual activities. Pornographic video production is obviously a "situation" in which sexual activity can take place: it provides access to sexual experiences for its participants.[31]

Gay-for-Pay as a Porn Career: Constructing the Persona

It is common practice that when anyone enters the porn industry they adopt a stage name—a *nom de porn*—by which they will be known to viewers. This protects the performer's privacy despite what is often a very visible public presence. In addition to taking the nom de porn, the performer must create his "character" as a performer. This persona is a "career script" through which the performer integrates traits of personality, physical characteristics, and sexual performance style.

The new porn star fashions himself from the cultural myths and social roles that define male sexuality or violate masculine roles or that affirm homosexual desire or draw upon ethnic or racial beliefs. Performers must obviously also draw upon their "intrapsychic" fantasies and beliefs. Thus, one performer may create his persona as the aggressive, dirty-talking "top" (the one who penetrates). In Rod Barry's case, his persona enables him to play the military man having sex in the barracks, a white-trash hillbilly who fucks his cousin Seth but who won't kiss (they are "fucking cousins, not kissing cousins"), or a man who, in his first scene as a "bottom" (the one who is penetrated), "aggressively" urges on the man who tops him. Another performer might create his persona as an exclusive top, a man with a large penis, and a man who never kisses—elements drawn from sexual scripts, from both cultural scenarios and intrapsychic fantasies or fears.

When any man, whatever his sexual preferences, seeks employment in gay pornographic video production, he must justify his choice from a number of perspectives. Participation in gay pornographic video production is, to some degree, a socially stigmatized activity (especially for those who do not identify as gay), not only because it is a form of sex work and because most people believe that public sexual performance negatively affects those who participate in it, but also because homosexuality is still a stigmatized form of sexuality. Thus, every new entrant into the porn business must give himself permission to engage in it.[32] Men who identify as heterosexual wanting to work in the gay porn industry must overcome the standard presumption that only gay men would want to perform in gay pornographic films. Obviously, the description of these performers as "gay-for-pay" presumes that the permission they require is primarily economic.

But economic permission is often entangled with other reasons, such as curiosity or latent homosexual fantasies, such as in the following example:

> Um, well, I was straight before I found out about gay videos, but I was a straight person with, like, thoughts and feelings. And through my twenties, they got real strong. I almost thought I would try to have an interlude or a contact with a man. I thought about it, yeah, I was, like, one of those straight-curious types. But then I got into gay video, and I decided I can simultaneously make money and fulfill a fantasy. The money's a perfect way to justify going into the sexual world. I guess I consider myself formerly straight and now I'm sexually bi with a lifestyle of straight.[33]

Permission for some performers can come from surprisingly odd sources. One performer, who had "danced" in local Latino gay bars in Jackson Heights in New York City, gave one of the more unusual forms of permission:

> INTERVIEWER: How did you get started in this business?
> TIGER TYSON: I just went in and did the video Tiger's Brooklyn Tails about two years ago. It turned out very successful. I didn't know I was going to become this whole character.
> I: Did making films come naturally?
> TT: It was something new, being that I'm bisexual. You could say I lost my virginity on video. . . .
> I: You haven't bottomed on film. Would you?
> TT: No, never. I would probably turn into a little punk . . . I wouldn't feel right being on the bottom.
> I: Do you now date guys?
> TT: No. Actually I'm engaged. She's very supportive. . . . I met her at Magic Touch while I was dancing for gay men, and she knows all about the videos. My mother is even supportive . . . that's why I don't bother to think I'm doing something wrong. If my mother doesn't feel disgraced, I feel good about it.[34]

Dancing or stripping in gay bars, as Tyson's story suggests, is a common way of entering the world of gay porn, where other dancers or agents will scout for producers of gay videos.[35] But many of the young straight men who enter the gay porn industry develop their permission to engage in homosexual activity in a video by using a surprisingly limited number of "scripts." One of the most common narratives that gay-for-pay performers tell of their entry into the industry is responding to a modeling ad or the approach of a recruiter who misleadingly offers to set up a photo shoot that turns out to be a nude photo shoot or porn audition. Brian Estevez, who worked in the industry in the late 1980s, gives this account of his recruitment:

> BRIAN ESTEVEZ: They wanted to see my whole body . . . and I thought: "What the fuck is this?" . . . At that point, I began to wonder what was going on and what the deal was. I turned to the old guy and said, "You told me modeling. What is this shit?" He then told me that these guys had big companies and that they made movies. I told him I didn't want to do movies—and then he started talking money and I swear . . . I don't know . . . I guess money manipulated me . . . I didn't want to do it!
>
> INTERVIEWER: And then the next step?
>
> BE: . . . and I went ahead, even though I'm very straight to this day.
>
> I: Now about being straight. . . .
>
> BE: . . . You know, I grew up very straight—never had any homosexual tendencies.
>
> I: You didn't connect it in any way to sexual pleasure?
>
> BE: I didn't get any sexual stimulation from it. Even to this day, even in a sexual act, even if I have a hard-on and everything—I still didn't connect it to "Wow, this feels good."
>
> I: And yet you started in films as a bottom?
>
> BE: Well, I didn't have a lot of choice.
>
> I: I'd think a straight boy would be a bit put off—that being a top would be more logical . . . more straight.
>
> BE: I know—and that's how I felt. I'd much rather be a top, and in my later movies I didn't do bottom anymore. It's just when they manipulated me into the business, they manipulated me into being a bottom. They told me that I wasn't big enough or buff enough to play a top role, so I was labeled a bottom—a small, hot guy who gets dick up his ass. After a few times around, I said, "Fuck it—I'm not doing that anymore."
>
> I: Was the fact that you were doing it eating away at you?
>
> BE: [quietly] Yeah—being a top would have been easier on my ego.
>
> I: Did you enjoy it while it was happening?
>
> BE: No, I didn't, because suddenly, out of nowhere, I was taking these big, hot monster dicks up my ass. It wasn't pretty.[36]

Estevez's construction of permission to perform in gay porn involves a series of disclaimers: "I'm very straight to this day," "I didn't get any sexual stimulation . . . even if I have a hard-on," and "I didn't have a lot of choice [to bottom]." Elaboration of permission and the construction of a persona often go hand in hand. Estevez's account illustrates this when he explains that "they manipulated me into being a bottom. They told me that I wasn't big enough or buff enough to play a top role, so I was labeled a bottom—a small, hot guy who gets dick up his ass . . . being a top would have been easier on my ego." Eventually, he refused to bottom, and in his later videos he only topped. However, it is clear from the permission Estevez gives himself and his ambivalence about the roles he performs in gay pornography that his persona is fashioned from other socially prevalent sexual scripts. Particularly noteworthy is his need to disclaim the evidence of erections as signifiers of sexual pleasure in a publication for gay men.

Constructing a persona is an important step for any new entrant in the gay porn industry, but for the straight performers it is probably the most important step. Gay men can rely to some extent on their private sexual personalities. For the heterosexual man, constructing a persona becomes the basis for navigating the demands of directors, agents, interviewers, and audience members and provides a foundation for determining what sexual acts and roles he will perform. In part, the persona is the self-conscious construction of a "personal" sexual script that draws on the individual's intrapsychic script as well as on grand cultural scenarios. The persona is a sort of sexual resume that the actor constructs around the kind of permission that he gives himself for entering the gay pornography business, but it is also based on the image that he wishes to project of whom he is as a sexual performer. The persona is what sociologist Erving Goffman has called (following certain vernacular uses) a "front": "that part of the individual's performance which regularly functions . . . to define the situation for those who observe the performance."[37] The actor's porn persona consists of a hodgepodge of beliefs about gender, sexuality, identity, acceptable sexual scripts that he may engage in, and his repertoire of acceptable sexual acts. Thus the actor's porn persona is a "situational sexual identity" that is constructed to be used within the confines of a porn career and the gay porno business. The persona is important because it enables the performer to have a self-concept that gives him permission to engage in homosexual activity and thus to sustain a credible sexual performance, to have erections, and to produce orgasms.

Once the actor has his porn persona, he will use it to negotiate auditions, interviews with the press, street encounters with fans and, most importantly, performances. He will use the persona to answer questions about why he started doing gay pornography (e.g., "I'm in it for the money"), his sexual orientation, his physical assets as a sexual performer (muscles, penis size, a "fuckable" ass), those particular sex acts he will or won't do, and to provide plausible excuses for any failure to turn in credible performances. Another aspect of a porn persona is whether the actor engages in professionally related activities like escorting or dancing. Usually people in the industry—agents, directors, journalists—help new entrants develop their porn personas. Often industry insiders inject a more palpable "marketing spin" into a new actor's persona. Insiders also supply standard terms like "top," "bottom," or "versatile" for roles involving anal intercourse, or more complex terms like "sex pig," "trade," or "straight bottom" to characterize the actor's porn performances.

When a gay-for-pay performer successfully conveys sexual pleasure, fans begin to question the performer's sexual orientation. Frequently a performer will concede that he is in fact bisexual. Describing himself as sexual is at least as common:

INTERVIEWER: Obviously, you think of yourself as heterosexual. . . .

ROD BARRY: [interrupting] I wouldn't say "heterosexual." I'd say "sexual."

I: What's the difference between being sexual and bisexual?

RB: I think bisexual means you're a switch-hitter, you like it both ways. Sexual is you like an orgasm and you don't care how you get it.[38]

Porn personas are intentionally constructed to facilitate work in the porn industry, but they often reflect intrapsychic investments. Rod Barry's description of himself as "sexual" may be more than a justification or permission to engage in homosexual sex. Over the course of his career he has insistently characterized himself as "sexual" or even "omni-sexual" rather than gay or bisexual: "Don't call me gay. Don't call me straight. Don't call me bisexual. Just call me sexual. I can cater to anybody . . . a gay male, a transsexual, or a female," he proclaimed in another interview.[39] He suggests a sexuality for himself that encompasses a wide range of "object choices" and roles (top or bottom); his image may embody an emerging style of masculine sexuality, one envisioned by Foucault: "What these signs and symbols of masculinity are for is not to go back to something that would be on the order . . . of machismo, but rather to invent oneself, to make oneself into the site of production of extraordinarily polymorphous pleasures."[40]

Virtually every actor who makes a name for himself as a top is challenged to bottom at some point in his career. Rod Barry, a former Marine and one of the top gay-for-pay porn stars in the late 1990s, was frequently asked if he would bottom. He always replied, "Where's the bucks?" The decision to bottom is justified in many ways but, like other aspects of the persona, involves repackaging symbolic resources, social roles, and culturally available sexual scripts:

I: Was "getting fucked" a big step or just another step?

RB: Another step. Obviously, it's a big step, because in the industry, everybody makes a big deal out of it. . . . That day was, to me, like any other day. Except for the fact that I was "getting fucked." . . . It's different from what I was doing, but it's just like any other day at the office.

I: Did you feel that you were playing a feminine role at that moment?

RB: No. No. No. And if you watch the movie, I don't think so, because I'm an aggressive top and I was also an aggressive bottom, playing the same way, like reaching around and grabbing his ass and pulling him: "Do it right!"[41]

Barry's performance as a bottom was very favorably reviewed by fans and critics. In a review in *Manshots*, director Jerry Douglas wrote, "Either Barry is one hell of an actor or he does delight in bottoming . . . his pleasure seems downright palpable. His energetic response to the rutting, the sparkle in his eyes, his joyous grin, and his rock-hard erection all confirm that he is indeed as exciting a bottom as he is a top."[42] Like many reviewers—in fact, it is the standard, perhaps even the expected, practice—Douglas elides porn's "documentary illusion" with the "acting" component of a sexual performance.

The actor's persona is both a marketing strategy and a personal statement about his relation to gay pornography. It is a kind of identity, helps him do his job, and acts as a "contract" with the social expectations of his significant others. An actor's persona may also have limits—he may not be able to successfully perform his persona at all times, or other people may not be aware of his persona or may choose to ignore it.[43] The longer their porn careers, the more actors are under pressure to revise their personas, to expand their repertoire of sex acts, and to put themselves into new situations in order to avoid becoming too predictable, and therefore boring to their fans. An integral dynamic of the porn industry, and for many forms of sex work, is a steady pressure for "fresh meat." In the 1930s sociologist Paul Cressey formulated the theory of retrogressive life cycles to explain the careers of young women who worked as taxi dancers ("dime-a-dance" girls). The young women who sought work as taxi dancers usually had left their families and communities to work in an occupation that was closely associated with prostitution. At first the young women found it exciting, but the longer they worked as taxi dancers the more difficult it was to compete with the newer and younger women who followed. Usually, the longer each woman worked, the less money she made and the more seedy the taxi halls she had to work in.[44] The life cycle of performers in the porn industry is subject to the same dynamic. Most porn actors are aware of this retrogressive dynamic and try to develop a career strategy to follow their porn career. Some leave the industry and go into other careers or businesses. Some work behind the scenes in porn, while others increasingly rely on escorting or some other form of sex work—which usually just stretches out the retrogressive dynamic over a longer period. Some performers will try to hold onto their fans by expanding their sexual repertoire—they will bottom or do a gang bang picture. But this progression usually leads to lower budget productions as well. "One interesting thing about this business," director Kristen Bjorn observed, "is that the longer you are in it, the less money you are paid. Once you are an old face, and an old body, forget it. You're through as far as your popularity goes."[45]

High-end companies like Falcon limit the number of times they'll use an actor. Thus, veteran actors are propelled into specialty videos (leather, golden showers, spanking, wrestling, etc.) and into situations not originally suggested by their personas. To some extent, the pressure to retain the interest of their fans also pushes many actors toward novel situations—they will bottom or do a gang bang picture. Eventually some actors' personas just wear out. The lower an actor's profile, the less necessary the persona.

The straight actor's development of a porn persona is a means by which heterosexual men can organize elements of their biographies, fantasized sexual scripts, and gender roles to perform homosexual sex acts and perhaps to achieve a minor sort of celebrity before an audience that is deeply engaged in the sexual significance and dramas of masculinity. The persona is, in part, a piece of bravado. Through the porn persona, the actor grants himself permission and elaborates the conditions under which he agrees to participate in the business. In addition, the persona can be easily parlayed into sex work—escorting and dancing—that is often an offshoot of performance in gay pornography. Nevertheless, the persona is relevant primarily to the pornography business and offers little help to straight actors who want to forestall the discrediting of their straight/heterosexual identities (by homosexuality and employment in sex work). An actor's persona also incites constant testing and probing by fans and other members of the audience—to confirm it, deny it, and reformulate a truer profile of the straight porn actor and his sexual identity.

Wood and Money Shots: Sexual Performance as Work

Working in the gay porn industry, as in other kinds of sex work, the actor is required to perform sex acts according to the direction of the paying party. While porn actors, like other sex workers, may exclude certain activities from their repertoire, their sexual behavior is governed by the demands and constraints of the video production context. Heterosexual actors in gay pornography must necessarily engage in homosexual sex acts. However, in the context of video production, three other factors help to define their sexual activities. One is the constant interruption of the homosexual activities in which they engage. A second is the use of various forms of heterosexual pornography—such as straight porn magazines or hetero porn videos shown on television monitors on the sidelines—as aids in maintaining their erections and stimulating orgasm. Third is postproduction and editing, which result in the illusion of an "authentic" sexual performance. The finished movie is the combined product of the credible sexual performances of the actors, the director's skill in motivating and preparing the actors to perform the sexual acts filmed, and the success of postproduction editing in sustaining the credibility and coherence of the sex portrayed and minimizing any discrepancies between the actors' personas and their sexual performances.

For the straight actor in gay pornography, it is the on-set performance of homosexual acts that defines his ability to successfully manage the situationally specific sexual demands. Many of these heterosexual actors claim that their first sexual encounter with another man was on the set of a gay porn video. Thus, even before his first homosexual experience, a straight actor must choose his repertoire of sexual acts. Certainly his most significant decision is whether or not he will engage in anal intercourse as a top or as a bottom. The repertoire of sex acts is very much a part of the actor's development of his porn persona. The shaping of his persona is dependent on those sexual scripts—those that exist in the culture at large, his own intrapsychic ones, or those he can imagine in his everyday life—in which he is able to invest his energy. Thus, for the straight actor, there is a continuum from the "trade" role, where the actor refuses all "gay" sex roles or reciprocity, to that of "sex pig," where he engages energetically in all aspects of sexual activities, to the "straight bottom" role, in which the straight actor engages primarily as a bottom.

The trade role is the gay porn role in which the actor presumably can maintain the most distance from the stigma of being labeled as homosexual, but ironically the straight bottom is a role that allows the performer to demonstrate that he is not aroused even though he is being penetrated—that is, he is not gay. The straight bottom, since he does not even need to produce an erection, requires even less of a libidinal investment than does an actor with a trade persona. However, the straight bottom role may also be adopted when an actor doesn't have the confidence or ability to maintain an erection in order to anally penetrate his costar. One such performer, Tim Barnett, during an interview questioning his choice of roles, responded,

> INTERVIEWER: Since you were relatively new to male-male sex . . . did you lay out any rules? . . . Was the whole menu of what you going to do discussed, or was it just "You're going to bottom"?
>
> TIM BARNETT: I think it was more or less discussed when I came out [to Los Angeles].
>
> I: The scene was filmed around what you were willing to do?
>
> TB: Right. And I'm very versatile. . . .
>
> I: Was there ever any question . . . whether you would top or if it would be a flip-flop?
>
> TB: . . . They wanted me to top Greg or do a flip-flop, and it just never came about . . . I just don't know if I'm comfortable enough with the sex yet that I would be a top.
>
> I: It's easier to be a bottom.
>
> TB: It's a lot easier to be a bottom.[46]

Despite the relative "ease" of bottoming, the *1996 Adam Gay Video Directory* was, nevertheless, critical of Tim Barnett's performances: "Tim is a big beefy blonde who just loves to get fucked. Unfortunately, he enjoys giving his co-stars pleasure so much he rarely has time to maintain his own erection."[47] (Here the reviewer maintains the public pretense of Barnett's libidinal investment, attributing his lackluster performance to his focus on giving pleasure to his costars.) Even gay actors, like straight actors, may have difficulties staying hard while being penetrated. That can be ignored if they project some form of libidinal engagement. Without any erections or effective engagement a straight bottom cannot give a credible performance.

Once the actor decides on the acts he is willing to perform, the major practical issue is the enactment of a credible performance of sexual acts. As I have already mentioned, heterosexual actors often use straight porn magazines, straight videos on monitors, or "fluffers" (performers who fellate the actor off camera) to help themselves achieve erections. Tim Barnett, the straight bottom quoted above, was asked if he used the person he was playing opposite to or if he drew on his own private world to get himself aroused. The actor answered, "Both. It really depends who it is. I really like my nipples played with, and sometimes the other person will be the kind of person I'd like to have playing with my nipples. A lot of times I'll use a magazine."[48]

Another adaptation is the development of what might be called a "professional" work ethic on the porn set. Still photographer Greg Lenzman discusses one such actor: "Usually, with the gay-for-pay, there are certain things they will not do or they don't have that energy. But there are some exceptions. Rod Barry, who started off more as a straight—I think he's now moved on to a lot of stages in his video career. . . . He will give all for his shoots and is very supportive of other performers. He's a joy to work with on a set, and you just know you're going to have a good scene with Rod Barry. The scene with Rod bottoming for the first time was just like an evolution."[49] Dirk Yates, the director-producer who discovered Rod Barry, concurred: "He seemed pro from the first day I met him. . . . He did twenty-nine scenes in a year. He started right off the bat. And I believe the guy's straight—maybe I'm wrong—but I've never seen such a performer. He would never turn you down on anything."[50] To porn video viewers, an important element is the sexual chemistry of the performers. It is unclear how often this is really the performers' chemistry or the result of editing and postproduction work. How do performers who are not gay manage to project the sexual appeal needed to attract viewers? Gay-for-pay performer Rod Barry insists that "porno is all about energy.[51]

Kristen Bjorn, probably the most successful contemporary director of gay porn, has made a series of videos using predominantly performers who do not identify, in any sense, as gay or homosexual.[52] While most of his actors are Latin American and European (and therefore from societies with different "sexual scripts"), they nevertheless have a large following of American gay men. Both Bjorn and his assistant director, who goes by the name of the Bear, have discussed the desirability of using straight actors many times. In one interview, the Bear notes,

> Straight men usually have less of a problem getting erections for still photography as well as video. I believe that they are better prepared to come to work knowing that sexual energy must come from themselves through fantasy, memories, erotic magazines, etc. Gay men often come to work thinking that their work is going to be a realization of a sexual fantasy that they have had for a long time. When they realize that they are not in control of the sexual activity, partners, and duration, they become detached and often bored with it and one another. When a gay model is turned on to another model, it can be great to film. In many cases the models are not that excited by each other, especially after four full days of filming the same sex scene. As one model put it at the end of a scene, "That was the longest trick that I ever had!" Once a gay model has decided that he is not sexually interested in the other models, it seems most difficult to bring him into the action and get him aroused. Straight boys don't seem to be as dependent upon the excitation of the other models nor as concerned whether or not they are exciting their partners. But when a gay model perceives that he is not arousing his partner, as often happens in scenes that involve gay and straight models together, it can make him feel insecure with himself. This affects his ability to get erections and ejaculate. Straight models are not as sensitive to the stimuli that can make or break a gay model's performance.[53]

The dynamics between gay men and straight actors is another important factor in the production of credible homosexual performances. Homophobic attitudes on the part of a straight actor often undermine the necessary "sexual chemistry." Gay actors often complain about working with straight performers. As the Bear notes, gay men are much more sensitive to the sexual chemistry between themselves and the straight actors. The identity issue frequently surfaces in gay men's assessment of working with heterosexual actors. Tommy Cruise, who explicitly identifies as a bisexual and as a bottom, comments,

> One of the things I hate is working with straight guys, because if they're not attracted to me, then I don't like it. People say, "What is your favorite guy like?" It doesn't matter, as long as they like me. That turns me on. If someone wants to fuck me really bad, that just turns me on—because they want me. Don't ask me why, I don't really know. That's what does it for me. It's not very enjoyable for me when I'm with a straight guy. A lot of straight guys, they don't even want me touching them. I'm like, "Why are you even in the business?" I've only worked with two straight guys who were okay—and one of them actually blew

my mind. He was the strangest dude I ever saw. He was like, "Okay, time to get a hard-on." Boom, he'd get a hard-on. It's like he's standing there like a friggin' robot. "Okay, time to come." Boom, he comes. He was so on-cue, it was kind of freaky, but he was so good to work with.[54]

Cruise's remarks point to the importance of the straight actor's attitude toward gay men and homosexuality, in addition to his intrapsychic need for his sexual partners to find him attractive. Buddy Jones, a gay man who has performed in several Kristen Bjorn movies, found it enjoyable to work with a straight actor: "It was a turn-on working with a straight boy . . . who was eating my ass and sucking my dick. And he was really good at that, especially the rimming. I was concerned about turning him on while he was fucking me, because I was really turned on. I thought that in his mind he was just working. But then his hard cock was up my ass and his hot cum shot all over me, and it kind of made me wonder if he was really enjoying it."[55] One gay man, Eric Hanson, who performs primarily as a top, says that his favorite costar is "straight bottom" Kurt Stefano: "He has a great persona about him. I think it's the straight thing going on with him. Straight-acting guys are a total turn-on."[56]

By itself, the porn persona is not sufficient for the successful management of sexual performances. The persona is only a strategy, a menu, and a resume. Sexual performances must project a certain degree of energy, enjoyment, and sexual heat to erotically stimulate their audience. Getting wood and producing orgasms are merely the certifying components of sexual performances in pornographic movies. Porn actors must convincingly play the roles of men engaged in sex in other ways in order to sustain a credible homosexual performance. As one porn actor after another iterates in interviews throughout the gay press and pornography magazines, making porn is hard work (no pun intended).

The Camera Frame: Sexual Scripts and Video Production

Pornography, both as a form of discourse and as a matter of practical production, invokes socially and culturally available sexual scripts in order to stimulate erotic expectations and fantasies.[57] Without being able to plug into culturally available scripts, neither the directors of porn videos nor the actors in the videos would be able to offer credible sexual performances. These socially available sexual scripts are utilized to create second-order scripts (screenplays) within the camera frame of video production during which the actors' sexual performances are transformed into screen performances.[58]

For straight performers, the gay porn video set provides highly structured access to homosexual activity. It is a social space dense with sexual cues.[59] Video production organizes the space (both physical and social) where sex will take place. But the making of pornography necessarily invokes the culture's generic sexual scenarios—the sex/gender scripts; racial, class, and ethnic stereotypes; dynamics of domination and submission; and various reversals and transgressions of these codes. Porn video scripts utilize these cultural and symbolic resources. These culturally significant symbolic codes help mobilize the actors' private desires and fantasy life in the service of the video's sexual narrative.

The making of a porn video requires not only the performance of real sexual acts but also the simulation of a coherent sexual "narrative." Real sex acts are usually performed, but the video representation of them is more coherent than the actual sexual activity being filmed. The shooting of any sexual scene is made up of an apparently simple sex act photographed from several different perspectives. In fact, the performed act is interrupted many times to arrange shooting angles and lighting and to allow the actors to "get wood"—to regain their erections.[60] For example, the cameraman crawls under actors fucking doggie style, then shoots them from above to show penetration of the ass, then from behind the active party to catch yet another penetration shot of the hard penis going in and out. Then the "money shots" (shots of the actors ejaculating) of all the performers in the scene have to be choreographed, often at the end of many hours of filming. The actors may need help of various kinds to help them ejaculate—heterosexual porno magazines, porn videos on monitors, or manipulation by one of their co-actors such as biting their nipples, inserting a finger in their anus, or kissing them. Thus a fifteen- to twenty-minute sexual scene that the viewer sees is edited and patched together, with soundtrack added, from footage shot over a six- or seven-hour period.

The director choreographs the sexual combinations and the action. Working from a script that is more like a storyboard or a treatment than a conventional script, the director plots the sexual combinations (who tops whom, from oral to anal, from doggie style to missionary position, and so on) within a loose storyline. Even in a pornography video without any storyline to speak of, casting the actors and plotting the sexual combinations constitute its narrative. In most videos, the director's main job is casting the performers and teaming them up, planning their sequence of sex acts, and coaching them in their performances. "I think you can get the hottest sex out of somebody," one performer commented, "when you give 'em a good partner and you don't over-direct. I think hot scenes have to do more with the costar than the director, really." There is a wide diversity in the directing styles of video porn directors. Regarding one very successful director, the same performer went on to say, "I think Chi Chi [LaRue] encourages people to do good. But it's a double-edged sword. If you're too verbal and too commanding, it can take their wood away. Chi Chi can be kind of intense and that intensity can be kind of daunting."[61] Ultimately, it is the director's choreography of sexual performances and the effectiveness of the editing process that give pornography its quality as an idealization of sexual performance. Whatever shortcomings commercial pornography exhibits—the repetitiveness of sexual activities, inadequate performances (flaccid erections, lackluster orgasms, bored actors), and shoddy production values—they are exacerbated by the idealization that pornography as a medium promotes.

Porn "screenplays" frequently elaborate on or incorporate the culturally available sexual scenarios. The director fashions the sex scene in a video by deploying material drawn from cultural scenarios (where, for example, a very muscular, butch man will top a younger, slender man) and from everyday interpersonal social dynamics, as well as by relying on the actors' intrapsychic or personal identity scripts (gay, straight, bisexual, top, bottom, a man, etc.). The director shapes the video's script by exploiting and integrating these cultural resources.

The director uses the porn actor's persona as the raw material for the sexual plot when choreographing the sexual combinations. Of course, sometimes actors can't successfully manage the persona that they want to project. For example, if a straight performer whose persona presents him as "trade" (i.e., he will not perform oral sex, allow himself to be penetrated, or kiss) can't get an erection, making him unable to penetrate the performer assigned to play bottom, then he and the director must negotiate some modification in order to have a credible sex scene. If he isn't fired and replaced, the actor with the "trade" persona may have to perform outside his persona—perform oral sex or agree to bottom—in order to get paid. After 1998, Viagra has helped in achieving and maintaining erections, but there are still numerous other problems involving an actor's ability to live up to his persona and perform credible sex.

Conclusion

The making of gay male pornography provides an interesting example of the dynamics of situational homosexuality. Since performing in pornography is a kind of sex work, the performers' sexual conduct is a specific response to their customers' preferences and does not represent the preferred sexual responses of the performer. In other words, the sex that is performed is that for which the customer is willing to pay.[62]

In gay pornography, the participants have to develop a "persona" or "front" (a *nom de porn*, sexual histories, a repertoire of sex acts) to negotiate the social demands they must contend with as sexual participants. Like any front, it is more manageable if it is, to some degree, consistent with biographical attributes of the participant. But the persona also provides the performer with a way of invoking the potential cultural scenarios and sexual scripts that are compatible with his intrapsychic scripts.[63] The production process of gay pornography creates a situation that enables straight men to engage in homosexual sex for money. It is a highly organized commercial space that supplies sex partners, symbolic resources, and other erotic stimulants, and a video production technology that can produce coherent and credible sexual narratives and images.

The identitarian expectations of gay spectators shape both the making of a pornographic video and their interpretations of the sexual performances. It is commonly presumed that when an actor in a pornographic video has an erection while being penetrated he must be gay. In contrast, I have argued that credible homosexual performance, whether or not it sexually arouses the performer, can take place without conscious identification as a homosexual person or even without spontaneous preference for homosexual forms of activity. Situational homosexualities emerge when heterosexually identified individuals encounter situations that enable or reward homosexual behavior.

Situational homosexuality is socially constructed sexuality. All sexual performance is fundamentally situational and does not always result in long-lasting social psychological commitment to any one form of sexual activity. It is a process that draws on both intrapsychic scripts and cultural scenarios and integrates them into the interpersonal scripts of everyday social life. The theory of sexual scripts presumes that sexual performance is not about discovering and pursing one's intrapsychic desires (the presumptive core sexual self) but about defining and constructing scenarios of desire using cultural scenarios and negotiating interpersonal situations.[64] The men who work in the gay porn industry—whether gay, straight, or "sexual"—must all construct scripts in order to perform. In this way they are no different from any person engaging in sexual activity—since all sexual performance is situational.

7

The Wages for Wood

■ ■

Do Female Performers in the
Adult Film Industry Earn More
Than Male Performers?

The recession of 2008 hit the adult film industry, long thought to be immune to the vagaries of the business cycle, exceptionally hard, precipitating sharp drops in revenues (down an estimated 30 to 50 percent), production (the number of new titles cut by half), pay-per-view programming (a key source of revenue down 50 percent), and numerous shutdowns of smaller production companies. DVD sales, in particular, a significant source of revenues, plummeted. The industry's downturn was not only the result of a decline in demand for pornographic videos overall but also the result of a mix of technological challenges, piracy, and the growing abundance of free pornography on the Internet.[1]

In the early 2000s, the market for video porn was inundated with massive amounts of new product, not only from the five biggest producers (Vivid, Hustler, VCR, Evil Angel, and Digital Playground) but from numerous smaller studios and independent producers and through the availability of free content on "the tube sites," which show pirated clips and videos from amateurs who offer their homemade porn for free. At least five of the top one hundred websites in the United States are portals for free pornography (known as tube sites, e.g., x-tube) on which much of the content is pirated.[2]

The grand historical irony in all this is that the technologies that the porn industry pioneered and helped to introduce are now helping to undermine it. These technologies "democratized" the market for hardcore erotic content by reducing the barriers to entry and the transaction costs and in the process dramatically altered the market for pornographic videos. Low cost and easily accessible means of production and distribution have blurred the distinction between producers, distributors, and consumers.[3]

The downturn had a significant impact on both earnings and employment. Everyone was being paid less—from makeup artists to editors and performers. In 2009, porn star Savannah Stern told *Los Angeles Times* reporter Ben Fritz that she had gone from working four or five days a week to one, that producers had cut fees from $1,000 to $700 per scene, and that her annual income had declined from $150,000 a year to $50,000. Outside of reproduction and marketing, most employees (performers among them) have been treated as independent contractors. They receive no unemployment benefits or health insurance. With fewer productions there are also fewer opportunities. Yet competition for work was greater than ever—with the high unemployment rates after 2008, many more women entered the industry in order to make up for the loss of jobs by their husbands, boyfriends, or themselves in other sectors of employment. In fact, there was a mini-boom for middle-aged women as performers in productions for the MILF ("mothers I'd like to fuck") genre. Nevertheless, overall fees per scene for female performers were down by as much as 30 or 40 percent.

The 2008 recession had an even more devastating impact on male performers. Reporter Susanna Breslin, writing for *Salon*, believes that the recession hit the men in porn a lot harder than the women.[4] In an article in the *Guardian*, filmmaker Louis Theroux, who recently made a documentary about the current state of the porn business, reported that fees for scenes declined from $3,000 for big-name stars to $900 to $1,000 and for regular female performers down to $600; for men, it was even worse, as low as $150 per scene.[5] Women had the option of working in other sectors of the adult entertainment industry (such as stripping, live shows, or escorting); generally men did not.

It is widely believed that the adult film industry is one of the few industries in which women earn more than men. And in general, male performers on the average do earn lower fees per scene than female performers. Female performers' sex appeal and sexual performance are the main selling points for pornographic films. In fact, there's a standard jibe in the business that "male talent would pay producers for the opportunity" to have sex with the sexy women who are the main draw for consumers.[6] When asked about the pay disparity between men and women, male megastar James Deen, who played a major role attracting a female audience to straight porn, claimed that he was "overpaid . . . the girls get paid what they get paid because . . . most of the audience is buying the movie for the girl."[7]

In this chapter I examine the dynamics of the adult film industry's labor markets and the impact of these dynamics on performers' earnings. These labor markets combine both elements unique to the industry as well as the more common features of segmented labor markets.[8]

1 The labor market for adult film performers is distinctly "gendered work" and reflects the sexual division of labor in heterosexual inter-course. Thus no heterosexual "hardcore" scene can take place without male and female gendered performances (the classification of trans-sexual hardcore movies as a straight genre illustrate this principle). Both female and male performers are necessary to a successful representation of a heterosexual sex act.[9]

2 While both male and female are necessary to hardcore performances, sales are almost wholly dependent upon the appeal of female perform-ers. Their higher per scene fees reflect their greater market value (i.e., productivity) for revenue generation and profitability.

3 The career patterns of male and female performers are markedly different and are affected by the sexual division of labor, Cressey's retrospective dynamic, human capital investments by performers, and the availability of collateral markets for related skills and services.

Thus two separate labor markets developed for complementary work within a single production process: one for female performers and one for males. How-ever, each of those markets is stratified around economic and sexual factors: the female performer's sex appeal and willingness to perform transgressive sex-ual acts as well as the male performer's facility producing erections ("wood") and supplying orgasms ("money shot"). In addition, these two labor markets interact with other sectors (and labor markets) of the sex industry (strip clubs, escorting services, live websites, sex toy manufacturers, etc.) to generate sup-plemental income for performers.

Detailed, systematic, and consistent information about production, reve-nues, employment, and wages in the adult film and entertainment industry is almost nonexistent.[10] The adult video business and other sex-related businesses are not tracked with rigor or precision. Moreover, the definition of the busi-ness has always included different kinds of sexually explicit materials such mov-ies, magazines, sex toys, and other media. Almost all of the firms operating in the porn industry are privately held and have no compelling reason to disclose income or sales data. Those businesses that are publicly held and involved in the distribution of pornographic materials do not track their adult entertain-ment separately from their mainstream offerings.[11]

The quantitative information used in this study has been drawn from two online databases that provide fairly comprehensive information about the careers of adult film performers, directors, and studios and the films made. They differ however in terms of completeness and the various ways that the data can be sorted.

1 The Internet Adult Film Database (IAFD) is an online database of information pertaining to the American adult entertainment industry, covering male and female adult performers, directors, and movies. It is open to the public and is searchable. Films produced by the non-American porn industry are also found on the database if a U.S. release is available and the film concerned has a U.S. release date, not the original one. The predecessor to IAFD was a database of adult film actresses called Absverver that had been created by Dan Abend in 1993. Covering over 127,021 titles and 117,608 performers and directors, IAFD is maintained by a volunteer staff of editors. Quick checks have shown that this website is somewhat more accurate and complete in terms of listings of titles and number of titles in which performers have appeared than the Adult Film Database.

2 The Adult Film Database (AFD) is a website that also attempts to maintain complete records of all pornographic movies and adult film performers. This includes filmographies, partial biographies, and reviews, including labeled and categorized adult films. It was originally created in 1991. This database appears to be less complete and less extensive than IAFD, but it offers more sophisticated filtering and sorting.

Unfortunately, it has not been possible to systematically sample performers over time to determine more rigorous information on earnings. In fact, attempts to elicit earnings information directly from performers encountered strong resistance. One has to know a performer fairly well before they will divulge per scene fees (these vary dramatically by company, format, and status of performer) or annual earnings. Many performers do not want other performers to know much or how little they make. Much of the quantitative information provided here should be used heuristically.

Growth of the Adult Film Industry and the Emergence of Labor Markets

After World War II, two major changes occurred that transformed the economic and social conditions that enabled pornography—and particularly pornographic films—to enter the mainstream of American life and fostered

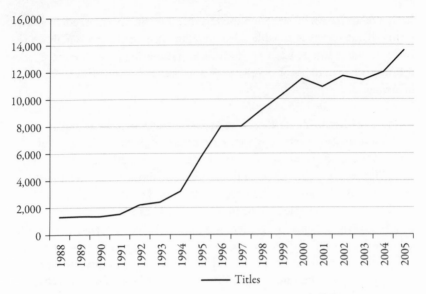

FIG. 7.1 Adult Film Titles, 1988–2005. (Source: http://www.internet-filter-review
.toptenreviews.com/internet-pornography-statistics.html.)

its economic growth. The first of the changes was the result of the U.S. Supreme
Court's decision in the 1948 *Paramount* case that required the major Hollywood studios to divest themselves of their theater chains. Television had already
cut deeply into weekly ticket sales; in the wake of the *Paramount* decision, theaters were no longer routinely provided with films to run. Every movie theater
was on its own. Theater owners turned initially to exploitation films and softcore movies and then eventually hardcore films in order to bring in audiences.
The second transformation was brought about by the Supreme Court's decisions
about obscenity and pornography during the 1950s and 1960s. In *Roth v. United
States* (1957), the most important of these decisions, the Court's majority opinion, written by Justice William Brennan, established a new definition of obscenity that went on to exercise a tremendous influence over legal issues of obscenity
and pornography in subsequent decades.[12]

Since the 1980s, the industry has grown enormously. During that time, pornographic filmmakers shifted production from shooting the X-rated features
on film designed for exhibition in theaters to video tapes that could be viewed
in homes. The new technology was cheaper to produce, cheaper to reproduce,
and more accessible to consumers (especially to those reluctant to attend porn
theaters). The advent of the AIDS epidemic and uncertainty about the transmission of HIV reinforced the appeal of home videos as a substitute for sex.
Video sales and rentals soared throughout the eighties and nineties. Growth

slowed down after 2000 despite the introduction of the DVD, a superior video technology, because of the increased availability of free or cheap porn on the Internet (see Figure 7.1).

The 2008 recession is a unique event in the history of a business that doubled more than ten times between the 1970s and 2007. Over the course of forty years, as the adult film industry grew and settled in the San Fernando Valley, where almost 90 percent of the porn produced in the United States was made, a distinctive labor market for performers emerged. From 1959 to 1969, when pornographic films were exclusively softcore, the industry often hired unemployed or aspiring actors as performers. But the conditions of employment changed with the transition to hardcore (sexually explicit) production in 1969.

The transition led to a dramatic shift in the production of pornographic films—both in how sex was portrayed on film and in the way the production of pornography was organized, who performed in it, and what other kinds of activities were associated with it. The defining characteristic of hardcore is insertion—oral, vaginal, or anal. It required new performance conventions and new cinematic production requirements. Whereas in the production of softcore cinema many standard cinematic conventions of genre, performance, and narrative held sway, virtually everything changed in hardcore production. The feature-length "nudie-cuties" (as softcore films were nicknamed) resembled Hollywood features with the addition of some female nudity.

The production of hardcore films required a new set of working conditions and new conventions of performance that allowed for the enactment of "real" sexual activity, which required erections and orgasms. Producers had to establish the social and physical conditions for sexual performances to be filmed: a bounded space where sexual performances would be filmed, a supply of sexual partners (via casting) who expected to perform sexual acts before a camera with other performers, and some sort of production crew. In addition, certain aspects of sexual performance became central to the production process. Thus, to be credible, the sexual encounters represented in hardcore movies require real erections and real orgasms—and those reality effects anchor the fantasy world that porn films offer to viewers. And whereas in softcore productions the performers are actors and the sex simulated, in hardcore porn the sex acts are "real" and performers are considered sex workers.

The shooting of any sexual scene is made up of an apparently simple sex act photographed from several different perspectives. The sexual activity being filmed is interrupted many times to arrange shooting angles, change the lighting, and allow the male performers to "get wood"—to regain their erections. The male performer is required to maintain an erection and refresh it easily. In the first three decades of the industry this required "fluffing," where someone was hired to stimulate the male performer; after 1998 it was possible to use

Viagra or some other pharmaceutical aid. The finished movie is the combined product of the credible sexual performances of the actors, the director's skill in motivating and preparing the actors to perform the sexual acts filmed, and the success of postproduction editing in sustaining the credibility and coherence of the sex portrayed and minimizing any discrepancies between the actors' personas and their sexual performances.[13]

When hardcore pornographic movies first began to be made, producers were often small business owners who were already involved in the porn business in some other capacity—for example, as photographers, bar owners, pimps, adult bookstore owners, theater managers or owners, or porn magazine publishers.[14] The challenge in its first stage was less production than distribution. Thus, in many cases some of the early investors came from those who controlled potential means of distribution. The porn business had been, up until that time, a mostly illegal activity and in which organized crime had played a significant role in both the distribution of products and the provision of protection. Eric Schlosser's profile of Reuben Sturman and Larry Revene's memoir *Wham Bam $$Ba Da Boom!* both provide vivid accounts of the role played by such figures.[15]

In the early period, from 1969 until the late 1970s, there was no routine way to recruit actors willing to perform in hardcore movies. Many early performers were unemployed actors, strippers, or musicians who entered the business in New York or Los Angeles as way to earn extra money. Initially, no one considered performing in adult films as a desirable career goal. Others entered the industry as an expression of sexual liberation in the wake of the counterculture and the sexual revolution—sex, drugs, and rock and roll.

During most of the 1970s, it was illegal in states like California to pay performers to have sex. "You cannot make a hardcore film without violating the prostitution laws," Captain Jack Wilson of the LAPD told Kenneth Turan and Stephen Zito. "When you pay actors to engage in sex or oral copulation, you've violated the laws. You've solicited individuals to engage in prostitution by asking them to exchange sex for money."[16] "When you get into hard core," one director of softcore films lamented, "you are dealing with a different class of people. You can't get actors or actresses anymore, but pimps and whores." Sex films were no longer merely products made on the margins of the Hollywood film industry; they were outside both the law and the film industry.[17] Thus casting for hardcore movies posed an entirely new set of issues for producers, finding people willing to perform "real" sex and avoiding the police.

The men and women of the first generation worked in an industry that slowly formed around them. Most production was haphazard. Harry Reems, who appeared in *Deep Throat* and numerous hardcore shorts made in the 1970s, claimed that he "never knew what I was being hired for. I just went and came. Some nights I'd literally limp home, I'd be so sore."[18] Nor was there an established or stable pay scale at the time. Women were paid $100 for a day's work and men $75. The women, however, would get an extra $25 if they did an anal scene. Reems and Georgina Spelvin (the star in the 1973 porn classic *The Devil in Miss Jones*) once protested that men should be paid the same rate and in that instance he was paid at the same rate that female performers were.[19]

As more and more of the adult film industry located to the San Fernando Valley on the northern end of Los Angeles County, a more formalized labor market emerged. It has remained a stigmatized, though somewhat glamorized, occupational activity that to some extent imposes a significant cost of entry into the labor market. The labor requirements for performers became more clearly delineated and led to the emergence of distinct submarkets. Initially, employment depended more on the willingness and ability to engage in sex on camera.

The labor market(s) for pornographic actors emerged only when certain conditions were met. Since few people, at the time, had aspirations to be a porn star as a career, it was necessary to identify potential performers more systematically. Initially, demand for performers was relatively small (probably in the hundreds) as well as contingent; talent scouts and agents were an effective means of supplying performers to producers. Male and female talent was often dealt with separately. Producers increasingly exercised more control over (and did not publicly disclose) the fees that were offered—plus female performers were paid at higher rates than males. The labor markets for female and male performers increasingly functioned independently of one another. And the constant demand for "fresh" or "new" female performers—for novelty of any sort—drives the demand for talent and new marketing opportunities.

The appeal of female stars emerged as the basis for marketing porn films. Physical attributes including especially breasts, buttocks, face, and hair (perhaps in that order) are very important, as well as what more transgressive acts they willing to engage in—and sometimes that matters even more than their sexual skills. While men are necessary to the production of a sex scene, they are not important to the marketing of a film. Nevertheless they have stringent physiological requirements. They have to be able to produce and maintain erections over the course of filming an entire sex scene, with breaks and retakes. And they have to be able to produce ejaculations practically on demand. In the early days of the industry male performers were not paid if they failed to produce a visible orgasm—thus the term "money shot." There are many accounts of the long hours (or days even) spent on sets by performers and film crews "waiting for wood" and money shots in order to wrap a film shoot.[20] The reliable male performers have a "physiological talent" that is not easily learned, and most men do not have. After 1998 Viagra and erectile disfunction pharmaceuticals have been used to help maintain wood, if not necessarily to stimulate initial arousal, which continues to require activation through desire. Of course both men and women also have to produce convincing performances of sexual pleasure, whether or not they are actually enjoying the sex they engage in during a scene.

Today the adult film industry has a highly developed infrastructure of production companies, distribution networks, and technical services as well as agents and scouts for performers. In 2008, the Free Speech Coalition, an adult industry lobbying group, estimated in their "State-of-the Industry Report, 2007–2008" that there were approximately one thousand performers actively seeking work at any given time.[21]

Employment and Earnings

In the intervening decades, employment in the adult film industry presumably followed the growth of production (shown in Figure 7.1). Production of adult films increased in the 1980s with the adoption of video (VHS), which was cheaper to produce than film and opened new distribution channels (porn could be played on television in private homes) and away from dependence on theaters. The introduction of the Internet during the nineties (the porn business pioneered the development of secure online business transactions) spurred production, and the introduction of DVDs in 2000 further accelerated the growth rate (because porn could be played on TVs and computers).

In Figure 7.2, the number of new entrants (i.e., the number of new performers cast each year in their first adult film) conveys the number of women and men actually hired, not necessarily the supply or demand. The growth in employment of new female performers closely reflects the growth of video production in the years between 1988 and 2005 (Figure 7.1), while the employment of male newcomers remains relatively flat. The years of rapid growth of production and female employment were the years that also saw the development of new subgenres (gonzo, bondage, strap-on) and availability of new media formats and channels of distribution (DVDs, Internet, mobile).

The impact of the 2008 recession is especially striking in Figure 7.2. Qualitative and anecdotal evidence suggests that the demand for female performers declined sharply. The number of new female performers had grown rapidly from 1990 up through 2008, after which it dropped precipitously. The demand (since the data are based on the annual number of performers in their first production) for male performers is in stark contrast. Some of this can be attributed to the wide gap in the fees and the physical and sexual requirements of new male entrants. There is no sign of comparable growth among the male performers during the period when women exhibited the greatest increase in the number of performers. The ratio of female to male new entrants (see Figure 7.3) is quite dramatic—increasing from a little more than two for every male to more than twelve per male in 2008.

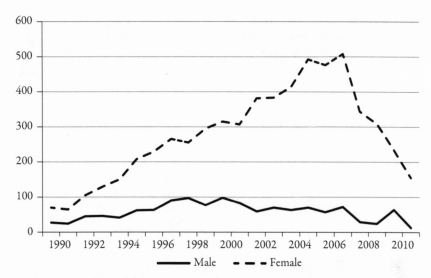

FIG. 7.2 Estimated New Entrants, Female and Male Performers, 1990–2010. (Source: Data are derived from http://www.adultfilmdatabase.com.)

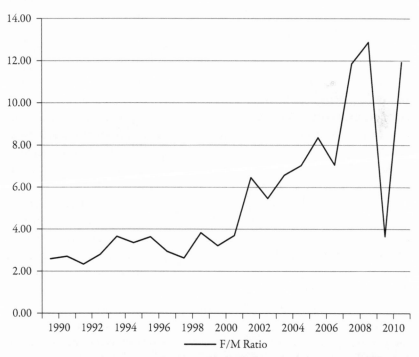

FIG. 7.3 New Entrants, 1990–2010, Female/Male Ratio. (Source: Data are derived from http://www.adultfilmdatabase.com.)

Table 7.1
Performer Fees and Female to Male Earnings Ratio, 1970–2010

Years	Female performer (basic "boy/girl" scene, vaginal)	Male performer (basic "boy/girl" scene)	Female to male earnings ratio (=female/male)
Early 1970s	$100/day	$75/day	1.33
Late 1980s / early 1990s	$400–$500/day	$300–$400/day	1.33–1.25
Mid-1990s	$800–$1,000/day		
Early 2000s	$800/scene	$400/scene	2.00
2007	$800–$1,000/scene	$250–$800/scene	3.20–1.25
2010	$700/scene	$250–$500/scene	2.80–1.40

SOURCE: 1970s data from Legs McNeil and Jennifer Osbourne, *The Other Hollywood: The Uncensored Oral History of the Porn Film Industry* (New York: HarperCollins, 2005); 1980s–2007 data from Mike Abo, Nelson X, and David Sullivan, "Rising Talent Rates: Welcome to the New Reality," *Adult Video News*, April 2007; 2010 data from http://www.good.is/posts/the-economics-of-porn-better -than-the-economics-of-other-stuff.

In the early days of the industry performers were paid a flat day rate. By the late 1990s most worked on a per scene basis as independent contractors. Female performers earned between $450 and $1,400 per scene, while male performers earned anywhere between $250 and $1,000. Talent rates in the gay sector of the adult industry for male performers were comparable to those of female performers.

As with other matters, there is no reliable or official data about fees, salaries, or employment in the adult entertainment industry. The data in Table 7.1 are more or less completely anecdotal. In practice, there are no standardized fees. Fees can vary enormously by the sex acts that performers are paid to do (blow jobs vs. double penetrations, etc.), the genre that is being made (features with plot vs. pro-amateur or gonzo), and the size and economic clout of the company producing the film (Vivid vs. White Ghetto).

Women dominate the occupational structure. Contract actresses are at the top of the pyramid in the porn workforce. Only the larger companies will sign popular actresses to exclusive long-term contracts. And few performers are under contract at any given time. They are the performers that companies put on the covers of DVDs. They can earn between $100,000 and $150,000 a year— which does not include the substantial earnings to be gained from collateral activities such as dancing (i.e., stripping), ownership of a personal website, or personal appearances. While all performers in the adult film industry are popularly called porn stars, contract actresses are the true stars of the adult film industry.[22] A female performer's pay depends on how closely she resembles the dominant standard of beauty, her willingness to engage in sex acts in addition to "vaginal boy/girl sex," the size of the production company, and how new she is to the business. A male's fee depends almost completely upon his "reliability"—his experience and his ability to produce wood and the money shot.

The female-to-male earnings ratios calculated above are, of course, extremely crude and thus give only a rough sense of the extreme disparities that can exist between female and male performers. In the United States as a whole, the female-to-male earnings ratio in 2010 was 0.81, which signified that American women earned 19 percent less than American men. The data in Table 7.1 suggest that in the adult film industry men could earn between 25 percent less up to more than 200 percent less—a much wider gender gap than existed between women and men at the end of the nineteenth century (0.463).[23]

I don't have an accurate estimate of the proportion of women (relative to men) working as performers; however, the ratio of female to male new entrants suggests that women constitute a significant majority of performers working at any one time. The adult film industry has what economist Claudia Goldin has called "the aura of gender," in which its most public occupation is categorized—rhetorically and normatively—as female.[24]

Porn Stars, Human Capital, and the Occupational Pyramid

The porn star—like the star in Hollywood, in music, or on television—is a major economic resource of the adult film industry. Stars sell movies. They are marketing tools that help stimulate and stabilize the demand for films.[25] Thus, for the companies that produce the movies and for customers who purchase or rent the movies, the star, however much that term may seem to be an exaggeration, is absolutely essential. Laurence O'Toole claimed that

> the most crucial strand of Vivid's capital investment has been in people. . . . It doesn't matter how good the script or the digitalia [sic—genitalia] are, whether it is film or videotape in the camera, this kind of adult entertainment depends upon bodies and beauty. Vivid is famous for its beautiful contract players, also known as the "Vivid Queens." It was the first company to offer exclusive contracts to performers, with Ginger Lynn the original Vivid Queen in the mid-eighties. Though other companies have followed suit, Vivid still leads the field. Wicked, VCA, Ultimate and Sin are all doing it, but still only with a maximum of three contracted players at any given time.[26]

The persona of a star is constructed around the personality and performances of individual performers, but the star is also a complex social role. The star is an iconic image that signifies something about sexuality and gender and also represents a distinctive personality or type. And the star is a worker, a person who earns his or her income as a performer. Last, but certainly not least, the star is an economic asset, an investment for the studio or company that has her under contract.[27] The term star is implicitly a term of value; not every movie actor is a star. However, in the adult entertainment industry porn star is often used much more broadly and loosely. Almost every performer in a pornographic film production is termed, at some point, a porn star—at least to fans and viewers—though industry insiders generally use the term "model" to refer to the performers in adult films. For the individual performer, star quality is something that can be consciously developed and is highly marketable. Performers will often make human capital investments (cosmetic surgery, breast enhancements, skin treatments, etc.) in order to increase their sexual appeal and thus earnings. Stars are an essential component of both the making of movies (as workers and images) and the marketing of movies (as assets that attract audiences). Stars sell movies—they are marketing tools that help to stimulate and stabilize the demand for films.[28]

Three of the most prominent contract actresses in the early 2000s were superstars Jenna Jameson, Tera Patrick, and Sasha Grey. In the late 1990s Jameson emerged as the dominant performer in the adult film industry. She signed an exclusive contract with Wicked Pictures, at that time a relatively small production house. She was paid $6,000 for each of the eight movies that she performed in for Wicked. By 2001 she earned $60,000 for her performance in a single DVD. On top of her performances in adult films, she earned $8,000 a night dancing in strip clubs. In 2000 she launched Club Jenna, her own adult entertainment company, on the Internet. In 2005, Club Jenna had revenues of $30 million (her profits were estimated at half of that).

Male performers usually do not have such economic opportunities. If the contract actresses are racehorses, reliable male talent (the "woodsmen") are work horses. Perhaps the closest male equivalent (in terms of renown if not wealth) to Jameson is James Deen, who started at age eighteen in 2004 and had by 2012 already made 1,322 videos and directed eleven movies. He is said to make over $20,000 a month from his video performances. He has played an important role in attempting to expand the heterosexual porn audience from its male base to include women. And by the early 2000s Deen had succeeded in attracting a large following among women and teenage girls. In 2013, he starred with Lindsey Lohan in an independent feature (*The Canyons*) directed by Hollywood auteur Paul Schrader. Some of the other more experienced male performers have started their own production companies (e.g., John Stagliano of Evil Angel) or married "contract actresses" and with them formed a production company and began directing adult productions.[29]

If the contract actresses are at the top of the pay scale and represent the top tier of the workforce, reliable male talent occupies the second tier. Reliable, as I mentioned earlier, means being able to produce, maintain, and refresh erections ("get wood") on demand as well as producing money shots, also on demand. Young, inexperienced, or ineffectual male performers' failure to produce wood and/or money shots can result in expensive production delays—the problem of "waiting for wood."[30] Reliable male performers earn higher fees than young female performers. There are, by one count, no more than thirty or forty men in that category.[31]

Under the reliable male talent in both status and pay are the vast sea of B-girls who perform in the productions of smaller companies or in low-status genres. Beneath the B-girls are the new male performers who have not yet proved themselves reliable. And on the very bottom are the "suitcase pimps," the boyfriends and husbands of young female performers. These men often claim to be managers or agents for their girlfriends and wives.[32] What performers are paid depends on where they are in the occupational hierarchy. The suitcase pimps and new male talent are generally paid very little (at the bottom of the range), while reliable male talent earns fees at the top of the range.

Agents play a central role in the smooth functioning of the labor markets for both male female and male pornographic actors. For many years, Jim South's World Modeling Talent Agency, served as the sole agent in the adult film industry. The agency regularly recruited new performers through ads in the local newspapers. In the course of recruiting a large talent pool, it helped to mold a more reliable workforce for the industry and, at the same time presumably, higher rates for performers. In recent years, other agencies have emerged, and many potential performers use the Internet to seek employment as adult performers.

Careers in the Adult Film Industry

It is widely assumed that the average length of a performer's career is typically assumed to be short—three years is a number commonly given. However, it is unclear what empirical grounds exist for this generalization about the length of careers in the adult film industry. For this study I took a sample of performers from the adult film databases to offer a more grounded estimate. In order to get a more accurate estimate of the length of careers in the adult film industry I drew a random sample of performers (females: $n = 74$; males: $n = 76$) from AFD. The sample consisted of female and male performers who appeared in a movie released in 2007(AFD allowed us to sort by year). That year was chosen in part because it was the last year of production before the recession of 2008–2009, but also because it standardized for the relative time period in the industry. The data from AFD were supplemented by data on age of birth, age started, years in the business, and number of titles from IAFD, which tended to have more comprehensive listings of adult films in which performers appeared.

Many of those who undertake work as performers in the adult film industry probably first begin to work in porn films as either a temporary source of

Table 7.2
Porn Career Patterns, Females and Males (as of 2012)

	Female (average) n = 74	Female (range)	Male (average) n = 76	Male (range)
Age started	23	18–33	28	18–40
Years in business	6	1–13	12	1–27
No. of titles made	110	1–364	669	1–1,205

SOURCE: Sample selected from performers who made at least one video in 2007 derived from http://www.adultfilmdatabase.com.

income during periods of unemployment or a way of supplementing their regular income. Few enter the workforce of the adult industry as part of a long-planned career move, although once engaged, many continue to work in the industry over a period of several years. Most make one movie: 54 percent of men and 29 percent of women make one movie and then go on to something else. A vast majority of the performers make ten videos or fewer (88 percent of men and 58 percent of women). Despite the high drop-out rate, male performers can have careers twice the length of female performers. The average length of time that men work as performers is twelve years, as opposed to six for women. The ratio of new male entrants to new female entrants suggests that women outnumber men in the industry's workforce. The longevity of male performers may serve to equalize to some extent the gender balance as a whole, though it is still likely that women outnumber men.

The other significant fact is that some male performers may not only outlast female performers but also work more often. The average number of titles that they appear in (it isn't possible to estimate how many scenes they appear in) is almost six times the number of titles in which female performers are cast.

If we compared only the income earned by female and male performers for their work in adult film, reliable male performers may actually earn more than female performers. Thus if E is the average annual potential income from film work,

$$E = (T \times P) \div Y,$$

where T is the average number of titles accrued throughout a performer's career, P is the basic fees per scene, and Y is the number of years that the performer was in the industry. Then the average annual earnings of male performers from their film work alone is $44,600, compared to $18,333 for female performers.[33] But many young porn actresses earn additional income by dancing in strip clubs, performing on websites, and escorting. Income from these sources is more substantial than that from the film work. Danni Ashe, founder of Danni's

Hard Drive, one of the first porn mega-websites, notes that "being a featured dancer is where the money is. You model and shoot movies just to earn the credits and name recognition that can be traded for large feature booking fees and headline status in the clubs."[34]

Compared to the female performers, male performers have limited options to increase their earnings within the industry. The most common is working behind the scenes, handling lighting, building sets, or working as a videographer. But the most lucrative income earning option for male performers is directing—directors potentially earn $20,000 to $60,000 for each film made. Approximately 46 percent of our sample of male performers had directed an average of fifty-six hardcore videos. While many of those who directed videos were among more "reliable" male talent (many of whom had performed in hundreds of videos), just as many of those reliable performers had not directed.

Another channel open to male performers is working in the gay porn sector of the industry. Only a small handful of performers have chosen that route, but performers in gay male porn earn fees comparable to female performers in the straight industry. And the gay porn industry has a category of performer known as "gay-for-pay"—heterosexual men who perform in gay porn movies for the money. Rough estimates suggest that in 2003 somewhere between 30 and 40 percent of gay porn performers, and many of the biggest stars, were gay-for-pay. However, for the most part, gay-for-pay performers are usually "reputably" straight or bisexual men who have never worked in the straight industry.[35]

It is not easy to move between gay and straight porn, especially since the AIDS epidemic began and before the introduction of the HIV prevention medication PrEP (pre-exposure prophylaxis), not only because of the stigma but also because of differing policies of condom use and testing.[36] Nevertheless, a small number of performers have been able to cross over to become recognized (reliable) performers in the straight industry side. Peter North (1,871 straight hardcore movies from 1983 to 2012) and Christian XXX (844 videos from 2003 to 2012) are two of the best known who followed that path. But the third option is that of a male performer who has worked for a number of years in the straight business who decides to work in gay porn. The gay-to-straight earnings ratio (see Table 7.3) is very favorable to those performers willing to work across the divide. During 1990s and early 2000s, among the straight performers who went into gay porn were Frank Towers (as Mark Slade; 453 straight videos and 36 gay videos), Jason McCain (as Jason McCain; 125 straight videos and 6 gay videos), T. J. Cummings (as Nick Steel; 352 straight videos and 34 gay videos), and Seth Dickens (as Cameron Sage; 553 straight videos and 65 gay videos).

The typical pattern of earnings over time for people working in the sex-related businesses differs sharply with the standard profile widely observed in

Table 7.3
Male Performer Fees in Gay and Straight Sectors of Adult Film Industry

Years	Gay adult	Straight adult	Gay to straight earnings ratio (=gay/straight)
Late 1980s–early 1990s	$1,000/scene	$300–$400/day*	3.33–2.50*
Mid-1990s	$400–$1,800/scene	n/a	n/a
Early 2000s	$400–$1,500/scene	$400/scene	1.00–3.75
2007	$500–$1,000/scene	$250–$800/scene	2.00–1.25
2010	$600–$800/scene	$250–$500/scene	2.40–1.60

SOURCE: Gay rates from J. C. Adams, "Less Bang for the Buck," *HX*, no. 447 (March 31, 2000): 29–30; J. C. Adams, "Pay 4 Porn," *Badpuppy*, no. 5 (2003); 1980s–2007 data from Mike Abo, Nelson X, and David Sullivan, "Rising Talent Rates: Welcome to the New Reality," *Adult Video News*, April 2007; 2010 data from http://www.good.is/posts/the-economics-of-porn-better-than-the -economics-of-other-stuff.

* In the late 1980s and early 1990s male performers were paid by the day and not by scene. For the sake of these calculations, scene and day are comparable.

many conventional forms of employment. The standard earnings profile shows as an upward sloping curve over several decades. This pattern reflects increases in productivity from on-the-job learning, training, and education and other human capital improvements. Of course, in the long run, after peaking, earnings decline with age. The steepness of the curve and the peak time span vary by gender, race, education, and other factors. In contrast, the standard career in sex work is fairly short, and the peak earning period occurs very early, and earnings drop off very quickly after the peak years.

Novelty is a central component of the adult film industry's relentless quest for new female talent and the fuel for its economic dynamism. "One interesting thing about this business," porn director Kristen Bjorn observed, "is that the longer you are in it, the less money you are paid. Once you are an old face, and an old body, forget it. You're through as far as your popularity goes."[37] Sociologist Paul Cressey was one of the first scholars to identify this distinctive socioeconomic pattern. In his 1932 ethnographic study of "dime-a-dance" girls, *The Taxi-Dance Hall: A Sociological Study in Commercialized Recreation and City Life*, he explored an occupation that employed young women to dance and socialize with young single men for a fee, which was widely seen as a step on the road to prostitution. Cressey found that the social and economic prospects of these young women followed a distinctive pattern that has been recognized by many of those working in the adult entertainment industry. The pattern was essentially one in which the longer an individual worked in the industry the less money that individual made—for the same work—over time. Cressey formulated his hypothesis as the "theory of retrogressive life cycle."[38]

Cressey explained the theory of retrogressive life cycles primarily in terms of social status and racial stratification. But the regressive stages of the taxi-dancer's career that Cressey identifies translate directly into economic consequences. Many of young women who entered the world of commercialized dance entertainment found that after an initial success as a novelty in the taxi-dance hall, they ceased to be the "new girl" and experienced a loss of favor and status that soon resulted in an exit from the job—"finding herself losing favor in one social world, the taxi-dancer 'moves on' . . . from taxi-dance hall to another, perhaps one of lower standing." This cycle continues in the young woman's life as long as she persists in her work—"her decline . . . may be rapid or slow, depending upon the personality, ingenuity, and character of the individual girl. But . . . a decline in status seems almost inevitable."[39]

While ultimately the retrogressive dynamic, as Cressey suggested, may be an inevitable process, it is possible for adult film actors to slow down its impact and stretch out their careers. Cressey cited "the personality, ingenuity, and character of the individual girl," but there are also a number of common work-based strategies that help to prolong a porn actor's career. This usually involves integrating new and different activities into the performer's sexual repertoire. Changes in appearance, clothes, hair color, weight, and physical fitness also contribute to enhancing the sex performer's erotic appeal.

The retrogressive dynamic is, in part, rooted in the psychological dynamics of fantasy that shapes consumers' sexual expectations. The successful sexual performance simulates a reality in which the subject controls the situation by virtue of the video's either commercial or fantasmatic nature, and without the emotional risks that attend everyday sexual encounters—which are often full of uncertainty, guilt, and anxieties.[40] Thus the repetitive playing out of a porn movie, a fantasy encounter, or experience with the same cast will eventually reduce the uncertainty, mystery, or suspense necessary for an erotic fantasy to remain vivid.[41] When the fantasy potential of an erotic scenario (and the objects of desire it plays with) is exhausted, the retrogressive dynamic emerges in full force as a challenge to the performer. Whether it is through overexposure, repetition, or stasis, the diminishing rate of fantasmatic investment produces boredom or irritability in the spectator. While the porn star's sexual heat is generated through a complex formula that includes personality, physical attributes, and sexual skills, the performer's fantasy potential increases only when the erotic scenarios reveal new aspects of the performer. Every performance that shows new or hitherto unknown skills, that demonstrates new physical attributes, and that is energetically performed enriches the porn star's fantasy potential.

The star's durability and appeal are prolonged if she can continue to reveal new possibilities, make new fantasies possible, and reinvent and renew herself without closing off the old fantasies that inspired her fans originally. Her failure to add to the new and maintain the old makes her vulnerable to the retrogressive dynamic. Performers who refuse to broaden their sexual repertoire must rely exclusively upon their screen partners and the scenarios in which they appear. Most of these performers will have short careers unless they adopt a strategy that limits their overexposure, diversifies their sexual services or related career activities, modifies their physical attributes, or engages in new promotional and other marketing efforts. In the straight porn industry, the Cressey dynamic has a significant impact on female performers, since they are an essential component of the marketing process. Male performers are exempt from this process in the straight industry, though they are not if they work in the gay male porn industry.[42]

Performers react to the retrogressive dynamic in different ways. On a practical level, most female porn stars (and successful gay male porn stars) worry, quite reasonably, about "overexposure"—that is, they are concerned that viewers will lose interest in them if they appear in too many movies too quickly or play roles that are too similar. The most common way to limit overexposure is appear in a limited number of productions, perhaps a handful a year, though most successful performers usually pursue a number of different activities.

Conclusion

The earning differentials in the labor market for the adult film performers reflect both (1) the productivity differences (the value of marketing vs. the value of "wood") between female and male performers and (2) the unequal distribution of earnings both between the male and female sectors as well as within the female sector itself. These types of distributions (which follow Zipf's law, also known as "power law distributions") have very long tails, which implies that very few performers receive a very large share of the rewards. These distributions typically occur when there are (1) a diversity of different kinds of services and skills offered in the same market, (2) with differing degrees of quality, and (3) which is exacerbated by network effects, such as word of mouth and star power (or reputation).[43]

Contract actresses are the industry's superstars and earn significantly more than the highest paid male performers. Their fees are driven by the demand of the predominately male audience for adult films. The male role, however, is necessary, and the male performance requires reliable erections and orgasms. Producing erections and orgasms on demand are difficult feats for most men, and one would think that the men—the "woodsmen"—who can perform such feats should be highly paid. Demand for their services is somewhat inelastic, and they are the highest paid male performers in the adult film business. While many might not purchase or rent a video specifically to see the average female performer (the B-girls), they are much better paid than the average male performer or the suitcase pimps. The introduction of Viagra and other erective pharmaceuticals may have improved the comparative advantage of these male performers vis-à-vis the reliable male, but not enough to completely replace reliable male performers. On the other hand, reliable male performers have active career spans twice the length of those of female performers. And they perform in six times as many films and can earn substantially more, through film work alone, than the average female performer.

Female performers potentially have sources of income other than film work—stripping, escorting, and personal appearances. The standard career path of female porn stars consists of a sequence of jobs that are allocated in overlapping but quite distinct labor markets (stripping, escorting, etc.).[44] These markets are heavily mediated by networks and brokers (e.g., recruiters, scouts, agents, and escorting services), each of them is loosely organized compared, say, to the labor market for school teachers.[45] The porn star as stripper and escort implicitly helps to organize these disparate and overlapping labor markets into a single hierarchical structure. Performing in porn movies is the most visible form of sex work on a national level—as well as the most prestigious. However, the three overlapping markets—for escorts, strippers, and porn stars—interact on a number of levels both nationally and locally. Porn performers operate in a quasi-national market, while both strippers and escorts who haven't worked in porn are hired in local markets. In the case of adult video performers who have moved along the career path, the markets for strippers and escorts tend to be more national because of the national distribution of pornographic movies. They serve as forms of publicity, provide potentially relevant information about sexual performance and capabilities, and may potentially enhance the performer's fantasy potential.

8

Porn Star / Stripper / Escort

■■■■■■■■■■■■■■■■■■■■

Economic and Sexual
Dynamics in a Sex Work
Career

"Sex work" and "sex worker" are broad and rather vague terms. Generally they
refer to work involving or a person engaged in any kind of economic exchange
for sexual services. While "prostitution" is the classical term for such economic
exchanges, "sex work" has emerged as a broader and more inclusive term for a
wide range of occupations—everything from the street prostitute or escort to
the phone sex actress, stripper, or porn star. Thus, at times, journalists or even
industry insiders identify the huge complex of businesses and individuals offering these services as the "sex industry." Escort services, strip clubs, phone sex
services, voyeur websites, and porn producers are all part of the sex industry, as
are the street hustler and prostitute. The services and products of the sex industry exist along a continuum: from pornographic videos that involve no direct
interaction to phone sex, stripping, lap dancing, and prostitution, all of which
involve some degree of interaction between customer and sex worker.[1]

Very few aspects of the sex industry have been extensively studied. There are
a number of reasons for this. One is the stigma attached to sex work generally,
another stems from the fact that some of the industry's activities are or have
been at times illegal or semilegal, and a third reason is that many participants

in the sex industry are self-employed or work for privately owned businesses (e.g., Vivid Studios, the largest producer of straight pornographic videos, and Falcon Studios, long the most profitable producer of gay videos); thus, there are no publicly reported sales statistics, annual reports, or income data.[2] In addition, certain activities—escorting is the best example—operate quite openly without ever explicitly alluding to its illegal status. This situation posed a certain dilemma in the composition of this chapter; I have referred to various performers who work as escorts indirectly, unless they have either publicly acknowledged working as escorts or advertised escorting services in local gay newspapers or on escorting websites. In this manner, I have carefully observed the fine line between discretion and empirical verification.

Since so little research has been conducted on the gay porn industry, I have relied upon numerous sources that scholars may consider unconventional or even, perhaps, questionable. The most important of these is *Manshots* magazine, which between 1988 and 2002, when it ceased publication, virtually operated as the "magazine of record" for the U.S. gay porn industry. Over the course of its twelve-year-plus history it published almost 400 substantive interviews with performers (not puff pieces—*Manshots* was not associated with any porn production company) and more than 130 interviews of directors and other assorted behind-the-scenes personnel. I also have inevitably drawn on other magazines and numerous websites as well as the more than fifty in-depth interviews that I have conducted since 2001 with individuals working in the gay porn business (including directors, film editors, producers, marketing directors, and performers). In addition, I have learned a great deal from many casual and more serious conversations with people working in the industry. These interviews, conversations, and relationships were developed in the course of conducting research for a previous book on the gay porn industry.[3] Much of the information and knowledge gleaned from these sources—such as personal conversations and acquaintances, internet discussion boards, or popular magazines aimed at gay men—is not available in scholarly publications.

Despite the huge revenues earned within the sex industry (revenues in the U.S. porn industry alone are estimated at ten billion dollars a year), very little is known about the careers of people who work in it.[4] The U.S. porn industry, according to one estimate, employs approximately twenty thousand people—though it is unclear whether this includes the many occasional and part-time workers employed in the porn industry or full-time equivalents.[5] The gay porn business probably employs some fraction (arguing from standard estimates of the gay male population: 5–10 percent) of those working in the industry as a whole.[6] These numbers are crude estimates to begin with, but they are useful just to suggest that the overall number of people employed in all branches of the sex industry is many times larger.

For many of the people employed in these jobs, sex work is a supplement to other forms of income, or if it is a primary source of income, it usually lasts for a short time period (months to several years) over the course of an individual's lifetime. Thus, it may seem somewhat paradoxical to speak of careers in the sex industry. The concept of career is usually applied to the sequence of jobs performed by individuals over the course of their work lives. But the term also has been applied metaphorically by Howard Becker, Erving Goffman, and others to the various stages in the development of social behavior that is not economic—such as the stages by which a person becomes a marijuana user, a patient in a mental hospital, a soldier, or a homosexual.[7] In this chapter I map one set of interlocking sex work roles that exists among performers in the gay porn industry—identifying the key decision points and the underlying sexual-economic dynamics. This set of interrelated jobs—porn star–stripper–escort— is a career path widely utilized by performers in the gay porn industry to create a more viable economic basis and, thus, constitutes a career, in both the occupational and subcultural senses of the term. This, however, is not the only possible career path; there are several others. One of the most common is the path that leads from stripper to porn star (and then perhaps to escort)—in which performing as a stripper serves as the means through which performers are recruited by scouts or porn company representatives. Another is a career path that opens up for veteran performers within the industry itself—as production assistants, videographers, producers, or directors. Each of these paths requires different kinds of skills, degrees of training, and, especially important in the porn industry, the psychological (or fantasmatic) investments on the part of the individual performer—resulting in the loss of glamour and public recognition, requiring different kind of engagement with sexual performance, and modifying one's own and one's fans' sexual fantasies. In this chapter I explore the issues surrounding one common career path followed by performers in gay pornographic films.

Porn Star: Fantasy and Human Capital

Porn stars, like movie stars or other celebrities, embody ideals and utopian fantasies, while at the same time serving as cultural fetishes and commodified public figures. In *Stars*, French philosopher Edgar Morin analyzes the psycho-cultural dynamics of stars and celebrities: "The star becomes the food of dreams; the dream, unlike the ideal tragedy of Aristotle, does not purify us truly from our fantasies but betrays their obsessive presence; similarly the stars only partially provoke catharsis and encourage fantasies which would like to but cannot liberate themselves in action. Here the role of the star becomes 'psychotic'; it polarizes and fixes obsessions."[8] Star personas crystallize both fantasies of identification (who we want to be) as well as fantasies of sexual desire (who we want)—a dynamic that is central to adult films.[9] In the complex dialectic between "active subject" and the passive "object of desire," most spectators of porn vacillate between the two positions, imagining themselves as both the active "desiring" party and the passive "desired" object.[10]

The idea of the porn star owes a great deal to Hollywood and the star system that originated in the film industry in the 1920s and 1930s. The star was and is both a featured performer and an iconic presence—and in the history of the movies the making of stars has exploited key aspects of film as a medium. Screen performers do not, like stage actors, create a role, but instead construct their personas—and the roles they play as actors—from their own psychological and physical characteristics.[11] As Leo Braudy has pointed out, "The film actor . . . works on his self-image, carries it from part to part, constantly projecting the same thing—'himself.' . . . The stage actor. . . . project[s] a sense of holding back, of discipline and understanding, the influence of head over feelings, while the film actor projects effortlessness, nonchalance, immediacy, the seemingly unpremeditated response."[12] Thus the emphasis on the role in a theatrical production is replaced on the screen by the persona with its sense of immediacy and its suggestion of authenticity—a characteristic absolutely essential, I would argue, to the success of video porn. The porn star's persona is like a character, but it is his character that he takes, at least partially, from his own sense of self (porn film as a medium requires certain reality effects, i.e., erections and orgasms) and from a certain projection of a marketable sustainable role (top, bottom, sex pig, etc.) across various movies.[13]

In the early days of the movie industry, the studios relied upon stars to distinguish between the films of various studios. Stars were then an important means by which to promote and market the studio's films. Each star offered a distinct personality and style that branded the studio that employed him or her. While stars exist in other performance media such as music, theater, and dance, movie stars in particular achieved wide recognition among the mass audience created by the film industry.

The persona of a star is constructed around the personality and performances of individual performers, but the star is also a complex social role. The star is an iconic image that signifies something about sexuality and gender and also represents a distinctive personality or type. And the star is a worker, a person who earns his or her income as a performer. Last, but certainly not least, the star is an economic asset, an investment or a form of human capital for the studio or company that has him or her under contract.[14] But also for the individual star, star quality is something that can be consciously developed and is highly marketable. Stars are an essential component of both the making of movies (as workers and images) and the marketing of movies (as assets that attract audiences). Stars sell movies—they are marketing tools that help to stimulate and stabilize the demand for films.

The term star is implicitly a term of value; not every movie actor is a star. However, in the porn industry—at least in the gay porn industry—porn star is often used much more broadly and loosely. Almost every performer in a pornographic film production is termed a porn star—at least to fans and viewers—though industry insiders generally use the term model to refer to the performers in adult films.

Since its beginning years in the early 1970s, the gay porn business has created several generations of porn stars who have become popular icons among gay men.[15] Casey Donovan, the star of both Wakefield Poole's *Boys in the Sand* and Jerry Douglas's *The Back Row*, was the first gay porn superstar. He made twenty-one films between 1970 and 1986. Well educated and culturally sophisticated, Donovan resembled and aptly represented the liberated gay man residing in New York City in the 1970s; he was both promiscuous and sexually versatile.[16] The other iconic figure of early gay porn was Al Parker, who represented the bearded masculine man in a work shirt and jeans—an image that became the dominant gay male style ("the clone") of the late 1970s and early 1980s. Like Donovan, Parker was sexually versatile.[17]

By the mid-eighties, a new type of gay porn superstar emerged in the person of Jeff Stryker. Identified as straight, Stryker was primarily known for his large penis. He performed exclusively as a top: he was the active partner in anal sex, was passive in oral sex, and did not engage in kissing.[18] The other superstar of the 1980s, Ryan Idol, was similarly identified as straight.[19] Among the few "gay" men who approached superstar status in the mid-eighties were Leo Ford, Jon King, and Joey Stefano. Both King and Stefano were exclusively or primarily bottoms.[20] Leo Ford's career was cut short from his death in a motorcycle accident (d. 1991), Stefano's from a drug overdose (d. 1994), and Jon King's by his arrest and incarceration for auto theft and his death from AIDS shortly after he resumed his career (d. 1995).

The era of superstars in American gay porn was passing, even though in the mid-eighties the market for gay porn was booming. The new video technology and the extensive ownership of VCRs had lowered the cost of production and made pornography more accessible. And it became cheaper to purchase and easy to rent. The new technology also enabled pornography to be viewed privately and at home. The AIDS crisis reinforced the privatized experience—some gay men turning to video porn in place of sex with another man.[21] However, by the mid-1990s, the market for gay porn had experienced some setbacks and the Internet was beginning to emerge as a competitor to scripted and produced porn films.[22] In the 1990s, only Ken Ryker (six foot four with a twelve-inch penis), who initially identified as a straight top, aspired to the status of a superstar, although he eventually expanded his sexual repertoire to include oral sex, kissing, and even bottoming (that is, the role of being penetrated during anal intercourse).

The gay porn superstars—Jeff Stryker, Ryan Idol, and Ken Ryker—were made by directors (Matt Sterling and John Travis for Stryker) or agents (David Forest with Idol and Dan Byers in Ryker's case) who self-consciously built a mystique around each of the prospective stars and heavily promoted their name recognition—these efforts paid off in sales (as far as we can gauge without reported earnings, etc.) and industry awards. In each case, the mystique rested on a calculated strategy of aloofness, presumed heterosexuality, and constricted sexual role that helped to sustain an air of mystery—their erotic charge created, in part, by what they would not do. Idol and Ryker found it is difficult to maintain that aloof Garbo-like presence over an extended period—in addition both Idol and Ryker contended with personal problems and experienced ambivalence about their roles in gay porn.[23] Neither one was able to achieve an economically secure career. Only Stryker achieved economic security, was able to maintain that aloofness, and enhanced it by working in the straight industry.[24] Though I doubt even he supported himself by making gay porn.

In the late 1990s, a new kind of gay porn star emerged—the "professional"—performers (both gay and straight) who were able to show variety in their sexual performances—who could top or bottom, who kissed, who sucked cock, who rimmed, and who used sex toys. The well-known veteran porn star Rod Barry exemplifies the new professional. As the 2003 *Adam Gay Video Guide* noted, "Rod is one of those remarkable performers who was so good from the beginning it was difficult to believe he was just a beginner."[25] Although he has been married twice and is involved with women in his private life, Barry defines himself as neither straight nor gay, but rather sexual—"sexual is you like an orgasm and you don't care how you get it."[26] But Barry was only one of the most notable of the new professionals to enter gay porn in the mid-nineties.

Other performers who entered the industry in the mid-nineties were Kurt Young and Matt Easton, two lovers who migrated to Los Angeles in order to work in the porn industry. Both became major stars. Young, who performed frequently as a top, was the most successful actor in the history of gay porn, winning fourteen industry acting awards in four years; Easton created a persona as a butch bottom, though eventually he left embittered at the lack of recognition by the industry. Other performers embodying the new professional orientation in the gay porn business include Dino Phillips, a popular versatile performer, who left college to pursue a career in porn; Jim Buck, a bookish young man from a small town in Louisiana who, fully aware of the feminine side in his personality and a talented comic actor, went on to create a persona (in the movies of Wash West and others) as a hot, masculine top; Dean Phoenix, a sailor who came out after leaving the Navy and emerged a notable top; Tanner Hayes, a cowboy from rural Montana who made his reputation as a power bottom; and Harper Blake, a popular drag performer in the Bay Area who transformed himself into a sexually versatile masculine body builder. In addition, there was Logan Reed, who built a career around the flip-flop (when two performers alternate between top and bottom), and Travis Wade, a Texas-born bisexual gym trainer who was one of the most successful of the "exclusives" signed by Falcon Studios. These performers were among the most popular porn stars in the last five years of the twentieth century. Almost every single one of these performers was sexually versatile, performing both top and bottom roles at some point in their careers. Few major stars have emerged in this period—in part because of the growing significance of live sex shows on the Internet.

Among the leading performers today, only Jason Adonis, a performer who has evolved from gay-for-pay into a self-acknowledged bisexual, and Matthew Rush, a professional body builder and a Lifetime Falcon exclusive, who is a self-identified gay man, approach superstar status. Neither pursued the high-profile promotional drive of Stryker and Idol, although both occupied the aloof role adopted by Stryker and Idol—however, unlike Stryker and his fellow superstars, both perform a wide variety of sexual activities. Yet neither supports himself solely by work in the porn industry.

In the gay porn film business, while male performers, on average, earn more (per scene) than male performers in the straight side of the industry, it is usually not possible to earn an adequate annual income exclusively by performing in gay pornographic movies. While major stars can earn anywhere from $10,000 to $50,000 per scene (as Jeff Stryker was reportedly paid several years ago), performers typically earn on the average between $500 and $2,500 (depending on their popularity, the sexual acts to be performed in the scene, and the prestige and wealth of the studio). Smaller companies generally pay much less—closer to $500 per scene. Thus, if a performer is paid $2,000 a scene and makes a movie every month, his annual income would be $24,000.[27]

In the gay porn industry, the development and maintenance of "exclusives" is much less common than it is in the straight sector. Veteran performer Rod Barry believes that both the performer and the studio lose out if the adult video companies fail to sign and nurture performers:

> I'm the biggest star that ever came out of All Worlds. And the biggest mistake that they ever made was not signing me to an exclusive contract.... They would have made much more money from my movies if they'd given me an exclusive contract.... They consider exclusives a lot of work, and lots of times they are, but you've got to create stars for your company. Straight porn companies are built on the followings of certain stars. In the gay business, only a few companies take advantage of that—Falcon, Jet Set, and Studio 2000 to an extent. You have to create followings and I don't know why the people who ran All Worlds never wanted that.[28]

Falcon Studios—the dominant and most economically successful of the gay porn companies—has long had a policy of having exclusive contracts with half a dozen or more performers whose careers they strictly regulate by controlling their access to the gay press, their repertoires of sex acts, and the roles and characters they play in their films. Other studios may sign one or two performers as exclusives, but few seriously devote resources to the development of exclusives or contract actors.

The star, however, is not only a performer but also a form of human capital, an investment, whether made by studios or by the performer himself, to help guarantee the sales of movies. In porn this can be achieved through the display of specific sexual skills and through construction of an image or persona that appeals to a wide audience of the gay men who purchase or rent porn videos. To be a successful porn star the performer must maintain his or her fantasy potential—the ability to suggest that erotic possibilities will not be exhausted.

An exclusive contract acknowledges the performer as an essential asset of the studio's promotional and marketing effort—a successful investment strategy for 'stars' and 'exclusives' is one that does whatever is necessary in order to maintain the erotic appeal of the performer, that protects a performer from overexposure and that carefully stages the expansion of a star's sexual repertoire. However, without an exclusive contract,—and in the gay porn industry, very few performers are signed to exclusive contracts—the performer must manage his career on his own. Unless they are working with an agent, very few performers that I have interviewed have a self-conscious investment strategy; instead, they must navigate by themselves, and usually without much awareness, the risks of overexposure and the trap of unlimited sexual accessibility, shaped by the psychoeconomic dynamics of fantasy and retrogression.

Pornography as a Career

It has often been said—more as an example of folk wisdom than as a demonstrable fact—that in the gay porn business a successful porn star must have two of three characteristics: a beautiful face, a beautiful body, or a big penis. Performers are absolutely central to the gay porn industry—casting is considered one of the most significant aspects of making a successful porn film.

However, despite the fact that "porn star" is used as a generic term, not all performers in porn become stars. Becoming a porn star is rarely something that young men—especially young gay men who must address the issue of their homosexuality—anticipate as a career to which they will devote their lives. The vast majority of the men interviewed by myself and others (e.g., Douglas, Spencer, and others in *Manshots*) become performers in porn movies without much premeditation—they knew a friend who was doing it or were approached by a scout or photographer or sent their photos on a lark to a porn company after they had become familiar with pornography.

The young gay men entering the gay porn business have frequently dropped out of college and often come from working-class backgrounds and from religious families and families uncomfortable or hostile to their homosexuality. Performing in porn is, for many gay men, a path to glamour or sexual exploration (many of the interviews in *Manshots* illustrate the points made above). The young straight men entering the gay porn world differ little from those Susan Faludi found in the straight porn business. "They had all bailed out," Faludi noted, "of sinking occupational worlds that used to confer upon working men a measure of dignity and a masculine mantle but now offer only uncertainty." The "easy" money exercises a major appeal.[29]

In the early days of gay commercial pornography, it was difficult to recruit performers because homosexual behavior was still highly stigmatized and production was illicit. The performers were frequently recruited by the filmmakers (who were primarily gay) themselves from friends, casual sexual partners, and boyfriends.[30] There was no preexisting network or agents to recruit performers for gay pornographic films. The gay pornography industry today has a highly developed infrastructure of production companies, distribution networks, technical services, as well as agents and scouts for performers.

Few performers enter the porn industry with any notion of what a career in the porn business really means—however, one of those who did was Jeff Stryker. He was fortunate to have John Travis and Matt Sterling, two of the most influential directors of gay pornographic films in the early 1980s, as his advisors. Travis initially responded to photos that Stryker submitted: "He had no concept of what anything was about in the big city of Los Angeles, and he was at first very untrusting. And in the first three months I knew him, we planned his future, the strategy—what could be done, how it could be done—and that strategy, that program still goes on today."[31] Stryker also was advised by Matt Sterling, a successful director for Falcon Studios in its early years and one of the most prominent directors of the 1980s. Sterling saw Stryker as "a young Marlon Brando" or "a young Elvis Presley." Sterling believed that Stryker closely resembled Presley and Brando in spirit, like "his passion for motorcycles . . . I felt it was the real thing, not a packaged thing. I just wanted to bring out as much as I could of the real, and it worked—he became a hero of sorts in the gay community."[32]

Performing in gay video pornography is a form of sex work and, like all sex work, requires the performance of sex acts according to the direction of the paying party. While porn actors, like other sex workers, may exclude certain activities from their repertoire, their sexual behavior on the set is governed by the demands and constraints of adult video production. Thus, even heterosexual actors in gay pornography must necessarily engage with other performers in homosexual activity. But the sexual acts that all performers must engage in are unlike those that they might perform in their everyday lives: the sexual activities that they engage in are constantly interrupted, and in order to maintain their erections and stimulate their orgasms, they are allowed to use various forms of pornography—gay or straight, depending on their sexual orientation. "It's not what you would think," performer Dino Phillips told *Unzipped* magazine. "It's a lot of contrived, regulated, stop-and-start sex."[33] The final product shows scenes that through editing and postproduction techniques appear as credible sexual encounters.

How individuals are recruited, their sexual orientation, and the limits they place in terms of which sexual acts they will perform determine the potential shape of their porn career. These factors together help a performer shape the persona that he will adopt as his character in the films he makes. The persona is a sort of sexual resume that the performer constructs in order to be cast in films in which he will feel most comfortable performing. It is based, in part, on his motivation for entering the gay pornography business—be it money, attention, and/or sex—but also on the image that he wishes to project as a sexual performer (an aggressive top, a submissive bottom, a sex pig, sexually versatile). The persona is the porn performer's identity as a sexual performer—the package of assets, physical appearance, sex roles, and personality. It is constructed from his beliefs about sex and sexual identity, from acceptable sexual scripts (romantic stories, leather, orgies, etc.) in which he may comfortably engage, and from his repertoire of acceptable sexual acts (active/passive oral, anal penetration, rimming).

The performer's porn persona is constructed to be used within the confines of a porn career and the gay porn business. He must maintain it in his on-screen sexual activities, in his public appearances, and in his interactions with fans. It is a kind of identity or character; it helps him do his job, and it helps define the social expectations of his significant others in the business. However, a performer's persona also may have its limits—he may not be able to successfully perform his persona at all times, or others may not be aware of his persona or may choose to ignore it. His backstage behavior may vary greatly from his public persona. It also is little help in negotiating encounters with the people in the actor's life who may not know of his participation in the world of gay pornography.[34] Whatever training new performers in gay porn receive often takes place relatively quickly. Usually the first few scenes expose the new performer to the knowledge and skills that are required. Learning to feel comfortable performing sexually in front of a camera and group of people is something a porn performer must adapt to relatively quickly or he would not be able to continue to work in the industry. Keeping an erection and regaining it quickly were essential skills in the days before Viagra. But since the introduction of erectile drugs, performers must discover the exact doses or brands that work for them. Several performers have told me of taking a whole pill, which gave them headaches and even made it more difficult to maintain their erections. They had to learn which dosage was most effective. However, performers have reported to me that not even Viagra can arouse a man if he feels no desire or attraction for his partner—or if there no other aids (e.g., pornographic magazines or videos) on the set to stimulate his arousal.

Also important is anal douching for the performer who will be bottoming or engaging in light anal penetration by fingers, tongues, and sex toys. Occasionally I have heard complaints from tops about inexperienced or careless bottoms who had not douched properly. The final orgasm is not called the money shot for nothing—performers must be able to achieve an orgasm and ejaculate after many interruptions and delays in the sexual action of the scene. And, again, one hears complaints about performers unable to hold off coming, but even more problematic are performers unable to come at the end of a sexual scene. The final ejaculation, by convention, brings closure to a scene. Sometimes a director may choose to ignore a performer's inability to come, but others may call in a "stunt dick" to fake the performer's final orgasm. One very successful gay-for-pay performer told me that in his first porn movie scene (a straight porn movie), he had been unable to get an erection and they had to fake his orgasm with a jet of hand cream on his partner's belly. These tricks of the trade must be learned relatively quickly if one wants to continue to perform in porn movies.

The most important career decision a new performer must make is whether he wishes to pursue a career in porn as his primary source of income or as a source of supplemental income on top of a steady paycheck from a more conventional job. The performer who chooses to make porn movies a source of supplemental income has more latitude on how he relates to the industry, but the performer who chooses, even temporarily, to pursue performing in porn videos as a primary source of income must face the dangerous currents of the retrogressive dynamic. As many performers have remarked, "Pornography is not a career." It has a very short life span, only as long as performers can compete with new and younger entrants into the business. "You can't do porn as your main career," performer Rod Barry warned. "If you do, you'll end up starving and on the streets, back with your family, sleeping on the couch—it's a supplemental income."[35]

The Retrogressive Dynamic

In the gay porn industry (and in many other occupations in the sex industry) there is steady demand for new, young, and attractive performers, for "new faces" or "fresh meat"; and the search for new performers is an integral dynamic of the porn industry.

In the 1930s, sociologist Paul Cressey formulated the theory of retrogressive life cycles to explain the careers of young women who worked as taxi dancers (dime-a-dance girls). The young women who sought work as taxi dancers usually had left their families and communities to work in an occupation that was closely associated with prostitution. At first the young women found it exciting, but the longer they worked as taxi dancers the more difficult it was to compete with the newer and younger women who started after them. Usually, the longer each woman worked as a taxi dancer, the less money she made and the more shabby the taxi halls in which she had to work.[36] The life cycle of performers in the porn industry is subject to the same dynamic.

Most porn actors are aware of the retrogressive dynamic and attempt to either postpone the ultimate impact of the dynamic or develop a strategy that goes beyond their porn career. Though there are no statistical analyses, industry folklore suggests that the average porn career lasts somewhere between two and four years.

In the porn industry, the performer who is considered an "old face" or an "old body" is either overexposed or sexually predictable. He has made too many movies in a too short period of time, he has been around too long, or his performances are too similar from movie to movie. Viewers are bored with him and expect nothing new from him. But this progression often leads to lower budget productions as well. The performers most victimized by the dynamic are those addicted to drugs or alcohol or otherwise locked in by class or economic limitations.[37]

The retrogressive dynamic is rooted in the psychological dynamics of fantasy (the "laws of desire") that shape viewers' sexual scripts. But the dynamic operates all along the fantasy/interaction continuum by which the goods and services of the sex industry are defined. The successful sexual performance in a strip show, with an escort, or in a porn movie allows the person entertaining the fantasy, watching the movie, or engaging in sex to protect his sexual excitement from being undercut by anxiety, guilt, or boredom, and it simulates a reality in which the subject controls the situation by virtue of either its commercial or fantasmatic nature and without the emotional risks that attend everyday sexual encounters—which are often full of uncertainty and performance anxieties.[38] The fantasy scenario itself, not its fulfillment or the satisfaction of the desire, stimulates a subject's desire, and for many people the erotic excitement is heightened when the fantasy's outcome is uncertain—when it includes an element of risk, danger, mystery, or transgression. Thus the repetitive playing out of a porn movie, a fantasy encounter, or experience with the same cast will eventually reduce the uncertainty, mystery, or suspense necessary for an erotic fantasy to remain vivid.[39]

When the fantasy potential of an erotic scenario (and the objects of desire it plays with) is exhausted, the retrogressive dynamic emerges in full force as a challenge to the performer. Whether it is through overexposure, repetition, or stasis, the diminishing rate of fantasmatic investment produces boredom or irritability in the spectator. While the porn star's sexual heat is generated through a complex formula that includes personality, physical attributes, and sexual skills, the performer's fantasy potential increases only when the erotic scenarios reveal new aspects of the performer. Every performance that shows new or hitherto unknown skills, that demonstrates new physical attributes, and that is energetically performed enriches the porn star's fantasy potential.

The star's durability and appeal are prolonged if he can continue to reveal new possibilities, make new fantasies possible, and reinvent and renew himself without closing off the old fantasies that inspired his fans originally. His failure to add to the new and maintain the old makes him vulnerable to the retrogressive dynamic. Performers who refuse to broaden their sexual repertoire must rely exclusively upon their screen partners and the scenarios in which they appear. The trade top who does not suck dick, kiss, or rim soon becomes boring—his fantasy potential is quickly exhausted after only a few movies. The exclusive top who always has a difficult time keeping his erection will not enhance his fantasy potential. The ambitious performer who starts out as an aggressive top, performs increasingly as a bottom (but without having an erection), then bottoms in a series of gang bang movies as a sex pig (a persona with an aggressive and insatiable enjoyment of all forms of sex) will soon deplete his fantasy potential if he doesn't maintain himself as an aggressive top—although other aspects of a performance may deplete a performer's fantasy potential. The muscle-bound performer who only bottoms and never gets an erection will never generate much fantasy potential. Most of these performers will have short careers unless they adopt a strategy that limits their overexposure, diversifies their sexual services or related career activities, modifies their physical attributes, or engages in new promotional and other marketing efforts.

Performers react to the retrogressive dynamic in different ways. On a practical level, most performers worry, quite reasonably, about "overexposure"—that is, they are concerned that viewers will lose interest in them if they appear in too many movies too quickly or play roles that are too similar. The most common way to limit overexposure is to appear in a limited number of productions, perhaps a handful a year, though most successful performers usually pursue a number of different activities. Veteran performer Jon Galt (who is widely considered an exciting and dependable performer, but not a major star) summarized his strategy: "If you want to have any kind of longevity in adult entertainment, it's probably better to do a couple of very good things a year and stretch your career out over a number of years, instead of doing 50 really bad films at once, shooting your wad and overexposing yourself. . . . Do a few things a year and keep it interesting. I have a full-time job outside of porn that I love that pays me very well, so I'm not doing movies or involved in an escorting career for my livelihood."[40] Such an approach is most feasible if one has chosen not to make one's career in the sex industry one's primary source of income.

Superstar Jeff Stryker is the most famous example of a prominent performer who prolonged his career by rationing his film appearances—approximately one a year. His sexual range was extremely limited—he only fucked, never kissed, never sucked a penis, and never rimmed or bottomed; yet he was able to maintain his popularity for more than a decade. Stryker explained his rationale to *Manshots*: "See, I never hustled or tricked on the side, and that way, I was unobtainable. The only way they could get it was on video. So with that in mind, my objective was to make as few movies as possible, but make sure they were the best. That's what I tried to do and to do that, you've got to start out from a position of power. I negotiated deals in which I was covered—my rent and everything, so that I wasn't having to take jobs to get by or to get food, rent or whatever."[41] Falcon exclusive Travis Wade is another example of a porn star who built his strategy around limiting the number of movies in which he appeared. Wade was discovered by Falcon Studios and signed with them to make five movies in his first year. When he completed his contract, he decided to re-sign after a short break because he decided that the "money is way too easy to make [at Falcon] for me to be . . . doing 20 films with all these different companies" and being forced to leave the business because "nobody cares who you are."[42] Over the course of his career, he gradually expanded his sexual repertoire from his original stance as a trade top, and eventually bottomed in *The Crush*, his last movie for Falcon. Bottoming, Wade said, "increased my overall worth in the business. It appeals to a different audience. Some people just want to see me as a top. And then there are those people out there that have been saying how beautiful my butt is. . . . I wanted *The Crush* to take me to that next level, so that when I'm ready to stop making movies, I'll still have the option of another year or two of performing in clubs, doing video signings and doing appearances."[43] Throughout the time period that he performed in porn movies, Wade also danced and escorted. He eventually left the business to work as a personal trainer—a common post-porn career for many of the more gym-conscious performers.

Periods of retirement and subsequent comebacks offer another strategy for avoiding overexposure. Any performer who has worked in the industry for more than five years has taken extended leaves from film production. They may continue to perform live on stage, escort, or work behind the scenes, but their absence from the screen can help rejuvenate their fantasy potentials. Because the turnover of performers is fairly rapid (two to three years), older high-profile performers can reenter the business and perform in new combinations with new partners. Comebacks are often associated with additions to the performer's sexual repertoire as well.

One common strategy adopted by performers to postpone the retrogressive dynamic's effect, enhance their fantasy potential, prolong their careers, and hold on to their fans is by expanding their sexual repertoire—tops will bottom or perform in transsexual movies, bottoms will engage in more extreme forms of anal play (gang bangs, large dildos, fisting, etc.). Rod Barry is an example of a performer who increased his fantasy potential and extended his fan appeal by adding new elements to his sexual repertoire. During his first year in the business, Barry developed a persona as an aggressive, verbally abusive, dirty-talking top. After about a year or two, he began to bottom and gave a new spin to his persona by performing as a similarly aggressive bottom, trash-talking and shouting such things as "Fuck me! Fuck me harder, you mother-fucker!" Then after taking a four-year break, he staged a comeback in 2003–2004, winning a GAYVN Award for his performance as an aggressive, trash-talking hillbilly top in *White Trash*. In performances on his own website, the Live and Raw website and Falcon TV, he expanded the range of his anal eroticism and bottoming, using a variety of dildos (including a baseball bat), and ultimately achieving orgasms while being fucked, without ever relinquishing his persona as an aggressive top.

Others will choose to stay in the industry and work behind the scenes in porn. And some will rely increasingly upon escorting or some other form of sex work—which often stretches out the retrogressive dynamic over a longer time period. But buying time is the primary form of leverage against the retrogressive dynamic. Many, of course, will leave the industry and go into other occupations or businesses.

Stripper: Fantasy and Tips

The retrogressive dynamic affects most seriously those performers who wish to rely on work in the adult film industry as their primary source of income. Performers become aware of the dynamic when they are offered less money to perform in a scene than they had received earlier in their career or when they encounter more subtle forms of the dynamic such as being hired and paid less for smaller roles or being asked to perform sexual acts they had rejected previously or to be an extra in an orgy scene (i.e., neither topping nor bottoming). Some performers may decide to leave the business at that point, while others may accept the lower paying jobs until they can diversify their sex work activities or find some other way to increase their fantasy potential.

Once the retrogressive dynamic kicks in, it affects the income that performers are able to earn from appearing in porn movies. At that point, some performers may choose to combat the decline in the economic potential of their porn career by engaging in other forms of sex work that are complementary to their continued employment as performers in porn movies. The most frequently exercised options are stripping and escorting, but others are not uncommon; many go on to work behind the scenes as videographer (Colby Taylor) or director (e.g., Gino Colbert, Michael Lucas, Dino Phillips, Doug Jeffries, Chad Donovan, Chris Steel). A number of performers have worked as personal trainers (e.g., Chad Conners, Travis Wade, Matthew Rush), which is not strictly a form of sex work but may draw on the fantasy potential of their porn careers.

Performing live, dancing, stripping, or whatever is the appropriate term (the word that is used depends often on local laws, whether the venue serves liquor or not, whether it's a club or theater, etc.) is probably the most common remunerative activity engaged in by porn stars to supplement their income. Whereas performers in porn videos are usually paid by the scene, the primary form of income for live performances comes from tips—dollar bills stuffed into briefs or thrown on stage. Female strippers can make thousands of dollars a night, but male strippers usually earn considerably less.[44]

As Travis Wade notes, the porn star comes with an advantage; his name recognition, or merely his status as a performer in porn, serves as an attraction for the club putting him on stage. The porn star, by virtue of the national distribution of porn videos or through adult sites on the Internet, has a reputation that reaches beyond the local gay community. In the clubs, he is a "featured entertainer" in contrast to the local talent or relatively anonymous dancers who routinely perform. As Travis Wade pointed out, "The money is not in the movies really. The money is good for movies, but if you're a dancer at the same time—which is what I was before I was a film star—it quadruples your money when you're performing in a club."[45] Thus, the porn star not only may be paid a fee (though more often, probably only travel and hotel are paid for) but also earns more in tips than strippers working locally and serves to promote his career as a porn performer. The recently closed Gaiety Theater in New York paid the travel expenses and a per diem fee to cover the cost of a nearby hotel room for its porn star headliners. At the Gaiety, most of the dancers were expected to earn their income through tips and/or escorting (thus the value of the nearby hotel room).

There is a fairly well-established circuit across the United States of gay clubs and bars that hire porn stars as featured dancers. Thus, dancing can enhance a porn star's income-earning ability by making him better known and by creating a broader fan base. However, giving live performances usually requires traveling extensively outside the area where the performer lives.

Many models are satisfied with the combination of performing in movies and live performances. However, such a combination of activities is difficult to sustain for any length of time if one has a regular job. It is difficult to schedule the travel required to appear in clubs and bars around the country, not to speak of the time required to perform in movies, if one has some kind of regular employment. And unless one has achieved considerable popularity very quickly after first entering the industry, performing in gay porn movies and stripping will probably not provide a reasonably stable income for very long.

Stripping and dancing on stage allows the porn performer to re-create, in the flesh, his porn persona. These activities also enable the porn star to elaborate on his persona and give his fans a chance to interact with him while he enacts it—though it is not actual sex. The degree of touching and physical interaction allowed depends on local laws, their enforcement, and house policies. Stripping, like porn, projects a fantasy—but with a difference: it is physically present to the spectator and permits a degree of interaction. The manager of a straight strip club explained the relationship between stripping to prostitution like this: "We sell the idea of sex. We do not sell the act of sex. We sell a sexual fantasy without actually copulating."[46] Live performances allow performers to take the fantasy persona that they create in their pornographic movies into a real-life scene in close proximity to their audience and fans. Thus, they can help to increase the performer's fantasy potential—although, of course, a lackluster performance can have a damaging effect.

I recently witnessed a performance by Rod Barry that both reenacted and elaborated on the aggressive sex pig persona he portrayed in his videos. He came out on stage and stripped relatively quickly, then presented his ass to the audience, spreading his anus and allowing spectators near the stage to finger it. Then he inserted a beer bottle in his ass and penetrated himself (and then afterward drank the beer that had remained in the bottle). After that he moved along the perimeter of the stage reaching out and pulling in the oldest or less attractive men to him, rubbing himself up against them. He spit on the bald head of one man dressed in leather, spreading the spittle out affectionately over the man's naked scalp, and kissed the man's head. Then, swinging from the pipes along the ceiling of the bar, Barry moved over the heads of the audience, landing and planting his naked ass on the faces of patrons who sought his attention. It was an extremely provocative and even shocking performance; the audience, however, was delirious with excitement and surprise.

For the most part, stripping is a way, like performing in porn, of earning extra cash. As a supplement to a career in pornographic movies, it can be, as Travis Wade suggested, quite lucrative. But by itself, even combined with performing in gay hardcore videos, it probably cannot produce a sustainable income. "Movies and dance gigs," observed Rod Barry, "they're just a little extra cash. I can go out and do a film—and get a motorcycle."[47] Only escorting can provide an adequate full-time income. In this regard, stripping is a somewhat ambiguous enterprise. While many strippers may not work as escorts, stripping can serve as a point of contact for escorting. Traveling around the country dancing in gay clubs and burlesque theaters allows the porn star to demonstrate his appeal and meet clients in the smaller markets away from the gay meccas of Los Angeles, San Francisco, and New York.

From Porn Star to Escort: Porn Movies as Advertising

When a performer decides to pursue work as an escort, his relationship to making porn and to work as a stripper changes; the economic weight of escorting in his employment portfolio transforms the work in porn and as a stripper into adjuncts of escorting. The appearances in porn movies become akin to infomercials, and the dancing and stripping at the clubs on the gay club circuit become a modern triple-X version of the traveling salesman. "I don't think that porn stars really make a living doing porn, they have to have some kinds of other income," notes director Kristen Bjorn. "They just cannot make that much money. So those who are totally into just doing porn movies are basically, prostitutes who use the porn movies as publicity for what they really do."[48]

The term "escort" has a broad significance, but it is only one kind of male prostitute.[49] Compared to hustlers who often work on the streets or out of bars, escorts more generally work by phone, through advertisements in the local gay papers, through escort agencies, or increasingly through websites like rentboy .com, male4malescorts.com, the Big Cock Society, or the escort's own site. When successful porn stars (those with some name recognition) become escorts, they have a degree of national recognition and a scope of operation that local escorts cannot match. A quick glance at a local gay publication reveals many ads for models/escorts that list non-porn escorts by their first name only (Adam, Luis) or by some descriptive phrase (Str8 Italian, Hot Black, Hard Body, Donkey Dick). Conversely, ads for porn star escorts usually supply the performer's entire name (Talvin Demachio, Ken Ryker, Billy Brandt). Ryker was one of the superstars of the gay porn industry; Brandt also is well known, though not very active. Demachio has not been a particularly active XXX performer in the last four or five years (the *Adam Gay Video Guide* shows him active from 1997 to 2000), but his ad suggests that he very clearly assumes there is an audience out there who knows who he is. The ads range from merely listing the porn star's name, cell phone number, or website to detailed information about availability. An advertisement for one porn star escort in an issue of *Frontiers* magazine (vol. 23, no. 12, October 2004) announces that "I will be escorting in the following cities: Toronto, Canada Oct. 4–6 (In/Out), Los Angeles, CA Oct. 7–10 (In/Out), Vancouver, Canada Oct. 11–12 (In/Out) . . . Berlin, Germany, Oct. 21–23. Return to the USA Oct. 24." This national or even international visibility puts the porn star (or even the former porn star) at the top of the hierarchy in the male prostitution market. This porn star escort is able to travel for his escort work without needing to reach potential customers through the retail marketing that stripping and dancing represent.

Fantasy is a significant component of any sexual encounter between the porn star escort and customer. As long as the porn star appears only in movies, he remains to some degree unattainable (à la Jeff Stryker) and exists only in a fantasy mode. For porn stars and mainstream movie stars, "audiences demand to hear more about the private life of the film actor than the stage actor because film creates character [i.e., the star's persona] by tantalizing the audience with the promise of the secret self, always just out of the grasp of final articulation and meaning."[50] The spectator's ability to imagine access to the star, whether by gossip, strip show, website, or escort ad, helps to sustain the fan's desire and fosters a fantasy scenario of connection with the star. Thus the mere possibility of hiring the porn star as an escort is integral to the spectator's fantasy (even if he never hires one) and to the economic link between working as a porn star and working as an escort.

Many spectators' fantasies are generated through interviews (sometimes completely fabricated) with their favorite porn stars in softcore porn magazines. However, interviews in local gay magazines and newspapers (when the porn star is in town dancing at a local club or promoting his latest film) also feed the fantasy of connection. Chat rooms, web cams, voyeur sites, and interactive websites like Live and Raw's 1-on-1 or Flirt-for-Free allow fans to engage in conversations and have contact with porn stars. On the Live and Raw's 1-on-1 sessions, fans can purchase "exclusive" time with the performer/star, interact with him, and together enact a fantasy scenario—while voyeurs, who pay a lower fee, can watch the interaction but not interact with the performer. In a typical interaction that I witnessed on the Live and Raw website, a fan (using the name Topman) bought exclusive time with one of his favorite porn stars and engaged in a fantasy scenario: Topman wanted to "top" the performer, so the porn star penetrated himself with a dildo and verbally played out the fantasy scenario, shouting "Fuck me harder, Topman," and masturbating until he reached orgasm. This is the cyber-fantasy equivalent of an escorting encounter.

In-person sexual encounters between porn star escort and their clients also involve a degree of fantasy—sometimes that fantasy is one of intimacy.[51] This sometimes can be disappointing if the porn star fails to live up to his persona, performs badly, is drunk, is high on drugs, or is uninterested in pleasing his customer, but porn escorts are often as professional in their escort work as in their video work. One prominent porn star told me that he experienced a comparable problem; he often found that his clients expected him to live up to his film persona and that he had difficulty sustaining that without the presence of the camera or an audience.

Some escort sites have review sections for clients to rate the men they hire—male4malescorts.com is one of the most popular. In the case of well-known porn stars, the reviews often seem to navigate between the fantasies that clients may have entertained before they hired the performer and the quality of the sexual encounter itself. One prolific reviewer on male4malescorts commented on his sexual encounter with a performer:

> I first saw Rick in a Lucas DVD where he played the b/f of Marco Rochelle. Marco is one very hot, sexy Frenchman. I never thought I would be watching and drooling over anyone else if I was watching a Marco DVD. Not to take anything away from Marco, I couldn't take my eyes off "the other guy." I had to look at the credits to find his name. It was Rick Gonzales. I never forgot it.
>
> The DVD was made a few years ago and his English was not the greatest. But I wasn't looking for a grammar lesson. . . . I wanted that thick hard cock and what he did with his mouth on the very very fortunate Mr. Rochelle. Rick at that time was a bit thinner and looked kinda like a little tough. And even though I didn't like the character he played, I fell in love with HIM and ALL that major equipment between his legs. I wanted him from that day on AND that bubble ass. I could just taste its sweetness.
>
> Last year Mr. Lucas was smart enough to hire Rick again and this time the body was a bit more mature and mmmmmm that dick and that bubble ass . . . well you can't improve on perfection. It was just as beautiful as I remembered. BETTER!!!! I was so hungry to suck that cock, but I though NAH, he's probably a snot nose kid . . . WRONG.
>
> A few months ago I saw his ad on RENTBOY. MMMMMM I said, nothing ventured, nothing gained. I wrote him thru RENTBOY and left my phone number as well as my e-mail address. For the life of me, I can't remember if he called or wrote. Doesn't matter. He answered me immediately and arrangements were made for him to come over and he was right on time when he came. . . .
>
> He greeted me at the door with a sweet kiss and hugged me and thanked me for asking him to come over. He appears to be in his late 20's or very early 30's. He apologized for wearing a kerchief on his head. BAD HAIR DAY. I thought it made him look so fucking sexy and hot. Oh my GOD yes it did. I think he blushed when I told him that. My knees were shaking. He looked like that boy in the DVD, but now a magnificent and very composed young man and he was mine for the next two hours. AND ALL MINE INDEED.

Let me tell you they were two hours of sheer joy and ecstasy. It was almost a religious experience. I was worshiping one of the most beautiful dicks I have ever seen. Rick had me standing up, laying down and ON MY KNEES as he fed that dick to me. He fucked my face over and over and over again. I was sucking and lapping at it as if I never saw one like this before. ALMOST RIGHT. There are not too many dicks to worship. I HAD IT THAT NIGHT. I could not stop moaning sucking Rick's cock. . . .

I lay there spent from this wonderful exhaustion. . . . All I could think of was I just rented and had Rick Gonzales, porn star in my bed. He just gave me the greatest cock, ass and time and my name is not Marco Rochelle.

NO, WRONG, he was not Rick Gonzales porn star. . . . He was Rick Gonzales my LOVER for two hours and he just made love to me. He lived to please me as if I was the only person in the world for him. So much so that I called him the next night to come over. He could not but we set a date for a few days later where we just picked up the pieces and started from where we left off.[52]

This was clearly a satisfying sexual experience, but Rick Gonzales, the porn star—and all the fantasies generated by him—is intertwined throughout the reviewer's account. Such accounts not only are extensions of the fantasy process, but also contribute to the fantasies of the review's readers. Two themes that recur in many reviews are how "authentic" the escort seems as a person ("not a stuck up porn star!") or how genuine the escort's enjoyment of the sex is—which may go some way to compensate for the fact that the escort has been paid to have sex with the client. One reviewer commented on that very dynamic:

With Porn star escorts you have seen them in action and you know a lot more about their looks and sexual expertise than other escorts. Still what they project on screen and what they do privately are not always the same thing. . . . My favorite part was just watching him since he always always into it. He smiled a lot too. That was great. Let's be real. They are doing it for money. Some are better at hiding that then others. Some just have a great time getting paid for something they find fun. I think Rod is in this group. I wanted to see him standing up cause I liked to look at his body. We kissed some more then explored other desires. One thing he did that I really like was the way he just wrapped his legs around me while we were standing and kissing. This was an intense fun session. Rod is really about pleasing his client. His ass was incredibly tight and I really enjoyed myself. At one point he surprised me by saying he liked the way my sweat smelled. That was a first for me. My favorite way to climax turned out to be something that he had never done. He thought it was cool. I was sorta pleased that I showed him a new trick.[53]

While working as an escort has a great deal more economic potential than working as a performer in porn, escorting can have a feedback effect on a porn career by enhancing the model's fantasy potential—the potential availability or accessibility of the performer as an escort may itself contribute to his erotic appeal. While information about a star's escorting circulates in a realm of innuendo and euphemism because of the illegality of prostitution, it also enhances its transgressive appeal. The fan's knowledge of the escorting may never result in an actual purchase of the porn star's escorting services, but it contributes to the fantasy of accessibility.[54] Thus, as it helps to make the porn career economically unnecessary, ironically, it also may help to prolong the career.

Conclusion: Careers, Networks, and Markets in Sex Work

I have explored the economic and sexual interrelations of a career path—porn star / stripper / escort—frequently adopted by performers in gay pornographic movies. The focus of this chapter has been on the individual; in particular, on the impact of the diminishing erotic appeal of the performer over time—called the retrogressive dynamic by sociologist Paul Cressey—and the measures that performers adopt in order to counteract the economic effects of the retrogressive dynamic. Performers have sought to counteract the economic effects in two different ways: (1) by enhancing their fantasy potential, a form of investment in human capital which includes such activities as elaborating one's persona, working out at a gym, dyeing one's hair blond, or expanding one's sexual repertoire; and (2) by engaging in complementary forms of sex work such as stripping (live performances) and escorting.

The career path—porn star / stripper / escort—however, consists of a sequence of jobs that are allocated in overlapping but quite distinct labor markets. These markets are heavily mediated by networks and brokers (e.g., recruiters, scouts, agents, and escorting services); each of them is very loosely organized compared to, say, the labor market for schoolteachers.[55]

Porn producers hire performers through a variety of sources, such as through recruiters and scouts visiting strip shows, body building contests, or wet underwear contests, through performers who recruit their friends and acquaintances, as well as through unsolicited photos submitted to production companies by men who want to be in porn movies and their friends. There are no systematic means by which performers for adult videos are hired. There are no want ads or adult employment agencies, no labor laws governing their employment, no minimum wage requirements. Only agents who sign promising or already successful performers are able to help models attain higher fees and strategize about their careers.

These markets function primarily through networks—individuals linked through informal or casual connections, often involving a certain degree of reciprocal relations, and embedded in social contexts that are not necessarily explicitly oriented to sex work—though they may be sexual.[56] For example, two men may meet at a club. One, let's call him Jake, who is porn star, is a friend of a friend and is introduced to another man at the club, let's call him Ed. Merely curious, Ed may inquire about working in porn, or Jake may be attracted to Ed, but if Ed expresses some interest in performing in a porn movie, then Jake may contact a recruiter, a scout, or even a director of one of the companies for which he performed. It is through these network traits that the labor market for performer emerges.[57] At some point a broker—a recruiter, scout, director, or agent—is brought into the situation.[58]

While the labor market for adult video performers continues to be loosely organized, the porn star as stripper and escort implicitly helps to organize these disparate and overlapping labor markets into a single hierarchical structure. Performing in porn movies is the most visible form of sex work on a national level—as well as the most prestigious. However, the three overlapping markets—for escorts, strippers, and porn stars—interact on a number of levels both nationally and locally. Porn performers operate in a quasi-national market, while both strippers and escorts who haven't worked in porn are hired in local markets. In the case of adult video performers, who have moved along the career path, the markets for strippers and escorts tend to be more national because of the nationwide distribution of pornographic movies. It serves as a form of publicity, provides potentially relevant information about sexual performance and capabilities, and may enhance the performer's fantasy potential. In the long run, the porn star / stripper / escort as a sequence of interrelated jobs thus may help to unify these overlapping markets.

9

Trans Porn, Heterosexuality, and Sexual Identity

■ ■

> In my distant past, as I was sorting out a variety of Freudian issues, I was attracted to pre-op transsexual prostitutes. I found them to be beautiful in this otherworldly way. I liked watching them in their clubs—it was theater, it was criminal, it was underground. To me, they were mythical, and being around them was my escape into a world of risk and eros and beauty and tragedy.
> —Jonathan Ames, interview,
> *Village Voice*

Over the Fourth of July weekend in 1999, PFC Barry Winchell was murdered, asleep in his bed, at Fort Campbell. The victim of constant homophobic taunts and slurs, Winchell became one of first martyrs of the U.S. military's "Don't Ask, Don't Tell" policy on homosexuals. Ironically, Winchell was probably not gay at all; he had previously identified as heterosexual. But he was romantically involved with Calpernia Addams, a transgender woman. Addams had begun to undergo hormone therapy and had some preliminary surgery, but she had not fully transitioned—she still had a penis. The welter of conceptual and psychological confusion surrounding Winchell's sexual relationship triggered the tragic events leading to his murder.

Addams lived her life as a woman, and Winchell considered her a woman and treated her like one. They had met at a gay bar in Nashville, where she was a regular performer. Winchell had never been to a gay bar before but had gone there with some other soldiers on weekend leave. He was introduced to Calpernia by his roommate, Justin Fisher, who seemed to have been infatuated with Calpernia himself. After they became involved, Winchell wondered if he was gay because he was sexually involved with her. When it became known that he was dating Addams, Winchell was repeatedly taunted and called a faggot by his fellow soldiers as well as his officers. On the Fourth of July weekend, he got into a fight with a fellow soldier over an unrelated issue, but the soldier was outraged that he had been beaten by a "faggot." And the following night that soldier took his revenge by bludgeoning Winchell to death with a baseball bat as he slept.[1] Winchell was undoubtedly a victim of the homophobic environment in his military unit, but more notably he was also one of the first martyrs as the male lover of a transgender woman with a penis.

More than twenty years have passed, and the sexual appeal of the trans woman with a penis is now more commonly accepted. According to the latest Internet statistics, traffic to trans female porn and dating sites has exploded, growing by more than 5,000 percent in the five years between 2005 and 2010. The business news website www.examiner.com estimated that in that time period more than 188 million men (worldwide) had gone to these sites. During the three summer months (June–August) of 2009 traffic to both trans porn and dating sites grew by 350 percent.[2] The consumers who go to these sites are, reportedly, predominately heterosexual men. *Adult Video News* (*AVN*), the porn industry's trade publication, reviews trans female porn as a straight genre.

If that seems improbable, the claim is supported by economic and marketing results. According to Steven Gallon, who founded one of first "transsexual" porn sites in the late nineties, "the majority of customers are straight men." Trans porn has no appeal for gay men, the other large audience for porn; Gallon notes that it garners "practically no response in the gay market at all. I don't even bother to promote it to the gay market, because it would be a waste of money."[3]

In this essay I explore the emergence of a form of sexual desire that did not strictly exist before the late twentieth century. It is a desire for a kind of person that did not exist before then—a partially feminized male-bodied person who typically has breasts developed through hormone therapy or breast augmentation and some other female characteristics but who has not yet undergone male-to-female sex-reassignment surgery. Previously such a person may have existed only in someone's fantasies, through a cross-dresser's performance, or with someone who was an intersex individual.[4]

Desire is not something given to us out of the blue but is constructed through fantasy—and it is through fantasy that we learn how to desire.[5] Porn lets us explore new fantasies. Gay porn director Wash West believes that pornographic movies are "passports" to *fantasy worlds* where sex exists without the everyday encumbrances of social convention, endurance, or availability.[6] To imagine a sexual performance in a fantasy or to see one in a porn movie enables us to experience sexual excitement without the side effects of anxiety, guilt, or boredom—and for many the erotic excitement is heightened when the fantasy includes an element of risk, danger, mystery, or transgression.[7] Pornographic films embody and even document these fantasies through the reality effects of filmmaking.[8]

The porn film industry is broadly organized into straight and gay sectors reflecting the patterns of heterosexual and same-sex gender roles. Nevertheless, two genres ("she/male" or "transsexual" films and bisexual films) that cross gender and sexual lines are classified to be exclusively in one sector or the other. Bisexual films are considered a "gay" genre, in part because same-sex activity takes place, while trans films are considered a straight genre. This is because the sexual activity takes place between a male and female—despite the fact that the female has a penis.

The historical development of this new form of sexual desire is documented, in part, by the emergence of the trans pornographic video as a "heterosexual" genre. The typical encounter in these videos is between transgendered women (i.e., male-to-female trans women who have undergone hormone treatment, developed breasts and other female characteristics, but haven't had reassignment surgery) and male performers who routinely identify as heterosexual. The sexual activity will often include mutual fellatio and anal intercourse in which either party can take the active or top position.

The primary focus of this essay is on the male spectator, with a secondary emphasis on the "male" performer. I explore how both male performers and consumers self-identify, what concepts of gender both performers and consumers hold, and how the adult entertainment industry organizes and reflects sex and gender conventions and practices.

The genre and its popularity among heterosexual men challenges our conception of straight male identity and the ways in which male heterosexuality is or is not a sexual orientation analogous to gay male identity. Most significantly, it unsettles received ideas of the relation between gender and heterosexual sex and its representation in pornographic films.[9]

Sex and the Transgender Woman

Erotic interest in the United States in trans women first emerged in 1953 following the publicity surrounding the male-to-female (MTF) sexual reassignment surgery of Christine Jorgensen, whose sex change operation introduced the transgendered woman ("transsexual" was the term used at the time) as a representative figure of modern life. Jorgensen had always sought to downplay the stigmatized sexuality (homosexuality) that often predated a successful surgically transformation, but it wasn't until the sexual revolution of the sixties and seventies that sex was more openly explored and accepted that the MTF trans woman was eroticized. Though Jorgensen was considered by the press and the public as glamorous and highly attractive, she downplayed her sex life. Yet throughout this period many transgender women sought to enhance their feminine sexual appeal by having hormone treatments to soften skin and reduce body hair, implants to enlarge their breasts, and plastic surgery to remove their Adam's apples or feminize their cheek bones.[10]

In the decade after Jorgensen's operation the female-to-male transgender woman emerged as a separate social identity—but it required sorting through both medical and quotidian conceptions of biological sex, the sexual self, and gender. Initially, these different conceptions were confusingly overlaid. When the concept of transsexuality first emerged in the 1960s it was closely associated with homosexuality—MTF trans woman were classified by many psychiatrists and clinicians as homosexual men. Many observers found it difficult to separate MTF transsexualism from homosexual desire since some MTF transsexuals engaged in same-sex sexual activity before their surgical transition. In addition, the gay male community had a long tradition of cross-dressing men, some of whom were effeminate in identification and behavior, who worked as performers (female impersonators) or prostitutes. There were also many heterosexual men who chose to cross-dress as an erotic fetish. Over time "sexual object choice" was differentiated from "gender identification" and both of them from "cross-dressing."

Thus, while homosexual desire and the desire to make a transgender transition may overlap, they are also separate psychological needs. And as a more precise nomenclature evolved, cross-dressers came to be identified as "transvestites," that is, as men or women who wear the clothes of the other sex. However, once sex reassignment surgery became readily available, men in some of these different groups began to consider making the surgical/medical transition from male to female. Thus transsexualism, transvestitism, and homosexuality emerged as analytically distinct identities, though in fact the social worlds of each group remained linked. However, interest in and anxiety about transsexualism were largely spurred on by its association with stigmatized forms of sexuality such as homosexuality.

During the sixties a significant change took place. The tactical need for transsexuals and their advocates to downplay explicit sexuality receded and there was an increased recognition and acceptance of transsexualism and its links to transgressive sexuality. One of the first signs of this shift was an explicitly pornographic memoir *Take My Tool*, by Vivien Le Mans, published in 1968. The book's back cover copy announced that "sexual surgery made *him* a complete woman capable of the ultimate in unbridled sexual desires."[11] Included in the book were pornographic accounts of oral and anal sex that Le Mans had engaged in as a homosexual before having her reassignment surgery. She concluded with graphic descriptions of heterosexual intercourse after her surgery. In the eyes of some readers, Le Mans's heterosexual activity demonstrated that she was a true woman. Other authors followed in Le Mans's footsteps. In 1972, Olympia Press, the Paris-based publisher of erotic and sexually provocative books by Henry Miller, Jean Genet, William Burroughs, and Vladimir Nabokov, published Lyn Raskin's *Diary of a Transsexual*, which described her sex life as a gay man and as a woman, after her operation. In *Man-Maid Doll* (1972), another author, Patricia Morgan, wrote about her life as a prostitute. "Let's face it," she wrote, "I'm a whore . . . I've hustled men as a boy, as a guy in drag, and as a woman."[12]

Despite the fact that reassignment surgery has become more available and less costly, it is nonetheless an expensive process to fully transition from male to female—especially for those from working-class and minority backgrounds. Prostitution and various kinds of sex work have helped many prospective MTF trans women to finance the necessary hormone treatments and surgery—as escorts, street-based prostitutes, strippers, and performers in pornographic films.[13] As sex workers, performers in the pornographic film industry occupy a particularly desirable niche—they are able to work on a pay scale somewhat comparable to that for women in the straight industry, which can be quite lucrative. They are perceived as stars and are considered more glamorous than other sex workers. If they also work as escorts, the films serve as promotional videos for their services. If successful, they are able to work as escorts anywhere in the world.

While the sexually explicit memoirs published in the sixties set the stage for the emergence of the transgender woman as a sexual heroine, they did not explicitly eroticize the MTF trans women who emerged later in pornographic films. The pornographic film industry is almost exclusively interested in MTF trans women with penises as performers. How the preoperative trans woman with a penis emerged as an erotic fetish around which a film genre would form is historically obscure. Initially as "chicks with dicks" or as "she/males" they played distinctive roles in the sexual marketplace. Transgender female sex workers occupy a distinct labor market from that of cis female sex workers. Their penises offer a significant comparative advantage. However, it is an advantage that is lost when an MTF trans woman completes reassignment surgery and has fully transitioned. For that reason, some trans female prostitutes and porn stars often chose not to have reassignment surgery.[14]

The Big Surprise

In the forty-plus years since porn has emerged as a major entertainment industry, there has been an extraordinary growth in the variety and range of sexual activities and genres represented.[15] As in any other industry, there is an economic imperative to reach the broadest audience possible. Genres and market niches emerge to cater to specialty interests—gay, BDSM, and sexual fetishes of all kinds. Since it was introduced in the early 1990s, "tranny porn" or "she-male porn" as it was known in the business has become extremely popular. Trans porn films are often shot in the gonzo style (a documentary style in which performers may directly address the viewer) and produced by small specialty studios such as Robert Hill Entertainment, Devil's Films, and Legend. By the late nineties, bigger studios like Evil Angel had also entered the market.

Director Joey Silvera probably did the most to popularize porn featuring pre-operative transgendered women and push the genre into the industry's mainstream. Active in the porn industry since the 1970s—first as a performer (he appeared in more than one thousand scenes) and then since the early 1990s as a director—his "Rogue Adventures" and "Big Ass She-Male Road Trip" series offered higher quality production. The first *AVN* award (the Oscars of the porn film industry) for a transsexual film was given in 1995.[16] In the last five years, more established straight male performers such as Rocco Siffredi and Kurt Lockwood have begun to make trans female videos.

As the genre grew, MTF transgender performers also began to achieve a level of recognition comparable to mainstream female porn stars. One of the first successful transsexual performers was Gia Darling. She was the first MTF transgendered model to appear in full-on magazine layouts as a Penthouse Pet and a Hustler Honey. She also started her own production company, Gia Darling Entertainment, and in 2006, the breakout year for trans porn, Darling won *AVN*'s "Transsexual Performer of the Year" based primarily on her "Transsexual Heartbreaker" series. "In their fantasies, there's always that girl-on-girl thing," Darling explained, "but the other thing they like is a girl topping a guy. For me, it's easier to be a top."[17] Carmen Cruz, Allannah Starr, Wendy Williams (not the radio and TV personality), and Danielle Foxx are some of the genre's major stars.

Sexual arousal and the performance of sexual acts depend upon the meanings and cues of the social and cultural context. Human sexual behavior is organized by structured expectations and prescribed interactions that are coded like scripts. The theory of sexual scripts formulated by John Gagnon and William Simon provides a useful analytical framework for exploring the dynamics of sexual performance in pornographic production. Scripts are metaphors for the narrative and behavioral requirements for the production of everyday social life. In their theory of sexual scripting, Gagnon and Simon suggest that these scripts, with cues and appropriate dialogue that are constantly changing and reflect different cultural groups, circulate in societies as generic guidelines for organizing social behavior. They distinguish three distinct levels of scripting: *cultural scenarios* provide instruction on the narrative requirements of broad social roles; *interpersonal scripts* are institutionalized patterns in everyday social interaction; and *intrapsychic scripts* are those that an individual uses in his or her internal dialogue with cultural and social behavioral expectations.[18]

For example, interpersonal scripts help individuals to organize their self-representations and those of others to initiate and engage in sexual activity, while the intrapsychic scripts organize the images and desires that elicit and sustain an individual's sexual desire. Cultural scenarios guide an individual's behavior as a participant of collective social life—providing prescriptions for various social, gender, or occupational roles, class and racial identities, sexual beliefs, popular cultural ideals and symbols, and broad social values and norms.[19] The working materials of pornographic movies largely derive from society's received cultural scenarios and rework them—in order to produce a transgressive effect.[20] Trans porn scripts play on the cultural assumptions of gender preference.[21]

Arousal "is stimulated by the scenario of presentation, by the mise-en-scène and the implied narrative."[22] The mise-en-scène of trans porn films is organized around a central encounter—a man makes a pass at woman, picks up a sexy woman, hires a babysitter, or arrives for a tryst with a prostitute—for what appears to be a routine heterosexual encounter. The man makes a pass at the sexy woman with large breasts or a big ass; he may fondle the woman's breasts or squeeze her ass. She grabs his penis and pulls it out. She may even start sucking it. Gradually, the man moves his hand toward the woman's crotch, but when reaches it he has a surprise! "This chick has a dick," he may say. The surprise—that is, the presence of an extra penis in a heterosexual encounter—is an underlying dramatic device in a vast majority of trans porn sex scenes. The surprise can take many forms—sometimes the surprise is intended only for the video's viewer, and at other times the surprise may be about the *size* of the transgender female's penis or the particular sex acts that the male partner hadn't expected to engage in such as fellatio or anal intercourse. In some scenes, it may even be a pleasant surprise when the male partner discovers the hefty package of the performer's large or erect penis. In many of these scenes, the arc of the male's acquiescence (i.e., what was called by some websites "the transsexual seduction") leads to the male partner taking the receptive role in anal intercourse. The Lacanian cultural critic Slavoj Žižek has suggested that psychologically the surprise is an inverse of the child's traumatic discovery that females have no penis.[23]

In real life, such a surprise would pose a small crisis for most heterosexual men. In the 1992 Oscar-nominated film *The Crying Game*, the male lead falls in love with another man's girlfriend. While the woman initially resists his approaches, she eventually responds positively, but when they go to bed together he suddenly sees her penis. He turns away in disgust. She assumed he knew that she was transgender. After an emotional struggle, he comes to terms with his infatuation, but in trans porn the surprise and the male's internal conflict are often rather perfunctory—an acknowledgment that things have already gone too far for the man to turn back—and produce a ratchet effect. It is impossible or difficult to reverse the surprise. The male partner keeps going, perhaps continuing to show some reluctance, but the trans woman has gained the upper hand and now leads the man on to go further (continuing with "the transsexual seduction"). She pushes his head down to her cock. Reluctantly, at least initially, he sucks her cock. He begins to play with her ass—and the trans porn sex scene usually finishes with anal intercourse. Half of the time, he fucks the trans woman in the ass. And ideally, they both display their erections as well as their orgasms at the end. Half the time, the trans woman will fuck the man. Again, at the scene's (and their sexual) climax, both will display their erections and optimally the male will ejaculate while he is being penetrated.

This typical scene illustrates a number of the standard rhetorical tropes that organize most trans porn. They are (1) the meet cute and the surprise, (2) the trans seduction process during which the trans woman seduces the man to suck her cock, and (3) the trans seduction process ultimately to fuck her or to get fucked himself—the transgender woman as top is the ultimate transgression of the heterosexual masculine code.[24] And (4) the orgasms of both the man and the woman are the resolution of the situation.

"Sexuality is constructed by seduction," argues film theorist Elizabeth Cowie. And trans porn scenes show the process of seduction of the heterosexual male (as well as the heterosexual spectator) and activate his "polymorphous desire" by stimulating his sexual arousal. The straight male viewer's *fantasy video script* is elaborated through an intrapsychic dialectic that oscillates between desire and identification—the movement between the arousal stimulated by the setup and the desirable objects (the active role) and the imagined substitution of oneself in place of the objects of desire (the passive role). It is the continued imagining of an unattained but possible sexual satisfaction that nurtures desire.

Trans porn scenarios violate some of the standard expectations of heterosexual sex—in this genre of heterosexual porn the woman has a penis, the man sucks her cock, and then she may fuck him. However, she IS a woman; she has breasts and appears to be a woman in every respect except one—she has a penis. To some degree, the trans woman's demonstrable feminine traits—her breasts, her makeup and dress, and her female presentation of self—help to neutralize any possible homophobic anxieties of the straight male spectator. As one internet trans female lover exclaimed, "They combine femininity with big-dickedness."[25] The ultimate impact of trans porn on heterosexual male spectators is reinforced by the kindred genre of heterosexual strap-on porn in which the woman, wearing a strap-on dildo, penetrates the male. Both genres are often classified as BDSM—because the male often plays a submissive role in both, though more unequivocally in the strap-on videos.

One of the ironies of straight pornographic videos in general is the common presence of the penis. Its size, erections, and ejaculations are routinely observed and are an accepted element of heterosexual representations. Male viewers of straight porn are not unfamiliar with penises—though they might not be familiar with other men's penises in their actual sex life. Whatever might be the case in an actual sexual encounter, in a porn scene the penis is not unusual. Of course, what is unusual is that the woman has a penis.

In trans pornography these contradictions are fairly substantial—not only between gender roles and identities but also in the repertoire of sexual activities associated with traditional gender scripts. Genre is organized by a small set of basic thematic oppositions that may not be present in any given film but underlie the entire genre: the presence of breasts and the presentation of the actor as female with the same actor having a penis and taking the active sex role. In addition, trans porn films mediate between two diametrically opposed categories of heterosexual sex: anal sex (perverse) and vaginal sex (normal). Though vaginal sex is absent, the sex in trans porn is often considered by the industry's definition to be heterosexual, that is, it involves a man and a woman.

Straight with a Twist

While the phenomenon has a clinical term ("gynandromorphophilia," i.e., literally "the love of males in the shape of females"), relatively little has been written about the men who have sex with trans women who have penises. There are a handful of scholarly studies that have touched on the topic; on the other hand, there are hundreds, perhaps thousands, of websites and discussion boards online that are open forums on the subject. It is a form of sexuality that has particularly benefited from the Internet.

Part of the erotic appeal of trans women with penises is their exoticism; they transgress conventional definitions of masculinity and femininity through their physical appearance and their sexual behavior. They are often both hyperfeminine in appearance and sexually aggressive. For some of the men attracted to MTF trans women, one side of the equation matters more than the other. I've heard many heterosexual men (many of whom had little or no experience with trans women) remark approvingly of their hyperfemininity. For example:

- Their femininity tends to be old school, the ones that I'm drawn to and interact with, but their masculine side tends to be very affirmative and aggressive, and I like the mix.[26]
- An exoticness, a uniqueness, something that can't be obtained elsewhere. They're just totally unique in their sexuality in that they're both . . . men and women and at the same time, neither men nor women. To me that's my fascination.[27]
- I found them to be beautiful in this otherworldly way. I liked watching them in their clubs—it was theater, it was criminal, it was underground. To me, they were mythical, and being around them was my escape into a world of risk and eros and beauty and tragedy.[28]

Others are excited by the sexual transgressiveness of trans women with penises:

- I like tits and I like dicks. . . . Something erotic about getting fucked by someone who is a woman.[29]
- I like the girls with a little something extra, you know what I mean. Pretty with a big dick.[30]

These comments capture the appeal that many men experience to trans women with penises.

Porn magazines such as *Hustler* and *Penthouse*, which typically address straight male audiences, often run advertisements for trans female porn and phone sex services. Many of the people who run trans porn sites characterize their customers as primarily straight. "A majority of the customers for the niche are straight men," claims one article. "The reason is simple: even though she/males have a penis, they look and act like women."[31] In an article on "How to Date a Pre-Op Transsexual Women," a commentator on www.tsgirlfriend.com expresses another opinion: "[Transsexuals] tell me that most of the guys who contact them are, in fact, bisexual or bi-curious. They say these men are often looking for a same-sex experience but packaged in such a way that they have deniability."[32] However, few gay-identified men express any interest in trans porn or having sex with trans women.

In one of the most recent studies of men who engage in sex with MTF trans women, most identified themselves at straight or bisexual (73 percent of forty-six men interviewed). This seems to be the case online as well. Those who identify themselves as straight (43 percent) usually offer a default explanation such as "I like women. I'm straight. I don't like men." A substantial number entertain the idea that their erotic interest is a form of bisexuality, that it brings the male and female together into one person: "My girl is TG [transgender] so I think of her as a girl, so in some ways I'm a straight person but in reality I guess some people would put me in the bisexual."[33] In addition another group characterizes themselves as "sexual."[34] Barry Winchell might have ultimately thought of himself in this way.

Male performers in trans porn films come to the genre along several different paths. In practice, adult film performers tend to work in a number of mixed or fetish genres, such as female strap-on, BDSM, transsexual, or bisexual movies. To some extent, the longevity of performers in the industry requires performers to constantly expand the envelope of their sexual activity.[35] Successful performers may turn to trans porn among others to extend their careers. Another prominent recruit to trans porn was Kurt Lockwood, one of the straight industry's leading male performers. Winner of four *AVN* awards between 2004 and 2007, he has appeared in over four hundred scenes. In 2008 he appeared in a handful or so female strap-on and trans female porn films as the male bottom. After performing in the trans and strap-on films, Lockwood went on to perform in some bisexual scenes.[36]

Another is gay-for-pay porn star Rod Barry. Throughout his career Barry has appeared in more than three hundred scenes in all genres. In 2004 he was cast in *Coming Out* (which wasn't released until 2007), a bisexual movie for Metro, a leading producer of straight adult videos, with a number of mainstream porn actresses—Shy Love and Arianna Jollee. Jollee, Barry's costar in one of his two scenes, Shy Love, the film's director, and the videographer all highly praised his performance with both women and men. Jollee and the others provided Barry with contacts on the straight side, and he went on to perform in numerous straight scenes, many of them for Devil's Films. Barry's versatility and sexual range also led to his performing in trans films as well as female-to-male strap-on and BDSM videos. Entrepreneur, producer, and director Tom Moore, himself a sexually complex figure with a sexual orientation very much like Barry's, cast him in a series of trans videos, shot mainly in Argentina. Moore and Barry shot more than eighty trans scenes. Barry developed a new persona as an adventurous and wacky sex-driven sidekick—fucking and getting fucked by trans women, as the bottom in female-to-male strap-on scenes, heterosexual creampie videos, and other transgressive fetish videos with hermaphrodite performers and trans men (with noted trans male performer Buck Angel). He also became widely known as an energetic and adventurous performer in fetish and BDSM circles. In early 2007, Barry was invited to perform for Kink, the leading producer of BDSM pornography on the Internet. He made a series of videos for Kink's *TS Seduction* and *Men in Pain* websites in which he took the submissive role. Although he has been married twice and is predominately involved with women in his private life, Barry defines himself as sexual rather than straight or gay. "I'm not gay or straight," he said.[37]

The erotic appeal of trans female porn to heterosexual men has posed a special challenge to the cis women who are involved with the men attracted to trans women. For cis women, their partners' interest in trans women raised doubts about their male partners' sexual identities. Magazine sex advice columnists and agony websites routinely handle letters from women who have discovered that their boyfriends or husbands watch trans female porn. Google Answers published a question posed in April 2004: "Why would a man in a committed, loving, sex (I'm his wife) relationship 'use' shemale and transgender porn?" and received numerous responses within days.[38] Recently, one young woman wrote to DearCupid.org that she had

> just discovered my boyfriend of 5 years has been looking at and jacking off to shemale porn. i discovered while using his computer. i was on google, and a little "memory typing" came up and said transvestite dating sites. i called my boyfriend as soon as i saw this and his reply was "i just wanted to see if it existed." Well, for some reason i felt he wasn't being honest. so i went through his history and found at least a hundred sites devoted to shemale porn, luckily, there was nothing to say that he was trying to meet these . . . women? anyways, when he got home i confronted him with it. it took a lot of coaxing to get it out of him, and it turns out he's been looking at and jacking off to this type of pornography for almost two years, and this whole time we have still been having sex i need to know, is this just a phase? is it that he's gay, or bi-sexual? is it normal for straight guys to be turned on by shemale porn?

These queries reflect a common doubt about the practical meaning of sexual fantasies or activities regarding trans women—DearCupid.org has a long list of similar enquiries from girlfriends, wives, and the men themselves.[39]

> Does liking transsexuals make me gay?
> My husband is into shemales.
> Is it weird that I'm a guy who likes to use dildos on himself when I'm with my girlfriend?
> Bf watches she-male videos every morning and is hardly interested in me now, help!
> Could my boyfriend be gay because he watches she-male videos?
> I found shemale videos in my husband's car! We've both tested positive for HIV.
> My boyfriend is a cross-dresser. Is he a time bomb waiting to go off?
> My manly man likes to see she-male porn! Is this a common fetish for men?
> My husband has been watching shemale porn.
> He has an obsession with "shemale" porn! What can I do?

He looks at Shemale Porn. Is this normal!?
My husband of 27 years looks at shemale porn. Should I be concerned?
I've recently found out he has registered on a site to meet a shemale!!!
I'm sure I'm not attracted to men, but I'm turned on by she-males!

One way to characterize men who are attracted to and who have sex with trans women with penises is that they are "heterosexual by default." They may not qualify as gay or bisexual if they are not sexually attracted to men; they are, as some of these men say, "straight with twist." But a twist of what? Is sexual involvement with trans women a clinical syndrome (gynandromorphophilia), a variety of BDSM, or a sexual orientation all its own? What about the men who enjoy passive anal intercourse with women or trans women? Nevertheless, the porn film industry has found an audience of men who purchase and watch videos and use them as passports into a fantasy world of women with penises who fuck men.

It is almost impossible to step outside of the Freudian discourse on fetishism and the phallic woman. Clearly, the trans female's penis is a fetish of some sort. As Robert Stoller observed, "A fetish is story masquerading as an object," though in fact the trans woman's penis as a fetish doesn't quite jell with Freud's account.[40] Or does the trans woman save "the fetishist from being a homosexual by endowing women with the attribute that makes them acceptable as sexual objects"?[41] Does the trans female penis restore the phallus to the woman and alleviate her sexual partner's castration anxieties? John Phillips, one of the few to write about "transsexual porn," has argued that the spectator of trans porn "'wants it all': the feminine and the masculine, the breasts and the penis, visible and incontrovertible signs of *jouissance* from the uncastrated woman."[42] Is the trans female an example of the Freudian concept of the phallic woman? In Freudian theory the phallic woman represents the fantasy of a woman, or more significantly a mother, endowed with the phallus or a phallic attribute—a symbolic representation, not a real penis.[43] Or is the trans woman with a penis in reality a new kind of phallic woman not envisioned by psychoanalytic theory? And how does the female with a strap-on dildo relate to this concept of the new phallic woman?

Fetishism plays a significant erotic role in all pornography, but it also works through a process of commodity fetishism and the creation of porn genres. Linda Williams argues that the powerful role that fetishism plays in pornography derives from the "substitutive nature of desire: the fact that anything and everything can come to stand in for the *original object of desire*."[44] The generic elements of trans porn scripts that frequently utilize tropes such as the surprise or the trans female with a hefty package serve as a trigger for the transsexual seduction of a heterosexual male. In what sense are these men heterosexual? Is the sexual identity of heterosexual males merely a default sexual orientation—as long as these men do not engage in sex with a man or a person who presents as a man, can they be considered straight?

Obscure Objects of Desire

Sexuality and gender may be analytically distinct, but they are intimately intertwined. Pornography is one of our society's most significant forms of popular discourses concerning sex and gender—it articulates and dramatizes our fantasies about sex *and* gender. Pornographic cinema is a passport into a fantasy world. It creates a safe space where sexual fantasies and gender roles can be enacted without the attendant anxieties, shame, and various physical limitations impeding sexual arousal and orgasmic resolution.

Moreover, pornography plays an important part in the social/historical process that Foucault has called "perverse implantation," through which peripheral sexualities and identities are socially articulated. It is no accident that the political mobilization around transgender issues, the emergence of transgender studies, and the development of trans pornography as a genre all exploded around the same time in 1990s.[45] From Christine Jorgensen's spectacular appearance on the public stage to the proliferation of new discourses on sex and gender that emerged in the course of the sexual revolution of the 1960s and 1970s, transgendered people have played an important part in how we think about gender and its relation to sexuality.[46] Pornographic film genres also serve to normalize the sexual fantasy and activities they represent. The porn film industry distinguishes between bisexual and trans movies. Bisexual movies are classified as a gay genre because despite the fact that in those films both men and women engage in sexual intercourse, sex also takes placed between males, while in trans porn films men engage in sex with females—yes, females with penises and no vaginas. Thus while trans porn seemingly breaks with the standard representation of gender on pornographic videos, perhaps even more importantly it disrupts the link between sexual object choice and sexual orientation or identity. Trans porn, in part, cultivates the desire for a transgendered sexual object. The viewer of trans porn, like the male performer in it, usually identifies as heterosexual, but their sexual object choices are not traditional or natural females but trans women—literally phallic women. The presence of penises and of males engaged in receptive anal intercourse does not affect the classification of the genre as straight. Trans porn represents heterosexual sex without vaginal intercourse.

The central sex act in trans female porn is anal sex—as the norm for both women *and* men. It also introduces heterosexual men to a fantasy of sexual surrender, to the intense pleasure of discharged tension, and ultimately to the psychic shattering of the self via the intensity of anal intercourse.[47] It enables a reconfiguring of male heterosexuality to experience, quoting Leo Bersani: "The pleasurable excitement of sexuality . . . when the body's normal range of sensation is exceeded and when the organization of the self is momentarily disturbed . . . by sensations somehow 'beyond' those compatible with psychic organization."[48] The erotic appeal of the preop transsexual woman and of transsexual porn is just one more example of movement along a "continuum of perversions which underlies human sexuality," the historical dynamic of a polymorphic sexual economy that allows for selection of diverse objects of desire.[49]

Epilogue

From the Secret Museum
to the Digital Archives

■■■■■■■■■■■■■■■■■■■■■■

Constructing the Sexual
Imaginary

In 1748 archaeologists discovered the town of Pompeii near Naples, which had been buried during an eruption of Mount Vesuvius three hundred years before the fall of the Roman Empire. The archaeologists found a very large number of erotic frescos, statues, and other lascivious objects—many representations of Priapus with a gigantic erect phallus. The king of Naples at that time decreed that all of the "obscene" artwork found at Pompeii was to be locked away in a secret museum. The entrance was bricked up and the secret chambers were almost completely inaccessible until 2000.

However, in the United States, by 2000 adult films had become the most important sector of the modern porn industry. Technological changes played an important part in that growth: in the 1980s pornographic filmmakers had shifted from shooting X-rated features on film designed for exhibition in theaters to videotapes (Beta and VHS) that could be viewed in homes on televisions. The new technology was cheaper to produce, cheaper to reproduce, and more accessible to consumers (especially to those reluctant to attend porn theaters or other public venues). The advent of the AIDS epidemic during the 1980s and uncertainty about the transmission of HIV reinforced the appeal of watching pornographic videos at home. Video sales and rentals soared throughout the eighties and nineties. Each technological shift made pornographic films and video more easily and cheaply available. With the shift from video pornography to the Internet, pornography became even more available and more frequently used as a source of knowledge about sex. Laura Kipnis has argued that porn is "an archive of data about our history as a culture and our own individual histories"—the pornographic archive created by the Internet is a perfect example.[1] Today, porn on the Internet has become a giant archive of sexual fantasies. Nowadays, with little or no sexual education, people search the many free porn sites looking for their exact scripts because, as psychoanalysts Robert Stoller, Jean Laplanche, Jean-Bertrand Pontalis, and Slavoj Žižek have pointed out, "it is precisely the role of fantasy to give coordinates of the subject's desire, to specify the object, to locate the position the subject assumes in it."[2]

The proliferation of pornography since 1970 has been driven by a "perverse dynamic," that is, the pursuit of ever more perverse and transgressive sexual scenarios. Pornography has a "short half-life"—exciting material quickly becomes boring—which can be attributed to the loss of a sense of risk, uncertainty, and transgression.[3] The perverse dynamic is both *an economic dynamic* and *a drive to maximize sexual excitement*—a "perverse implantation" to use Foucault's terminology for the cultural assimilation of perverse sexual desire.[4] Under the banner of sexual intercourse outside of the heteronormative marriage, pornography harnessed voyeurism and exhibitionism (both forms of perverse behavior found among porn performers) to portray sex with multiple partners, group sex, fellatio and cunnilingus, anal intercourse, lesbianism, male homosexuality, all kinds of sexual fetishisms, sex toys, BDSM, and other sexual practices. "The pornography industry," Robert Stoller observed, "is built around the problem of protecting its consumers from boredom . . . the result of loss of a sense of risk."[5]

Through the operation of the perverse dynamic and its acceleration and amplification by the Internet, the pornographic film industry has accumulated a huge archive of perverse fantasies and scripts. In the late 1980s, the industry produced fewer than two thousand videos (VHS tapes) a year—many available at local video stores. The Internet has led to a massive archival accumulation and facilitated the digital cataloguing of thousands of fantasies and scripts.[6] Pornhub, for example, is the fortieth most trafficked website in the world. It has more than ten million videos available for viewing and serves seventy-five million visitors a day.[7] Pornhub and other sites like it have replaced the "secret museum" of the nineteenth century as the library of sexually explicit images, fictions, and personal testimonies.[8]

The proliferation and concentration of porn scenes on huge porn sites like Pornhub allows Internet users to fine-tune or match their unconscious fantasy scripts with the perverse scripts produced by the porn industry to an unprecedented degree. Most porn genres, like perverse fantasies or the sexual scripts that circulate in society, are fairly heterogeneous—sharing only minimal thematic content and emphasizing perhaps certain cultural stereotypes, but others are highly organized. On the one hand, porn genres evolve because they are subject to the creative and spontaneous reformulations by directors and/or performers to satisfy their fantasies or expressive needs, while on the other hand the commercial drive to produce ever more perverse pornography (or some new edgier pornographic material) has expanded society's sexual imaginary—the repertoire of perverse sexual fantasies available to porn customers.[9]

This historical situation has three significant effects:

First, the porn customer must spend time to search for the porn script in which there are enough matching details to their own fantasies.[10] Thus, within the context of social media, consumer ratings, and online sexual communities, the process of identifying one's perverse fantasies has ceased to be based on direct personal (face-to-face) experience in the course of sexual encounters (perverse, neurotic, or not) or in therapeutic engagement; the search process is now more "social" or impersonal than in the past and has given rise to the emergence of online porn communities in which spectators can discuss and share their responses to the pornographic representations.[11] Other forms of porn have become more available—"cam porn," where the performer and spectator have some sort of direct address (or even communicate with one another) or "jerk-off instructions," which is more directly an interpellation (calling out to the spectator as "a subject").

Second, porn can also have a mimetic effect—it initiates a process of imitation and learning. It is a form of sex education and is increasingly pedagogic. A hot sexual scene can spur imitation. Spectators can be introduced to *new* fantasies or scripts that were not necessarily encoded in their infantile "microdots" or perverse fantasies.[12] Whether this material activates unused material from our own fantasies or implants altogether new material is unclear. "Pornography's favorite terrain is," Laura Kipnis has pointed out, "where the individual psyche collides with the historical process of molding social subjects."[13]

Third, repeated exposure to pornography also familiarizes perversity.[14] By mining the continuum of perversions that underlies human sexuality, the industry sought to produce fantasies that represented ever more "perverse" sexual combinations in order to sustain erotic excitement among its "bored" fans. The sexual fantasies supplied grow out of a complex intrapsychic dynamic between the familiar and the new, the normal and the taboo, the ordinary and the perverse. Operating within its masculine "reality effects" (that is, men's real erections, ejaculations, and orgasms), porn films demonstrate the potential viability of perverse sexual fantasies—traditionally for men and increasingly for women. Over the past fifty years, pornography, dominated as it is by its largely male audience and orientation, has, as Stoller noted, "condoned" and helped to normalize masculine perversity.[15] The dynamic of a polymorphic sexual economy promotes the process of fetishization and the selection of "risky" objects of desire.[16] It serves to normalize not only perverse sexual fantasies but also some of the activities they represent.

The proliferating pornographic "public sphere" on the Internet—whether it is (1) "finding one's script," (2) "adopting or learning a new script or how to have sex," or (3) completing the process of familiarization—has created a new sexual dreamscape that has taken us beyond the Kama Sutra, Krafft-Ebing, and Freud.[17]

As pornography is increasingly integrated into the contemporary psychological and social world, it has become a widely accessible form of social knowledge. This suggests that the perverse dynamic of the porn industry relies not only on the perverse fantasies as characterized by Stoller, but also on historical and social processes of learning. The developments on the Internet have taken place in a new social and cultural context. Pornography is increasingly integrated into the contemporary psychological and social world—it has become a widely accessible form of social knowledge. From the study of how his patients used pornography over time, Stoller concluded that individuals develop new scripts as their erotic dynamics change and are reflected in both their daydreams and their favorite pornographies. In the future, historical changes in parental practices will generate new historically specific injuries to the gender and sexual identities of children in subsequent generations—which may lead to the development of new identities, new sexual scripts, and new daydreams, and perhaps even new patterns of sexual behavior.[18]

Acknowledgments

As most writers know, writing is both a solitary occupation as well as a collective endeavor. We rely on the people who have inspired us, on our friends who talk about it with us, and on other people who publish us.

Writing the acknowledgments for a book is one of most pleasant aspects of preparing a book for publication. I've been thinking and/or writing about porn for more than forty years, so a great number of people have played a valuable role in the process. I first began to think about pornography during the feminist "sex wars" of the 1970s. Much of my early thinking on pornography (and sex, of course) was shaped by my friends, Amber Hollibaugh, Gayle Rubin, Carole Vance, Lisa Duggan, Allan Berube, and Judith Levine, all of whom were combatants (as "pro-sex" feminists) in the battles over sex and pornography. The pioneering works of Linda Williams and Laura Kipnis have been constant sources of inspiration and insight. Their books on pornography are truly great works.

The other strand of intellectual inspiration has derived from the work of John Gagnon and William Simon, both of whom over the course of years became friends. While Gagnon and Simon's conception of sexuality as socially constructed predated the work of Michel Foucault, it is not possible to think about the sociology and history of sexuality without all three—one needs Foucault's broad historical analysis as well as Gagnon and Simon's focus on the individual's scripting of sexual behavior. I am also indebted to the work of Robert Stoller and Jean Laplanche for their thinking about sex, sexual excitement, and fantasy.

Of course I could not have written the essays in this book without the people I have met and befriended in the porn business: my mentor and guide to the world of porn, director and writer Jerry Douglas; director Wash West, who has thought deeply about porn and influenced my own thinking; and my dear friend, Donald (aka Rod Barry). None of this would have happened if my friend Loring McAlpin hadn't introduced me to *Manshots*—considered by many to be the magazine of record for the gay porn industry—founded and edited by Jerry Douglas. There are too many others to give all their names.

Dagmar Herzog, Regina Kunzel, Cirus Rinaldi, Alain Giami, Eric Schaefer, Janice Irving, Ashley Mears, Gilbert Cole, Todd Morrison, Marco Seidelmann, Robert Phillips, and Brian A. Adams all have encouraged or solicited me at one time or another to write on some aspect of pornography. I am deeply grateful for the opportunities they have given me.

More important than anyone else are, of course, the friends who have supported me in my work, put up with impertinent questions, read numerous messy drafts of my essays, and given me good advice that I probably failed to take frequently enough, and who invariably influenced my thinking. One is the group of friends, known as the "tupperware group for perverts" (so nicknamed by performer Rod Barry), who themselves have also written about porn and who met monthly for almost two years to talk about it: Whit Strub, Kevin Bozelka, Howard Moore, Joe Rubin, April Hall, Ashley West, Benjamin Adam, Chris Baum, Devin McGheehan Muchmore, Alan Bounville, and Brandon Arroyo. It was/is a wonderful group. We even once went on a field trip to visit the last porn theater in Newark just before it closed.

Above all I owe a huge debt to Andrew Spieldenner, who has been reading my papers, using them in his courses, and talking with me about porn for more than twenty years; to Chris Mitchell, who teaches my work and knows it better than anyone; and to Jeffrey Colgan, who in the last two and a half years has been my most thorough reader, given me a continuous stream of valuable editorial guidance, and repeatedly challenged me to help me hone my ideas. This book has benefited enormously from his thoroughness, his conscientious readings, and his skepticism. I'm afraid all the faults are mine.

Last but not least, I am thankful for the company, the intelligence, and the beauty that Hector Lionel has brought into my life.

Notes

Introduction

1 Michel Foucault, *The History of Sexuality Volume 1: An Introduction* (New York: Pantheon, 1978), 103–104.
2 Andre Bazin, "The Ontological Status of the Photographic Image," in *What Is Cinema*, Vol. 1 (Berkeley: University of California Press, 1967), 9–16.
3 Siegfried Kracauer, *The Theory of Film: The Redemption of Physical Reality* (Princeton, NJ: Princeton University Press), 46.
4 William Simon and John H. Gagnon, "Sexual Scripts: Permanence and Change," *Archives of Sexual Behavior* 13 (1986): 97–120.
5 Pierre Bourdieu, *Outline of a Theory of Practice* (Cambridge: Cambridge University Press, 1977), 78.
6 Robert J. Stoller, *Sexual Excitement: The Dynamics of Erotic Life* (New York: Simon & Schuster, 1979), 166–167.
7 Jean Laplanche and Jean-Bertrand Pontalis, "Fantasy and the Origins of Sexuality," in *Formations of Fantasy*, ed. Victor Burgin, James Donald, and Cora Kaplan (London: Methuen, 1986); Stoller, *Sexual Excitement*, 207–209.
8 See Jeffrey Escoffier, "Every Detail Counts: Robert Stoller, Perversion and the Production of Pornography," *Psychoanalysis and History* 22, no. 1 (April 2020): 35–52; and Jeffrey Escoffier, "The Pornographic Object of Knowledge: Pornography as Epistemology," in *Sexologies and Theories of Sexuality: Translation, Appropriation, Problematization, Medicalization*, ed. Alain Giami and Sharman Levinson (Houndmills: Palgrave Macmillan, forthcoming).

Chapter 1   Pornography, Perversity, and Sexual Revolution

A revised version of this chapter was presented at "Sexual Revolution: A Seminar," Institut National de la Santé et de la Recherche Medicale (France) and the Faculty of Social and Behavioural Sciences, University of Amsterdam, Amsterdam, April 8–9, 2011, and published in Alain Giami and Gert Hekma, eds., *Sexual Revolutions in the West* (London: Palgrave Macmillan, 2014). Reproduced with the permission of Palgrave Macmillan. I would like to thank Alaim Giami, John Gagnon, Gert

Hekma, Dagmar Herzog, Rostom Mesli, Massimo Perinelli, and the other participants in the Amsterdam seminar on sexual revolutions for their comments and
suggestions.

1 "The Second Sexual Revolution," *Time*, January 24, 1964.
2 John Levi Martin, "Structuring the Sexual Revolution," *Theory and Society* 25 (1996): 105–151.
3 Wilhelm Reich, *The Sexual Revolution: Towards a Self-Governing Character Structure* [original edition 1933] (London: Vision Press, 1951).
4 Richard King, *The Party of Eros: Radical Social Thought and the Realm of Freedom* (Chapel Hill: University of North Carolina Press, 1972), 51–115; Christopher Turner, *Adventures in the Orgasmatron: How the Sexual Revolution Came to America* (New York: Farrar, Straus and Giroux, 2011).
5 Michel Foucault, *The History of Sexuality: An Introduction*, vol. 1 (New York: Pantheon, 1978), 15–49.
6 Daniel Scott Smith, "The Dating of the Sexual Revolution: Evidence and Interpretation," in *The American Family in Social-Historical Perspective*, ed. M. Gordon (New York: St. Martin's, 1978), 435.
7 Julia A. Ericksen, *Kiss and Tell: Surveying Sex in the Twentieth Century* (Cambridge, MA: Harvard University Press, 1999).
8 Ericksen, *Kiss and Tell*, 30–48.
9 Ericksen, 49–61; John Madge, *The Origins of Scientific Sociology* (New York: Free Press, 1962), 133–376.
10 Albert D. Klassen, Colin J. Williams, and Eugene E. Levitt, *Sex and Morality in the U.S.* (Middletown, CT: Wesleyan University Press, 1989).
11 Tom W. Smith, "American Sexual Behavior: Trends, Socio-demographic Differences, and Risk Behavior" (NORC Digital Library 1998, GSS Topical Report 25).
12 Tom Smith, "American Sexual Behavior,"Table 1A; Smith, "Dating of the Sexual Revolution"; C. F. Turner, R. D. Danella, and S. Rogers, "Sexual Behavior in the United States, 1930–1990: Trends and Methodological Problems," *Sexually Transmitted Diseases* 23, no. 3 (1995): 173–190.
13 Smith, "American Sexual Behavior," Table 1B; Turner, Danella, and Rogers, "Sexual Behavior in the United States."
14 Smith, "Dating of the Sexual Revolution," Table 1C.
15 Jeffrey Escoffier, *American Homo: Community and Perversity* (Berkeley: University of California Press, 1998; repr., New York: Verso, 2018).
16 Turner, *Adventures in the Orgasmatron*.
17 Turner, *Adventures in the Orgasmatron*.
18 Klassen, Williams, and Levitt, *Sex and Morality*, 4.
19 Klassen, Williams, and Levitt, 17.
20 Klassen, Williams, and Levitt, 134–135.
21 John H. Gagnon and William Simon, *Sexual Conduct: The Social Sources of Human Sexuality* (Chicago: Aldine, 1973); John H. Gagnon and William Simon, "Sexual Scripts: Permanence and Change," *Archives of Sexual Behavior* 15, no. 2 (1986): 97–120.
22 John H. Gagnon, *An Interpretation of Desire: Essays in the Study of Sexuality* (Chicago: University of Chicago Press, 2003), see Jeffrey Escoffier, "Foreword," xiii–xxvi.
23 Martin, "Structuring the Sexual Revolution."

24 Walter Kendrick, *The Secret Museum: Pornography in Modern Culture* (New York: Viking, 1987), 134.

25 Pierre Bourdieu, *Language and Symbolic Power* (Cambridge, MA: Harvard University Press, 1991), 43–65.

26 Jeffrey Escoffier, Whitney Strub, and Jeffrey Patrick Colgan, "The Comstock Apparatus," in *Intimate States*, ed. Margot Canaday, Nancy Cott, and Robert Self (University of Chicago Press, 2021).

27 Whitney Strub, *Obscenity Rules:* Roth v. United States *and the Long Struggle over Sexual Expression* (Lawrence: University Press of Kansas, 2013), 27–48.

28 Edward de Grazia, *Girls Lean Back Everywhere: The Law of Obscenity and the Assault on Genius* (New York: Vintage, 1992), 322.

29 de Grazia, *Girls Lean Back Everywhere*, 322.

30 Strub, *Obscenity Rules*, 22–23.

31 Strub, 162–169.

32 Strub, 162–169.

33 Gagnon and Simon, *Sexual Conduct*, 260–282.

34 Jeffrey Escoffier, ed., *Sexual Revolution* (New York: Thunder's Mouth Press, 2003), xi–xxxvi, 321–464.

35 Linda Williams, *Hard Core: Power, Pleasure and the "Frenzy of the Visible"* (Berkeley: University of California Press, 1989), 96–97.

36 Legs McNeil and Jennifer Osborne, *The Other Hollywood: The Uncensored Oral History of the Porn Film Industry* (New York: HarperCollins, 2005), 10–11.

37 Kenneth Turan and Stephen F. Zito, *Sinema: American Pornographic Films and the People Who Make Them* (New York: Praeger, 1974), 77–80.

38 Turan and Zito, *Sinema: American Pornographic Films*, 78–80.

39 Paul Alcuin Siebenand, "The Beginnings of Gay Cinema in Los Angeles: The Industry and the Audience" (PhD diss., University of Southern California, 1975), 27.

40 John Lewis, *Hollywood v. Hard Core: How the Struggle over Censorship Saved the Modern Film Industry* (New York: New York University Press, 2000), 1–10.

41 Eric Schlosser, *Reefer Madness: Sex, Drugs, and Cheap Labor in the American Black Market* (Boston: Houghton Mifflin, 2003), 112–115.

42 Jonathan Dollimore, *Sexual Dissidence: Augustine to Wilde, Freud to Foucault* (Oxford: Clarendon, 1991), 169–230; Foucault, *History of Sexuality*, 34–49.

43 Samuel R. Delany, *Times Square Red, Times Square Blue* (New York: New York University Press, 1999), 78.

44 Laurence Senelick, "Private Parts in Public Places," in *Inventing Times Square: Commerce and Culture at the Crossroads of the World*, ed. William R. Taylor (Baltimore: Johns Hopkins University Press, 1991), 329–353; Jose Bernard Capino, "Homologies of Space: Text and Spectatorship in All Male Adult Theaters," *Cinema Journal* 45, no. 1 (2005): 50–65; Rich Cante and Angelo Restivo, "The Cultural-Aesthetic Specificities of All-Male Moving Image Pornography," in *Porn Studies*, ed. Linda Williams (Durham, NC: Duke University Press, 2004); Amy Herzog, "In the Flesh: Space and Embodiment in the Pornographic Peep Show Arcade," *Velvet Light Trap* 62 (2008): 29–43.

45 Jean-Luc Baudry, "Ideological Effects of the Basic Cinematographic Apparatus," in *Narrative, Apparatus, Ideology: A Film Theory Reader*, ed. Phillip Rosen (New York: Columbia University Press, 1986), 286–318; Linda Williams, "Film Bodies: Gender, Genre and Excess," in *Film Genre Reader III*, ed. Barry K. Grant (Austin: University of Texas Press, 2003), 154.

46 Delany, *Times Square Red*; Laud Humphreys, *Tearoom Trade: Impersonal Sex in Public Places* (New York: Aldine, 1975), 1–16.
47 Humphreys, *Tearoom Trade*.
48 Delany, *Times Square Red*, 74–75.
49 Capino, "Homologies of Space."
50 Delany, *Times Square Red*, 78.
51 Williams, *Hard Core*, 272–273.

Chapter 2   Beefcake to Hardcore

This chapter was originally published in Eric Schaefer, ed., *Sex Scene: Media, Popular Culture and the Sexual Revolution* (Durham, NC: Duke University Press, 2014). Republished by permission of the copyright holder, Duke University Press. I am indebted to my friends Jerry Douglas, Rod Barry, Wash West, and Michael Stabile who have worked in the porn industry for their advice, suggestions, and information; to Joe Rubin for his amazing knowledge of pornographic film history; to John Gagnon and Alain Giami for valuable discussions about the sexual revolution; to Christopher Mitchell for reading several drafts carefully and offering historical clarification; and above all to Eric Schaefer for his patience, steadfastness, and many sage and practical editorial suggestions.

1 Jon Lewis, *Hollywood v. Hardcore: How the Struggle over Censorship Saved the Modern Film Industry* (New York: New York University Press, 2000), 192–195.
2 See Richard Dyer, "Coming to Terms, Gay Pornography," in *Only Entertainment* (London: Routledge, 1992).
3 Thomas Yingling, "How the Eye Is Caste: Robert Mapplethorpe and the Limits of Controversy," *Discourse* 12, no. 2 (1989): 3–28.
4 Earl Jackson, *Strategies of Deviance: Studies in Gay Male Representation* (Bloomington: Indiana University Press, 1995), 129–132.
5 For an exploration of the significance of the shift in the representation of sex by hardcore films, see Linda Williams, *Hard Core: Power, Pleasure and the "Frenzy of the Visible,"* exp. ed. (Berkeley: University of California Press, 1999); and her *Screening Sex* (Durham, NC: Duke University Press, 2008).
6 Jeffrey Escoffier, "Scripting the Sex: Fantasy, Narrative and Sexual Scripts in Pornographic Films," in *The Sexual Self: The Construction of Sexual Scripts*, ed. Michael Kimmel (Nashville: Vanderbilt University Press, 2007), 61–79.
7 Christian Metz, *The Imaginary Signifier: Psychoanalysis and Cinema* (Bloomington: Indiana University Press, 1982), 42–57.
8 Jeffrey Escoffier, "Pornography, Perversity and the Sexual Revolution" (paper, Seminar on the Sexual Revolution, Amsterdam, April 8–9, 2011).
9 Joseph W. Slade, *Pornography in America: A Reference Handbook* (Santa Barbara, CA: ABC-CLIO, 2000), 209–215.
10 John D'Emilio, *Sexual Politics, Sexual Communities: The Making of a Homosexual Minority in the United States, 1940–1970* (Chicago: University of Chicago Press, 1983), 115.
11 Slade, *Pornography in America*, 212–213.
12 Thomas Waugh, *Hard to Imagine: Gay Male Eroticism in Photography and Film from Their Beginnings to Stonewall* (New York: Columbia University Press, 1996), 413–417. Also see Christopher Nealon's chapter on the broader political and

cultural significance of beefcake magazines, "The Secret Public of Physique Culture," in *Foundlings: Lesbian and Gay Historical Emotion before Stonewall* (Durham, NC: Duke University Press, 2001), 99–140.

13 Laurence O'Toole, *Pornocopia: Porn, Sex, Technology and Desire* (London: Serpent's Tail, 1999), 7–10.

14 Barry Werth, *The Scarlet Professor, Newton Arvin: A Literary Life Shattered by Scandal* (New York: Anchor Books, 2001).

15 Slade, *Pornography in America*, 212–213; Werth, *Scarlet Professor*, epilogue.

16 On the criminalization of homosexuality after World War II, see Allan Berube, *Coming Out under Fire: The History of Gay Men and Women in World War Two* (New York: Free Press, 1990), 228–279.

17 Helen Lefkowitz Horowitz, *Rereading Sex: Battles over Sexual Knowledge and Suppression in Nineteenth-Century America* (New York: Knopf, 2002), 299–318.

18 For the history of the physique magazines, see F. Valentine Hooven III, *Beefcake: The Muscle Magazines of America, 1950–1970* (Cologne: Taschen, 1995); for an excellent account of the commercial and legal aspects of physique magazines from 1945 to 1963, see Waugh, *Hard to Imagine*, 215–283; and on the availability of illegal images, see 284–365.

19 Hooven, *Beefcake*, 1–51; Waugh, *Hard to Imagine*, 215–252; Nealon, *Foundlings*, 99–140.

20 Hooven, *Beefcake*, 74.

21 Waugh, *Hard to Imagine*, 215–283.

22 Nealon, *Foundlings*, 99–140; See also Dian Hanson, *Bob's World: The Life and Boys of AMG's Bob Mizer* (Cologne: Taschen, 2009).

23 Waugh, *Hard to Imagine*, 215–227; Hooven, *Beefcake*, 27–32.

24 Nealon, *Foundlings*, 1–23.

25 Nealon, 99–140.

26 Waugh, *Hard to Imagine*, 215–219.

27 Hooven, *Beefcake*, 52.

28 Waugh, *Hard to Imagine*, 217–219.

29 On sexual activity in porn theaters and arcades, see Samuel R. Delany, *Times Square Red, Times Square Blue* (New York: New York University Press, 1999); Brendan Gill, "Blue Notes," *Film Comment*, January–February 1973, 10–11; C. A. Sundholm, "The Pornographic Arcade: Ethnographic Notes on Moral in Immoral Places," *Urban Life and Culture* 2, no. 1 (1973): 85–104; Jose B. Capino, "Homologies of Space: Text and Spectatorship in All Male Adult Theaters," *Cinema Journal* 45, no. 1 (2005): 50–65; and Amy Herzog, "In the Flesh: Space and Embodiment in the Pornographic Peep Show Arcade," *Velvet Light Trap* 62 (2008): 29–43.

30 On desire and sexual identification, male spectatorship, and pornographic film, see Williams, *Hard Core*, 80–83; Elizabeth Cowie, "Pornography and Fantasy: Psychoanalytic Perspectives," in *Sex Exposed: Sexuality and the Pornography Debate*, ed. Lynne Segal and Mary McIntosh (New Brunswick, NJ: Rutgers University Press, 1993), 133; and Thomas Waugh, "Homosociality in the Classical American Stag Film: Off-Screen, On-Screen," in *Porn Studies*, ed. Linda Williams (Durham, NC: Duke University Press, 2004), 127–141.

31 Linda Williams, "Film Bodies: Gender, Genre and Excess," in *Film Genre Reader III*, ed. Barry K. Grant (Austin: University of Texas Press, 2003), 154.

32 Laurence Senelick, "Private Parts in Public Places," in *Inventing Times Square: Commerce and Culture at the Crossroads of the World*, ed. William R. Taylor

(Baltimore: Johns Hopkins University Press, 1991), 329–353; see also Delany, *Times Square Red*.

33 William Leap, ed., *Public Sex, Gay Space* (New York: Columbia University Press, 1999), 1–22; see also Laud Humphries, "Tearoom Trade: Impersonal Sex," in *Public Place* (New York: Aldine De Gruyter, 1975).

34 See Delany, *Times Square Red*; and Richard Cante and Angelo Restivo, "The Cultural-Aesthetic Specificities of All-Male Moving Image Pornography," in Williams, *Porn Studies*.

35 For a discussion of the theater as an integral component of the cinematic apparatus, see Jean-Louis Baudry's classic articles "Ideological Effects of the Basic Cinematographic Apparatus" and "The Apparatus: Metapsychological Approaches to the Impression of Reality in Cinema," in *Narrative, Apparatus, Ideology: A Film Theory Reader*, ed. Philip Rosen (New York: Columbia University Press, 1986), 286–298 and 299–318.

36 Capino, "Homologies of Space," 58–64.

37 Gill, "Blue Notes," 10–11.

38 Delany, *Times Square Red*, xiii–xx.

39 Eric Schaefer, *"Bold! Daring! Shocking! True!" A History of Exploitation Films, 1919–1959* (Durham, NC: Duke University Press, 1999), 210–214.

40 See Juan A. Suárez, *Bike Boys, Drag Queens and Superstars: Avant-Garde, Mass Culture, and Gay Identities in the 1960s Underground Cinema* (Bloomington: Indiana University Press, 1996).

41 Alice Hutchison, *Kenneth Anger: A Demonic Visionary* (London: Black Dog, 2004), 136.

42 Steven Watson, *Factory Made: Warhol and the Sixties* (New York: Pantheon, 2003), 72; Sally Banes, *Greenwich Village 1963: Avant-Garde Performance and the Effervescent Body* (Durham, NC: Duke University Press, 1993), 172.

43 See chap. 4 in Stephen Koch, *Stargazer: The Life, World and Films of Andy Warhol*, rev. ed. (New York: Marion Boyers, 2002); and Wayne Koestenbaum, *Andy Warhol* (London: Phoenix, 2003), 72–74.

44 Watson, *Factory Made*, 336–337.

45 Jeffrey Escoffier, *Bigger Than Life: The History of Gay Porn Cinema from Beefcake to Hardcore* (Philadelphia: Running Press, 2009), 47–88.

46 Escoffier, *Bigger Than Life*, 47–48.

47 Escoffier, 57–58.

48 Jerry Douglas, "Interview with Tom De Simone," *Manshots*, June 1993, 12.

49 Paul Alcuin Siebenand, "The Beginnings of Gay Cinema in Los Angeles: The Industry and the Audience" (PhD diss., University of Southern California, 1975), 50.

50 Williams, *Hard Core*, 93–100.

51 Thomas Schatz, *Hollywood Genres: Formulas, Filmmaking and the Studio System* (New York: Random House, 1981), 14–41.

52 Kenneth Turan and Stephen F. Zito, *Sinema: American Pornographic Films and the People Who Make Them* (New York: Praeger, 1974), 77–80.

53 Turan and Zito, *Sinema*, 77–80.

54 Douglas, "Interview with Tom De Simone," 12.

55 Turan and Zito, *Sinema*, 128.

56 Siebenand, "Beginnings of Gay Cinema in Los Angeles," 85.

57 Turan and Zito, *Sinema*, 128.

58 Whereas some sexploitation films included synch-sound dialogue, others featured awkwardly postdubbed "dialogue"; still others were essentially silent with narration.

59 Escoffier, "Scripting the Sex."

60 Siebenand, "Beginnings of Gay Cinema in Los Angeles," 27.

61 See Thomas Waugh, ed., *Out/Lines: Underground Gay Graphics from before Stonewall* (Vancouver: Arsenal Pulp Press, 2002).

62 Siebenand, "Beginnings of Gay Cinema in Los Angeles," 92.

63 Schatz, *Hollywood Genres*, 37–38.

64 Sebastian Figg, IMDb, www.imdb.com/name/nm0276544/.

65 David Carter, *Stonewall: The Riots That Sparked the Gay Revolution* (New York: St. Martin's, 2010).

66 Wakefield Poole, *Dirty Poole: The Autobiography of a Gay Porn Pioneer* (Los Angeles: Alyson Books, 2000), 145–164.

67 Escoffier, *Bigger Than Life*, 47–116.

68 Jerry Douglas, "The Legacy of Jack Deveau," *Stallion*, April 1983, 22–25, 46–47.

69 Douglas was the author of *Rondelay* (1969), a musical version of Arthur Schnitzler's *La Ronde*; *Score* (1970); and, under the pseudonym A. J. Kronengold, *Tubstrip* (1973), which was set in a gay bathhouse.

70 Ted Underwood, "Raw Country," *Stallion's Hot 50: All-Time Best Male Films and Videos 1970–1985*, special issue no. 4 (1985): 46.

71 Escoffier, *Bigger Than Life*.

72 Siebenand, "Beginnings of Gay Cinema in Los Angeles," 231. For accounts of Fred Halsted's life and work, see chap. 6 in Patrick Moore's *Beyond Shame: Reclaiming the Abandoned History of Radical Gay Sexuality* (Boston: Beacon, 2004); and William E. Jones, *Halsted Plays Himself* (Los Angeles: Semiotext[e], 2011).

73 Siebenand, "Beginnings of Gay Cinema," 222.

74 Siebenand, 211.

75 For example, the documentary film by director Joseph Lovett, *Gay Sex in the Seventies* (2006), uses clips from porn films by Jack Deveau and Peter Romeo to illustrate the gay sexual mores of the 1970s. See also chapter 3 of this book.

76 Or does the "perverse dynamic" include symbolic containment? No, commercial success both fed a perverse dynamic and established strategies of symbolic containment.

77 Brian Pronger, *The Arena of Masculinity: Sports, Homosexuality, and the Meaning of Sex* (New York: St. Martin's, 1990).

78 Henning Bech, *When Men Meet: Homosexuality and Modernity* (Chicago: University of Chicago Press, 1997); Jeffrey Escoffier, "Gay-for-Pay: Straight Men and the Making of Gay Pornography," *Qualitative Sociology* 26, no. 4 (2003): 531–555.

79 See Michael Bronski, *Culture Clash: The Making of Gay Sensibility* (Boston: Alyson Books, 1984), 166–174; Dyer, *Only Entertainment*, 121–134; Jackson, *Strategies of Deviance*, 126–172; Waugh, *Hard to Imagine*, 402–416; and Pronger, *Arena of Masculinity*, 125–150.

80 Edmund White, *States of Desire: Travels in Gay America* (New York: Plume, 1980), 45–46.

81 See Leo Bersani's *Baudelaire and Freud* (Berkeley: University of California Press, 1977) and *The Freudian Body: Psychoanalysis and Art* (New York: Columbia University Press, 1986).

82 Austin Foxxe, "Home Bodies," *Unzipped*, August 31, 1999, 40.

83 Sigmund Freud, "'Civilized' Sexual Morality and Modern Nervousness," in *Sexual Revolution*, ed. Jeffrey Escoffier (New York: Thunder's Mouth Press, 2003), 557–577.

84 Jonathan Dollimore, *Sexual Dissidence: Augustine to Wilde, Freud to Foucault* (Oxford: Clarendon, 1991), 219–230; Michel Foucault, *The History of Sexuality*, vol. 1: *An Introduction*, trans. Robert Hurley (New York: Vintage, 1980), 36–50; Williams, *Hard Core*, 272–273.

85 Michel Foucault, "'Omnes et Singulatim': Toward a Critique of Political Reason," in *Power, Essential Works of Foucault, 1954–1984*, vol. 3, ed. James D. Faubion (New York: New Press, 2000), 298–325.

Chapter 3   Sex in the Seventies

This chapter was originally published in *Journal of the History of Sexuality* 26, no. 1 (January 2017): 88–113. Copyright 2017 by the University of Texas Press. I would like to thank Benjamin Adam, Etienne Meunier, Christopher A. Mitchell, Andrew Spieldenner, and the anonymous reviewers and the journal's editor, Annette Timm, for their excellent comments and many valuable suggestions.

1 Brad Gooch, *The Golden Age of Promiscuity* (New York: Knopf, 1996).

2 Patrick Moore, *Beyond Shame: Reclaiming the Abandoned History of Radical Gay Sexuality* (Boston: Beacon, 2004).

3 Jeffrey Escoffier, "The Invention of Safer Sex: Vernacular Knowledge, Gay Politics, and HIV Prevention," *Berkeley Journal of Sociology* 43 (Spring 1999): 1–20.

4 For reviews of this literature, see Edward King, *Safety in Numbers: Safer Sex and Gay Men* (New York: Routledge, 1993); Gabriel Rotello, *Sexual Ecology: AIDS and the Destiny of Gay Men* (New York: Dutton, 1997); see also Douglas Crimp, ed., *AIDS: Cultural Analysis, Cultural Criticism* (Cambridge, MA: MIT Press, 1988) and Ben Gove, *Cruising Culture: Promiscuity, Desire and American Gay Culture* (Edinburgh: Edinburgh University Press, 2000) for an exploration of gay male writing on promiscuity. For a discussion of the debates in the early days of the epidemic, see Jennifer Brier, *Infectious Ideas: U.S. Political Responses to the AIDS Crisis* (Chapel Hill: University of North Carolina Press, 2009).

5 For a discussion on the significance of increased sexual expression in popular culture and the media, see Jeffrey Escoffier, "Beefcake to Hardcore: Gay Pornography and the Sexual Revolution" and other essays in *Sex Scene: Media and the Sexual Revolution*, ed. Eric Schaeffer (Durham, NC: Duke University Press, 2014), 319–347.

6 Martin P. Levine, *Gay Macho: The Life and Death of the Homosexual Clone* (New York: New York University Press, 1998), 10–29.

7 Moore, *Beyond Shame*, 4.

8 Moore, 6.

9 Moore, 16–33.

10 Moore, xxi–xxii. Two early pieces that treated the period as shameful are Bruce Bawer, "Sex Negative Me," *Advocate*, August 1994, and Larry Kramer's "Sex and Sensibility," *Advocate*, May 27, 1997.

11 Arthur Danto, *Playing with the Edge: The Photographic Achievement of Robert Mapplethorpe* (Berkeley: University of California Press, 1995), 7.

12 Danto, *Playing with the Edge*, 8.

13 This is confirmed by ethnographic studies conducted during the 1970s. For example, see Edward William Delph, *The Silent Community: Public Homosexual Encounters* (Beverly Hills, CA: Sage, 1978).

14 Joseph Lovett, dir., *Gay Sex in the 70s: A Steamy Romp*. To view the film and find more information, go to http://www.gaysexinthe70s.com.

15 Gove, *Cruising Culture*, 1–19.

16 Lovett's film captures the emotional aura of his subjects' memory images. Siegfried Kracauer explored the antagonistic relationship between emotional-laden *memory images* and the more reified photographic images in his essay "Photography," in *The Mass Ornament*, ed. Thomas Y. Levin (Cambridge, MA: Harvard University Press, 1995), 47–63. See also Miriam Bratu Hansen, *Cinema and Experience: Siegfried Kracauer, Walter Benjamin and Theodor W. Adorno* (Berkeley: University of California Press, 2012), 27, 31–32.

17 Andre Bazin, "An Aesthetic of Reality: Cinematic Realism and the Italian School of Liberation," in *What Is Cinema?*, vol. 2 (Berkeley: University of California Press, 1971), 16–40.

18 Jeffrey Escoffier, *Bigger Than Life: The History of Gay Porn Cinema from Beefcake to Hardcore* (Philadelphia: Running Press, 2009), 89–116.

19 David Halperin, "Is There a History of Sexuality?," *History and Theory* 28, no. 3 (1989): 257–274, reprinted in Henry Abelove, Michele Aina Barale, and David M. Halperin, eds., *The Lesbian and Gay Studies Reader* (New York: Routledge, 1993).

20 Eve Kosofsky Sedgwick, *Epistemology of the Closet* (Berkeley: University of California Press, 1990), 67–90; "Sources," in Anna Clark, *Desire: A History of European Sexuality* (New York: Routledge, 2008), 8–9.

21 Julian Carter, "Introduction: Theory, Methods, Praxis: The History of Sexuality and the Question of Evidence," *Journal of the History of Sexuality* 14, nos. 1/2 (2005): 1–9.

22 Carole S. Vance, "Anthropology Rediscovers Sexuality: A Theoretical Comment," *Social Science and Medicine* 33 no. 8 (1991): 878.

23 Michel Foucault, *History of Sexuality: An Introduction*, vol. 1 (New York: Pantheon, 1978); Clare Lyons, *Sex among the Rabble: An Intimate History of Gender and Power in the Age of Revolution, Philadelphia, 1730–1830* (Chapel Hill: University of North Carolina Press, 2006), 7–8.

24 Foucault, *History of Sexuality*, 53–73.

25 For a classic exploration, see Georges Bataille, *The Tears of Eros*, trans. Peter Connor (San Francisco: City Lights Books, 1989); Gilles Neret's volumes of erotic art provide a rich archive of visual (nonphotographic) representations of sex: *Erotica: 17–18th Century: From Rembrandt to Fragonard* (Cologne: Taschen, 2001); *Erotica 20th Century: From Rodin to Picasso* (Cologne: Taschen, 2001).

26 Stephen Garton, *Histories of Sexuality: Antiquity to Sexual Revolution* (New York: Routledge, 2004), 1–29; David M. Halperin, *How to Do the History of Homosexuality* (Chicago: University of Chicago, 2002), 1–23; Richard Godbeer, *Sexual Revolution in Early America* (Baltimore: Johns Hopkins University, 2002), 11; Clark, *Desire*, 4–8; Angus McLaren, *Twentieth-Century Sexuality: A History* (Oxford: Blackwell, 1999), 2–3.

27 Gove, *Cruising Culture*, 1–40; see also Douglas Sadownick, *Sex between Men: An Intimate History of the Sex Lives of Gay Men, Postwar to the Present* (San Francisco: HarperCollins, 1996).

28 Kramer, "Sex and Sensibility," 59.

29 Joseph Sonnabend, "Looking at AIDS in Totality: A Conversation," *New York Native*, October 7, 1985.

30 Escoffier, *Bigger Than Life*, 177–178 and Jeffrey Escoffier, "Sex, Safety and the Trauma of AIDS," *Women Studies Quarterly*, 39, nos. 1–2 (2011): 129–138.

31 Both Hans Licht in *Sexual Life in Ancient Greece* (London: Routledge & Kegan Paul, 1932; repr., London: Panther Books, 1969) and K. J. Dover in *Greek Homosexuality* (New York: Vintage, 1980) make extensive use of both erotic literature and vase paintings in their discussions of sexuality in classical Greece. Gilles Neret's volumes of erotic art provide a rich archive of visual (nonphotographic) representations of sex: *Erotica: 17–18th Century* and *Erotica 20th Century*.

32 Dover, "Problems, Sources and Methods," in *Greek Homosexuality*, 4–17.

33 Bataille, *Tears of Eros*.

34 Steven Marcus, *The Other Victorians: A Study of Sexuality and Pornography in Mid-Nineteenth-Century England* (New York: Basic Books, 1966). Marcus's Freudian view of sexual repression and the counteraction to it presumed a simple hydraulic model as the basis for a psychosocial interpretation of the history of sexuality. It was Marcus's book that provoked Michel Foucault to mount his scathing critique of the "repressive hypothesis" and thus effectively change forever how the history of sexuality might be written. Anonymous, *My Secret Life*, vols. 1–11, introduction by G. Legman (New York: Grove Press, 1966).

35 Lisa Z. Sigel, *Governing Pleasures: Pornography and Social Change in England, 1815–1914* (New Brunswick, NJ: Rutgers University Press, 2002).

36 Paul R. Deslandes, "The Cultural Politics of Gay Pornography in 1970s Britain," in *British Queer History: New Approaches and Perspectives*, ed. Brian Lewis (Manchester: Manchester University Press, 2013).

37 In Charles Sanders Peirce's semiotic typology, photographic images are indexical signs, that is, signs whose referents actually produce the signs—such as a weather vane signifying the direction of the wind or a knock on the door signifying a visitor. In predigital photographic or cinematic media, images are indexical because they are produced by the action of light reflected from objects in front of a camera onto a chemical emulsion.

38 Kracauer, "Photography," 47–63; Andre Bazin, "The Ontology of the Photographic Image," in *What Is Cinema?*, vol. 1 (Berkeley: University of California Press, 1967), 14; Philip Rosen, *Change Mummified: Cinema, Historicity, Theory* (Minneapolis: University of Minnesota Press, 2001), 133–135; Hansen, *Cinema and Experience*. Jacques Ranciere, in *Figures of History* (Cambridge: Polity, 2014), makes a similar argument about European political history and photographic media (3–30).

39 Linda Williams, *Hard Core: Power, Pleasure and the "Frenzy of the Visible"* (Berkeley: University of California Press, 1989).

40 Thomas Waugh, *Hard to Imagine: Gay Male Eroticism in Photography and Film from Their Beginnings to Stonewall* (New York: Columbia University Press, 1996).

41 Tim Dean, *Unlimited Intimacy: Reflections on the Subculture of Barebacking* (Chicago: University of Chicago Press, 2009).

42 Miriam Bratu Hansen, "Introduction," in Siegfried Kracauer, *The Theory of Film: The Redemption of Physical Reality* (Oxford: Oxford University Press, 1960; repr., Princeton, NJ: Princeton University Press, 1997), ix, and Kracauer, *Theory of Film*, 18–23, 46–74.

43 Kracauer, *Theory of Film*, 77–92; Roland Barthes, *Camera Lucida*, trans. Richard Howard (New York: Hill & Wang, 1981); John Tagg, *The Burden of Representation: Essays on Photographies and Histories* (Amherst: University of Massachusetts Press, 1988), 1–33.

44 Roland Barthes, "The Reality Effect," in *The Rustle of Language*, trans. Richard Howard (New York: Hill & Wang, 1986), 141–148; on reality effects in pornographic films, see Jeffrey Escoffier, "Scripting the Sex: Fantasy, Narrative and Sexual Scripts in Pornographic Films," in *The Sexual Self: The Construction of Sexual Scripts*, ed. Michael Kimmel (Nashville: Vanderbilt University Press, 2007), 60–79.

45 Linda Williams, "Pornography, Porno, Porn: Thoughts on a Weedy Field," in *Porn Archives*, ed. Tim Dean, Steven Ruszczycky, and David Squires (Durham, NC: Duke University Press, 2014), 41. On the use of porn as ethnography, see Dean's *Unlimited Intimacy*, 97–144.

46 Escoffier, "Scripting the Sex."

47 Escoffier, 63–64.

48 William Hughes, "The Evaluation of Film as Evidence," in *The Historian and Film*, ed. Paul Smith (Cambridge: Cambridge University Press, 1976), 49–79.

49 William Simon and John Gagnon, "Sexual Scripts: Permanence and Change," *Archives of Sexual Behavior* 15, no. 2 (1986): 97–120.

50 Escoffier, "Scripting the Sex."

51 Williams examines this rhetorical convention in her book *Hard Core*.

52 See Erving Goffman, "Interaction Order," in *The Goffman Reader*, ed. Charles Lemert and Ann Brannan (Malden, MA: Blackwell, 1997), 233–261; and the introduction to Michael Hviid Jacobsen, ed., *Encountering the Everyday: An Introduction to the Sociologies of the Unnoticed* (Houndmills: Palgrave Macmillan, 2009), 1–41.

53 George Chauncey, *Gay New York: Gender, Urban Culture and the Making of the Gay Male World, 1890–1940* (New York: Basic Books, 1994); Mark W. Turner, *Backward Glances: Cruising the Queer Streets of New York and London* (London: Reaktion Books, 2003); John Rechy, *The Sexual Outlaw: A Documentary* (New York: Grove Press, 1978); John Howard, *Men Like That: A Southern Queer History* (Chicago: University of Chicago Press, 1999); David Allyn, *Make Love, Not War: The Sexual Revolution: An Unfettered History* (Boston: Little, Brown, 2000), 149–151; Allan Berube, "The History of Gay Bathhouses," in *Policing Public Sex*, ed. Dangerous Bedfellows (Boston: South End Press, 1996); Samuel R. Delany, *Times Square Red, Times Square Blue* (New York: New York University Press, 1999); Laud Humphreys, *Tearoom Trade: Impersonal Sex in Public Places* (New York: Aldine, 1975); and Delph, *Silent Community*.

54 Jeffrey Escoffier, "Sexual Revolution and the Politics of Gay Identity," in *American Homo: Community and Perversity* (Berkeley: University of California Press, 1998); see also Turner, *Backward Glances*.

55 See Erving Goffman, *Stigma: Notes on the Management of Spoiled Identity* (Englewood Cliffs, NJ: Prentice Hall, 1963), 81–83; and his "Where the Action Is," in *Interaction Ritual: Essays in Face-to-Face Behavior* (New York: Pantheon Books, 1967), 141–270. See also the introduction to Martin Meeker, *Contacts Desired: Gay and Lesbian Communications and Community, 1940s–1970s* (Chicago: University of Chicago Press, 2006), 1–29.

56 Erving Goffman, *Relations in Public* (New York: Basic Books, 1971); Delph, *Silent Community*, 35–42. See the wonderful discussions of spatial practices and tactics

in Michel de Certeau, *The Practice of Everyday Life* (Berkeley: University of California Press, 1984), xvii–xxiv, 115–130.

57 For a discussion of these issues in the 1990s, see William Leap, "Introduction" and Michael C. Clatts, "Ethnographic Observations of Men Who Have Sex with Men in Public: Toward an Ecology of Sexual Action," both in *Public Sex, Gay Space*, ed. William Leap (New York: Columbia University Press, 1999), 1–21, 141–156; also see Marc E. Elovitz and P. J. Edwards, "The D.O.H. Papers: Regulating Public Sex in New York City," in Dangerous Bedfellows, *Policing Public Sex*, 295–316.

58 For an interesting discussion of the social psychological dynamics of the dyad and the quantitative aspects of social interactions, see the classic essay by Georg Simmel, "Quantitative Aspects of the Group," in *The Sociology of Georg Simmel*, ed. Kurt H. Wolff (New York: Free Press, 1950), 87–179.

59 Interview with Rodger MacFarlane, in Lovett, *Gay Sex in the 70s*.

60 Interview with Tom Bianchi, in Lovett, *Gay Sex in the 70s*.

61 Michael Warner, *The Trouble with Normal: Sex, Politics and the Ethics of Queer Life* (New York: Free Press, 1999), 173–181.

62 Samuel Delany, *Motion of Light in Water: Sex and Science Fiction Writing in the East Village, 1957–1965* (New York: New American Library, 1988), 174.

63 Lovett, *Gay Sex in the 70s*.

64 Allyn, *Make Love, Not War*, 149–151.

65 See the essays by Jonathan Weinberg and Darren Jones for the exhibition "The Piers: Art and Sex along the New York Waterfront" (Leslie Lohman Museum of Gay and Lesbian Art, Curated by Jonathan Weinberg with Darren Jones, April 4–May 10, 2012), https://leslielohman.org/exhibitions/2012/piers/. See the photographs in Alvin Baltrop, *The Piers* (Madrid: TF Editores, 2015). Also see the essays by Rich Wandel, Jonathan Weinberg, and Thomas Schoenberger and the photographs of Leonard Fink, in Leonard Fink, *Coming Out: Photographs of Gay Liberation and the New York Waterfront* (Biel: edition clandestine, 2014).

66 Barton Benes's and Joseph Lovett's conversation in *Gay Sex in the 70s*; see also Patrick Hinds, *The Q Guide to NYC Pride* (New York: Alyson Books, 2007), 95.

67 For a personal account, see Delany, *Times Square Red*; on the social impact of the porn theater as a sexual space, see Jeffrey Escoffier, "Pornography, Perversity and the Sexual Revolution," in *Sexual Revolutions*, ed. Gert Hekma and A. Giami (Houndmills: Palgrave Macmillan, 2014), 203–218.

68 Baltrop, *Piers*; and Tom Bianchi, *Fire Island Pines: The Polaroids, 1975–1983* (Valenza, Italy: Damiani, 2013).

69 "The Curious Closets of Barton Benes," *POZ*, August 1999, www.poz.com/article /The-Curious-Closets-of-Barton-Benes-11353-4477.

70 Kracauer, "Photography," 54–58; Gertrud Koch, *Siegfried Kracauer: An Introduction* (Princeton, NJ: Princeton University Press, 2000), 100–101.

71 James Sanders, *Celluloid Skyline: New York and the Movies* (New York: Knopf, 2001), 367.

72 For a similar development in straight porn, see Whitney Strub, "From Porno Chic to Porno Bleak: Representing the Urban Crisis in 1970s American Pornography," in *Porno Chic and the Sex Wars: American Sexual Representation in the 1970s*, ed. Carolyn Bronstein and Whitney Strub (Amherst: University of Massachusetts Press, 2016).

73 Sanders, *Celluloid Skyline*, 341–342.

74 Escoffier, *Bigger Than Life*, 60–74; Escoffier, "Beefcake to Hardcore," 331–342.

75 Escoffier, "Beefcake to Hardcore."

76 I would like to thank Andrew Spieldenner for suggesting the term *homo-realist*.

77 Delph, *Silent Community*, 19–34.

78 Delph, 24.

79 Jerry Douglas, "The Legacy of Jack Deveau," *Stallion*, April 1983, 22–25, 46–47.

80 The way that sociality can evolve in certain venues where public sex is taking place is explored and discussed in Etienne Meunier, "Organizing Collective Intimacy: An Ethnography of New York's Clandestine Sex Clubs" (PhD diss., Rutgers University, October 2016).

81 See Meunier, "Organizing Collective Intimacy."

82 Leo Braudy, *The World in a Frame: What We See in Films* (Garden City, NY: Anchor Books, 1977), 44–51.

83 For contemporary analyses of how a specific physical space may shape the sexual activity in locker rooms, saunas, or sex parties, see Etienne Meunier, "No Attitude, No Standing Around: The Organization of Social and Sexual Interaction at a Gay Male Private Sex Party in New York City," *Archives of Sexual Behavior* 43, no. 4 (2014): 685–695 and also William Leap, "Sex in 'Private' Places: Gender, Erotics, and Detachment in Two Urban Locales," in Leap, *Public Sex, Gay Space*, 115–139.

84 Siegfried Kracauer, "The Mass Ornament," in Levin, *Mass Ornament*, 75.

85 Kracauer, "The Mass Ornament, in Levin, *Mass Ornament*, 75.

86 Simon and Gagnon, "Sexual Scripts," 5.

87 Jeffrey Escoffier, "Sex O'Clock in America: Sexual Scripts in Historical Perspective, 1890–1930" (in Italian), in *I copioni sessuali. storia, analisi e application*, ed. Cirus Rinaldi (Milan: Franco Angeli, 2016); see also "Sexual Revolution and the Politics of Gay Identity," 52–57; de Certeau, *Practice of Everyday Life*, 34–42, 92–110.

88 Delph, *Silent Community*, 36.

89 Goffman, "Interaction Order," 240.

90 Erving Goffman, *Encounters: Two Studies in the Sociology of Interaction* (Indianapolis: Bobbs-Merrill, 1961; repr., Mansfield Centre, CT: Martino, 2013), 7–84; see also Erving Goffman, *Behavior in Public Places: Notes on the Social Organization of Gatherings* (New York: Free Press, 1963).

91 Delph, *Silent Community*, 157.

92 Leap, "Sex in 'Private' Places."

93 In *Gay Macho*, Levine's ethnography of the gay male sexual subculture in the 1970s, he does not single out public sex specifically.

94 Goffman, *Encounters*, 26–27.

Chapter 4   Porn's Historical Unconscious

I would like to thank Marco Seidelmann and Robert Alvarez for their encouragement and advice about Jack Deveau, Robert Phillips and Brian A. Adams for their perceptive and useful comments on Joe Gage, and especially Jeffrey Colgan for his editorial guidance, excellent comments, and valuable suggestions.

1 Jeffrey Escoffier, *Bigger Than Life: The History of Gay Porn Cinema from Beefcake to Hardcore* (Philadelphia: Running Press, 2009), 1–37.

2 Jeffrey Escoffier, "Sex in the Seventies: Gay Porn Cinema as an Archive for the History of Sexuality," *Journal of the History of Sexuality* 26, no. 1 (2017): 88–113.

3 Andre Bazin, "An Aesthetic of Reality: Cinematic Realism and the Italian School of Liberation," *What Is Cinema?*, vol. 2 (Berkeley: University of California Press, 1971), 16–40; see also Escoffier, "Sex in the Seventies."

4 Escoffier, *Bigger Than Life*, 89–116.

5 Siegfried Kracauer, *Theory of Film: The Redemption of Physical Reality* (Oxford: Oxford University Press, 1960), 304.

6 Escoffier, "Sex in the Seventies"; Bazin, "Aesthetic of Reality."

7 Linda Williams, *Hard Core: Power, Pleasure, and the "Frenzy of the Visible"* (Berkeley: University of California Press, 1989), 93–119.

8 Escoffier, *Bigger Than Life*, 95–101.

9 Escoffier, 121–124.

10 James M. Saslow, *On the Domestic Front: Scenes of Everyday Queer Life* (New York: Leslie-Lohman Museum of Gay and Lesbian Art, 2015), 13.

11 Charles Silverstein, *Man to Man: Gay Couples in America* (New York: Morrow, 1981), 114.

12 Michael Bronski, "How Sweet (and Sticky) It Was," in *Flesh and the Word*, vol. 2, ed. John Preston (New York: Dutton, 1992), 74.

13 Dennis Altman, *Coming Out in the Seventies* (Sydney, Australia: Wild & Woolley, 1979), 16–17. See also Dennis Altman, *Homosexual Oppression and Liberation* (New York: Outerbridge & Dienstrey, 1971).

14 Andrew Holleran, *Dancer from the Dance* (New York: William Morrow, 1978); Larry Kramer, *Faggots* (New York: Grove Press, 1978); see also Ben Gove, *Cruising Culture: Promiscuity, Desire and American Gay Culture* (Edinburgh: Edinburgh University Press, 2000), 81–131.

15 Comment from the transcription of an anonymous patron from Alan Bounville, *Adonis Memories* (IN OUR WORDS Theatre Group, production December 2016– June 2017, New York, unpublished script, 2016).

16 David Laderman, "What a Trip: The Road Film and American Culture," *Journal of Film and Video* 48, nos. 1–2 (1996): 41.

17 Joe Gage, "Interview with a Legend: Part I," by Jerry Douglas, *Manshots*, June 1992, 13.

18 Gage, "Interview with a Legend," 13.

19 Jerry Douglas, "The Kansas City Trilogy (1976–79)," *Stallion 50 Best: All-Time Best Male Films and Videos 1970–1985*, special issue no. 4 (1985): 49.

20 Jerry Douglas, "Heatstroke (1982), *Stallion 50 Best*, 22.

21 Joe Gage, "Interview with a Legend: Part II," by Jerry Douglas, *Manshots*, August 1992, 15.

22 Frank Rodriguez, "Joe Gage," *Butt: A Quarterly Magazine*, Spring 2007, 18–19.

23 Rodriguez, "Joe Gage," 19.

24 Raymond Williams discusses how feelings are shaped by the historical and social forces in *Marxism and Literature* (Oxford: Oxford University Press, 1977), 128–136.

25 Douglas, "Kansas City Trilogy," 49.

26 Rodriguez, "Joe Gage," 19.

27 Alan Hollinghurst, "Robert Mapplethorpe," in *Robert Mapplethorpe, 1970–1983* (London: Institute of Contemporary Art, 1983), 11.

28 Edmund White, *States of Desire: Travels in Gay America* (New York: Plume, 1980), 45–46.

29 Escoffier, *Bigger Than Life*, 129–146.

30 See Michael Bronski, *Culture Clash: The Making of Gay Sensibility* (Boston: Alyson Books, 1984), 166–174; Brian Pronger, *The Arena of Masculinity: Sports, Homosexuality, and the Meaning of Sex* (New York: St. Martin's, 1990), 125–150.

31 Escoffier, *Bigger Than Life.*

Chapter 5 Scripting the Sex

This chapter was originally published in Michael Kimmel, ed., *The Sexual Self: The Construction of Sexual Scripts* (Nashville: Vanderbilt University Press, 2007). Reprinted with permission from Vanderbilt University Press. I am indebted to John Gagnon, Matthew Lore, Lesley Fine, Andrew Spieldenner, and Wash West for their comments on earlier drafts. And I especially want to thank the many people in the gay porn industry who have talked with me over the years. Above all I owe an enormous debt to Jerry Douglas, director of many fine porn films and from whose many interviews of directors and performers I learned so much. He has been my teacher and mentor on the subject of making pornography. I would like to thank also Doug Jeffries, Chi Chi LaRue, Michael Lucas, and Wash West, each of them successful and talented directors of porn movies, for talking candidly and in depth about the business of making pornographic movies; Andrew Rosen, who has illuminated the process of editing porn films; my friends Jim Green and Moshe Sluhovsky, for giving me a place to stay in Los Angeles, encouraging me, and talking with me about it all. Last but not least I want to thank John Gagnon for the many thoughtful and enjoyable conversations over the years about sex, pornography, scripts, and my experiences doing research and writing about the gay porn industry.

1 John H. Gagnon, *An Interpretation of Desire: Essays in the Study of Sexuality* (Chicago: University of Chicago Press, 2003), 138–139.

2 Linda Williams, *Hard Core: Power, Pleasure and the "Frenzy of the Visible"* (Berkeley: University of California Press, 1989), 100–119.

3 Alexandre Astruc, "What Is *Mise-en-Scène*?," Andre Bazin, "On the *politique des auteurs*," and Jim Hillier, "Introduction," all in *Cahiers du Cinéma: The 1950s: Neo-Realism, Hollywood, New Wave*, ed. Jim Hillier (Cambridge, MA: Harvard University Press, 1985).

4 John H. Gagnon and William Simon, *Sexual Conduct: The Social Sources of Human Sexuality* (Chicago: Aldine, 1973); William Simon and John H. Gagnon, "Sexual Scripts: Permanence and Change," *Archives of Sexual Behavior* 15, no. 2 (1986): 97–120; Gagnon, *Interpretation of Desire*.

5 Williams, *Hard Core*.

6 Jeffrey Escoffier, ed., *Sexual Revolution* (New York: Thunder's Mouth Press, 2003).

7 Cindy Patton, "The Cum Shot: Three Takes on Lesbian and Gay Sexuality," *OUT/LOOK* 1 (1988): 72–77; Williams, *Hard Core*, 93–119; Roland Barthes, "The Reality Effect," in *The Rustle of Language*, trans. Richard Howard (New York: Hill & Wang, 1986).

8 Elizabeth Cowie, "Pornography and Fantasy: Psychoanalytic Perspectives," in *Sex Exposed: Sexuality and the Pornography Debate*, ed. Lynne Segal and Mary McIntosh (New Brunswick, NJ: Rutgers University Press, 1993), 133; Jean Laplanche and Jean-Bertrand Pontalis, "Fantasy and the Origins of Sexuality," in *Formations of Fantasy*, ed. Victor Burgin, James Donald, and Cora Kaplan (London: Methuen, 1986), 4–34.

9   Slavoj Žižek, *Looking Awry: An Introduction to Jacques Lacan through Popular Culture* (Cambridge, MA: MIT Press, 1991), 6.

10 Robert J. Stoller, *Observing the Erotic Imagination* (New Haven, CT: Yale University Press, 1985), vii–viii.

11 Andrew Ross, "The Popularity of Pornography," in *No Respect: Intellectuals and Popular Culture* (New York: Routledge, 1989), 196–197.

12 Jerry Douglas, interview by the author, New York, October 1, 2001.

13 Ross, "Popularity of Pornography," 196–197.

14 Erving Goffman, *Frame Analysis: An Essay on the Organization of Experience* (New York: Harper & Row, 1974), 123–155.

15 John Gibbs, *Mise-en-Scene: Film Style and Interpretation* (London: Wallflower Press, 2002), 5–27.

16 Simon and Gagnon, "Sexual Scripts," 109–110.

17 Escoffier, *Sexual Revolution*.

18 Doug Jeffries, interview by the author, Los Angeles, March 15, 2005.

19 Goffman, *Frame Analysis*, 40–82.

20 Hillier, "Introduction," 8–11; Gibbs, *Mise-en-Scene*, 5–26.

21 Laurence O'Toole, *Pornocopia: Porn, Sex, Technology and Desire* (London: Serpent's Tale, 1999), 8.

22 O'Toole, *Pornocopia*, 8, 84–89, 209–210.

23 *Adult Video News*, October 2003.

24 O'Toole, *Pornocopia*, 209–210.

25 Frank Rich, "Naked Capitalists," *New York Times Magazine*, May 20, 2001.

26 Žižek, *Looking Awry*, 199.

27 Žižek, 111.

28 Linda Williams, "Porn Studies: Proliferating Pornographies On/Scene: An Introduction," in *Porn Studies*, ed. Linda Williams (Durham, NC: Duke University Press, 2004), 5–6.

29 Williams, *Hard Core*, 130.

30 Williams, 120–134.

31 Benjamin Scuglia, "Art, Heart and Porn: Interview with Wash West" (2002), www.nightcharm.com/habituals/video/wash/index.html, accessed October 13, 2006.

32 Douglas interview.

33 Mandy Merck, "More of a Man: Gay Porn Cruises Gay Politics," in *Perversions* (New York: Routledge, 1993), 234.

34 Jack Shamama, "Gus Mattox: an Interview," in *Adam Gay Video XXX Showcase* 12, no. 3 (October 2004): 8.

35 For a discussion of traditional film genres, see Thomas Schatz, *Hollywood Genres: Formulas, Filmmaking and the Studio System* (New York: Random House, 1981).

36 Simon and Gagnon, "Sexual Scripts," 102–105.

37 Simon and Gagnon, 105.

38 Foster Hirsch, *Film Noir: The Dark Side of the Screen* (New York: Da Capo, 1983), 182.

39 Hirsch, 190.

40 Chi Chi LaRue, interview by the author, Los Angeles, October 7, 2004.

41 LaRue interview.

42 Doug Lawrence, *The Top 40 Films of Chi Chi LaRue* (Adam Gay Video Erotica) (Los Angeles: Knight, 1999), 46.

43 Douglas interview.

44 Lawrence, *Top 40 Films*, 46.

45 LaRue interview.

46 Toby Miller, *Sportsex* (Philadelphia: Temple University Press, 2001), 13, 51–52; Brian Pronger, *The Arena of Masculinity: Sports, Homosexuality, and the Meaning of Sex* (New York: St. Martin's, 1990), 177–214.

47 Steve Zeeland, *Military Trade* (New York: Harrington Park Press, 1999), 175–186.

48 Kaja Silverman, *The Subject of Semiotics* (Oxford: Oxford University Press, 1983), 46–53.

49 Rod Barry, interview by the author, Los Angeles, March 12, 2005.

Chapter 6   Gay-for-Pay

A version of this chapter was originally presented at a session of the American Studies Association on Situational Sexualities in Montreal on October 31, 1999. Reprinted by permission from Nature/Springer/Palgrave, *Qualitative Sociology* 26, no. 4 (Winter 2003), copyright 2003. I want to thank Terrence Kissack, Regina Kunzel, Matthew Lore, Andrew Spieldenner, and Aaron Tanner for their comments on earlier drafts of this chapter and Janice Irvine for her editorial guidance and encouragement. I also want to thank John Gagnon for many conversations on these topics over the years and offering ways of thinking about them; Jerry Douglas, playwright, journalist, and director of many award-winning porn movies, and one of the earliest commercial gay porn movies, *Back Row* (1974), for his many hours of conversation about the porn industry and for his many wonderful interviews with performers from which I drew in this chapter; and Michael Lucas, director of *Fire Island Cruising* and other porn videos, for his comments and his suggestion that I try writing a few porn scripts, which I found to be a very useful exercise for thinking about porn.

1 John H. Gagnon and William Simon, *Sexual Conduct: The Social Sources of Human Sexuality* (Chicago: Aldine, 1973); Mary McIntosh, "The Homosexual Role," *Social Problems* 16, no. 2 (1968): 182–192, reprinted in Kenneth Plummer, *The Making of the Modern Homosexual* (Lanham, MD: Rowman & Littlefield, 1981); Frederick L. Whitham, "The Homosexual Role: A Reconsideration," *Journal of Sex Research* 13 (1977): 1–11; Regina Kunzel, "Situating Sex: Prison Sexual Culture in the Mid-Twentieth-Century United States," *GLQ* 8 (2002): 253–270.

2 Sigmund Freud, *Three Essays on the Theory of Sexuality* (1905; New York: Basic Books, 1962), 36.

3 Peter Weatherburn et al., *Behaviourally Bisexual Men in the UK: Identifying Needs for HIV Prevention* (London: Sigma Research/Health Education Authority, 1996); New York City Department of Health, *Immigrant Men Who Have Sex with Men (MSM): HIV Prevention Needs Assessment* (New York: New York City Department of Health, Office of Gay and Lesbian Health, 1997); G. Goldbaum, T. Perdue, and D. Higgins, "Non-Gay-Identifying Men Who Have Sex with Men: Formative Research Results from Seattle, Washington," *Public Health Reports* 3, suppl. 1 (1996): 36–40; Jeffrey Escoffier, "Non-Gay Identified: Towards a Post-identitarian Theory of Homosexuality" (paper, Eastern Sociological Society, March 6, 1999).

4 Laud Humphries, *Tearoom Trade: Impersonal Sex in Public Places* (Hawthorne, NY: Aldine, 1970); Peter Nardi, "Reclaiming the Importance of Laud Humphries'

Tearoom Trade: Impersonal Sex in Public Places," in *Public Sex, Gay Space*, ed. William Leap (New York: Columbia University Press, 1999, 23–27.

5   Gagnon and Simon, *Sexual Conduct*; John H. Gagnon and William Simon, "Sexual Scripts: Permanence and Change," *Archives of Sexual Behavior* 15, no. 2 (1986): 97–120.

6   Escoffier, "Non-Gay Identified."

7   Albert Reiss, "The Social Integration of Queers and Peers," *Social Problems* 9 (1961): 102.

8   J. Antalek, "Porn in the USA," *Q San Francisco*, October/November 1997, http://qsfmagazine.com/9711/index.html; Frank Rich, "Naked Capitalists," *New York Times Magazine*, May 20, 2001, 51–56, 80–81, 92; John A. Thomas, "Gay Male Video Pornography: Past, Present and Future," in *Sex for Sale: Prostitution, Pornography and the Sex Industry*, ed. Ron Weitzer (New York: Routledge, 2000), 49–66.

9   Thomas Waugh, *Hard to Imagine: Gay Male Eroticism in Photography and Film from Their Beginnings to Stonewall* (New York: Columbia University Press, 1996).

10 Christopher Adam Mitchell, *Gay Ghetto to "Free" Market: Entrepreneurship and the Transformation of Queer Life in New York City* (Philadelphia: University of Pennsylvania Press, forthcoming).

11 Jerry Douglas, "Jaguar Productions: Interview with Barry Knight and Russell Moore," *Manshots*, pt. 1: June 1996, 11; pt. 2: August 1996, 72. See also Finley Freibert "Homorealist Uplift: Jaguar Productions' Synthesis of Production Value with Intersectional Class Politics in a Gay Film," *Peephole Journal* (June 2019).

12 Richard Dyer, "Coming to Terms: Gay Pornography," in *Only Entertainment* (London: Routledge, 1992), 121–134.

13 Laura Kipnis, "How to Look at Pornography," in *Bound and Gagged: Pornography and the Politics of Fantasy in America* (New York: Grove Press, 1996), 161–206; David Loftus, *Watching Sex: How Men Really Respond to Pornography* (New York: Thunder's Mouth Press, 2002).

14 Gagnon and Simon, *Sexual Conduct*, 260–265.

15 Cindy Patton, "The Cum Shot: Three Takes on Lesbian and Gay Sexuality," *OUT/LOOK* 1 (1988): 72–77; Linda Williams, *Hard Core: Power, Pleasure and the "Frenzy of the Visible"* (Berkeley: University of California Press, 1989), 93–119; Roland Barthes, "The Reality Effect," in *The Rustle of Language*, trans. Richard Howard (New York: Hill & Wang, 1986), 141–148.

16 Austin Foxxe, "Home Bodies," *Unzipped*, August 31, 1999, 40.

17 Williams, *Hard Core*, 93–119; Robert J. Stoller, *Porn: Myths for the Twentieth Century* (New Haven, CT: Yale University Press, 1991); Kipnis, "How to Look at Pornography"; Loftus, *Watching Sex*.

18 Michael Bronski, *Culture Clash: The Making of Gay Sensibility* (Boston: Alyson Books, 1984), 166–174; Dyer, "Coming to Terms"; Earl Jackson, *Strategies of Deviance: Studies in Gay Male Representation* (Bloomington: Indiana University Press, 1995); Waugh, *Hard to Imagine*.

19 Brian Pronger, *The Arena of Masculinity: Sports, Homosexuality, and the Meaning of Sex* (New York: St. Martin's, 1990), 125–176.

20 Bronski, *Culture Clash*, 166–174; John R. Burger, *One-Handed Histories: The Eroto-Politics of Gay Male Video Pornography* (Binghamton, NY: Harrington Park Press, 1995); Daniel Harris, "The Evolution of Gay Pornography: Film," in *The Rise and Fall of Gay Culture* (New York: Hyperion, 1997), 111–133.

21 Donald Suggs, "The Porn Kings of New York," *Out*, June 1999, 85–89.

22 Richard Dyer, *Stars* (London: British Film Institute, 1998), 17–19.

23 Patton, "Cum Shot"; Williams, *Hard Core*.

24 Pronger, *Arena of Masculinity*, 125–154.

25 Henning Bech, *When Men Meet: Homosexuality and Modernity* (Chicago: University of Chicago Press, 1997), 17–84.

26 Gagnon and Simon, *Sexual Conduct*, 15.

27 Gayle Rubin, "Studying Sexual Subcultures: Excavating the Ethnography of Gay Communities in Urban North America," in *Out in Theory: The Emergence of Lesbian and Gay Anthropology*, ed. Ellen Lewin and William Leap (Urbana: University of Illinois Press, 2002), 17–68.

28 Gagnon and Simon, *Sexual Conduct*; Gagnon and Simon, "Sexual Scripts."

29 Gagnon and Simon, *Sexual Conduct*, 98–104.

30 Erving Goffman, *Gender Advertisements* (New York: Harper, 1976).

31 Gagnon and Simon, "Sexual Scripts," 104–107.

32 Gagnon and Simon, "Sexual Scripts"; Sharon A. Abbott, "Motivations for Pursuing an Acting Career in Pornography," in *Sex for Sale: Prostitution, Pornography and the Sex Industry*, ed. Ron Weitzer (New York: Routledge, 2000), 17–34.

33 William Spencer, "Interview with Paul Morgan," *Manshots*, December 1998, 52–57, 72–73.

34 Thomas Straube, "Porn Profile: Tiger Tyson," *HX*, May 14, 1999, 68.

35 Joseph R. G. DeMarco, "The World of Gay Strippers," *Gay and Lesbian Review* 9 (March/April 2002): 12–14.

36 Robert W. Richards, "Interview with Brian Estevez," *Manshots*, April 1999, 53–58, 79.

37 Erving Goffman, *The Presentation of Self in Everyday Life* (New York: Doubleday Anchor, 1959), 22–30.

38 Jerry Douglas, "Interview with Rod Barry," *Manshots*, June 1998, 53–57, 72–73.

39 Antalek, "Porn in the USA."

40 Foucault, quoted in David Halperin, *Saint Foucault* (Cambridge, MA: Harvard University Press, 1995), 89–90.

41 Douglas, "Interview with Rod Barry."

42 J. Douglas, *Beach Buns* (review), *Manshots*, November 1998, 38–39.

43 Goffman, *Presentation of Self*.

44 Paul G. Cressey, *The Taxi-Dance Hall: A Sociological Study in Commercialized Recreation and City Life* (1932; New York: Greenwood, 1969).

45 Mark De Walt, "The Eye of Kristen Bjorn," *Blueboy*, January 1998, 52–55.

46 Jerry Douglas, "Interview with Tim Barnett," *Manshots*, February 1996, 30–33, 72–73.

47 Anonymous, *Adam Gay 1996 Video Directory*, 7–8.

48 Jerry Douglas, "Jaguar Productions: Interview with Barry Knight and Russell Moore," *Manshots*, pt. 1: June 1996, 10–15; pt. 2: August 1996, 72.

49 Jerry Douglas, "Behind the Camera: Interview with Greg Lenzman," *Manshots*, August 1998, 10–15, 81–82.

50 Doug Lawrence, *The Dirk Yates Collection: Adam Gay Video Erotica* (Los Angeles: Knight, 1999).

51 Douglas, "Interview with Rod Barry."

52 Jamoo, *The Films of Kristen Bjorn* (Laguna Hills, CA: Companion Press, 1997).

53 The Bear, "Interview with Buddy Jones," *Manshots*, November 1999, 30–33, 80.

54 Jerry Douglas, "Interview with Tommy Cruise," *Manshots*, October 1999, 66–71, 78–79.

55 The Bear, "Interview with Buddy Jones."

56 J. C. Adams, "The Adams Report" (1998), www.radvideo.com/news/adamhans .html.

57 Gagnon and Simon, *Sexual Conduct*, 260–265.

58 Erving Goffman, *Frame Analysis* (New York: Harper & Row, 1974), 124–155; Leo Braudy, *The World in a Frame: What We See in Films* (Garden City, NY: Anchor Books, 1977), 191–217.

59 Gagnon and Simon, "Sexual Scripts," 105–107.

60 This has changed to some degree since the introduction of Viagra in 1998. Maintaining erections is now much easier.

61 Spencer, "Interview with Paul Morgan."

62 M. Adams, *Hustlers, Escorts, Porn Stars: The Insider's Guide to Male Prostitution in America* (Las Vegas: Insider's Guide, 1999), 102–121.

63 Goffman, *Presentation of Self*.

64 Gagnon and Simon, *Sexual Conduct*; Michel Foucault, "Sex, Power and the Politics of Identity," in *The Essential Works of Michel Foucault, 1954–1984*, vol. 1: *Ethics, Subjectivity and Truth*, ed. Paul Rabinow (New York: New Press, 1997), 165–173.

Chapter 7   The Wages for Wood

This chapter is a revised version of a paper presented at the Social Science History Association, November 3, 2012, Session 12: "Gender and Value: Pay Gap Paradoxes and Puzzles." This chapter would never been written without the provocative invitation from Ashley Mears to participate in a Social Science History Association panel about one of the few industries in which women are presumed to earn more than men. I would like to thank Ashley Mears, Cati Connell, Tsu-Yu Tsao, and Jeffrey Colgan for their comments and excellent suggestions.

1 Ben Fritz, "Tough Times in the Porn Industry," *Los Angeles Times*, August 10, 2009.

2 See Fritz, "Touch Times."

3 See Fredrick S. Lane III, *Obscene Profits: The Entrepreneurs of Pornography in the Cyber Age* (New York: Routledge, 2001); Jonathan Coopersmith, "The Role of the Pornography Industry in the Development of Videotape and the Internet" (paper, International Symposium on Technology and Society, 1999); and Coopersmith, "Does Your Mother Know What You Really Do? The Changing Nature and Image of Computer-Based Pornography," *History and Technology* 22, no.1 (2006): 1–25.

4 Susannah Breslin, "They Shoot Porn Stars, Don't They?," *Salon*, October 16, 2010.

5 Louis Theroux, "How the Internet Killed Porn," *Guardian*, June 5, 2012, www .guardian.co.uk/culture/2012/jun/05/how-internet-killed-porn.

6 Mike Abo, Nelson X, and David Sullivan, "Rising Talent Rates: Welcome to the New Reality," *Adult Video News*, April 2007, 64.

7 Tracy Clark-Flory, "A Male Porn Star Speaks," July 21, 2011, https://www.salon .com/2011/07/28/porn_13/.

8 Alfonso Sousa-Poza, "Labor-Market Segmentation and the Gender Wage Differential," *Cahiers Économique de Bruxelles* 45, no. 2, (2002): 91–118.

9   Jeffrey Escoffier, "Imagining the She/Male: Pornography and the Transsexualization of the Heterosexual Male," *Studies in Gender and Sexuality* 12, no. 4 (2011): 268–281; see Lisa Adkins, *Gendered Work: Sexuality, Family and the Labour Market* (Buckingham: Open University Press, 1995).

10 Neither Kevin Heffernan, "Seen as a Business: Adult Film's Historical Framework," in *New Views on Pornography: Sexuality, Politics and the Law*, ed. Lynn Comella and Shira Tarrant (Santa Barbara, CA: Praeger, 2015), nor Shira Tarrant, *The Pornography Industry: What Everyone Needs to Know* (New York: Oxford University Press, 2016), has been able to provide this.

11 Lane, *Obscene Profits*, 24–30.

12 Lane, 1–40.

13 See Jeffrey Escoffier, "Gay-for-Pay: Straight Men and the Making of Gay Pornography.," *Qualitative Sociology* 26, no. 4 (2003): 531–555; Mark Granovetter, "Economic Action and Social Structure: The Problem of Embeddedness," *American Journal of Sociology* 91, nos. 3–4 (1985): 81–510.

14 See Legs McNeil and Jennifer Osbourne, *The Other Hollywood: The Uncensored Oral History of the Porn Film Industry* (New York: HarperCollins, 2005); Jeffrey Escoffier, *Bigger Than Life: The History of Gay Porn Cinema from Beefcake to Hardcore* (Philadelphia: Running Press, 2009); Robert Rosen, *Beaver Street: A History of Modern Pornography* (London: Headpress, 2010).

15 See Eric Schlosser, *Reefer Madness: Sex, Drugs, and Cheap Labor in the American Black Market* (Boston: Houghton Mifflin, 2003), 111–221; and Larry Revene's memoir *Wham Bam $$Ba Da Boom!* (New York: Hudson Delta Books, 2012).

16 Kenneth Turan and Stephen Zito, *Sinema: American Pornographic Films and the People Who Make Them* (New York: Praeger, 1974), 127–128.

17 Paul Alcuin Siebenand, "The Beginnings of Gay Cinema in Los Angeles: The Industry and the Audience" (PhD diss., University of Southern California, 1975), 85.

18 McNeil and Osbourne, *Other Hollywood*, 42.

19 McNeil and Osbourne, 42.

20 See Susan Faludi, "Waiting for Wood," in *Stiffed: The Betrayal of the American Man* (New York: William Morrow, 1999), 530–574.

21 Free Speech Coalition, *State-of-the-Industry Report 2007–2008* (Canoga Park, CA: Free Speech Coalition, 2008).

22 See Sharon Abbott, "Motivations for Pursing an Acting Career in Pornography," in *Sex for Sale: Prostitution, Pornography and the Sex Industry*, ed. R. Weitzer (New York: Routledge, 2000); Jenna Jameson with Neil Strauss, *How to Make Love Like a Porn Star: A Cautionary Tale* (New York: Regan Books, 2004).

23 See Claudia Goldin, *Understanding the Gender Gap: An Economic History of American Women* (New York: Oxford University Press, 1990), 73–82.

24 See Goldin, *Understanding the Gender Gap*, 81–82; Adkins, *Gendered Work*, 1–20.

25 See Sherwin Rosen, "The Economics of Superstars," *American Economic Review* 71, no. 5 (1981): 845–858.

26 See Laurence O'Toole, *Pornocopia: Porn, Sex, Technology and Desire* (London: Serpent's Tail, 1999), 184.

27 See Richard Dyer, *Stars* (London: British Film Institute, 1998); Gary S. Becker, *Human Capital* (New York: National Bureau of Economic Research, 1964).

28 See Rosen, "Economics of Superstars."

29 Jared Rutter, "The Evil Empire Turns 20," *Adult Video News* 25, no. 1 (January 2008): 98–127.

30 See Faludi, "Waiting for Wood."

31 Faludi, 546.

32 See Faludi.

33 This assumes that performers appear in only one scene in each title.

34 Danni Ashe, "On Learning How to Launch the Most Popular Adult Website from Working at a Strip Club," in *Naked Ambition: Women Who Are Changing Pornography*, ed. Carly Milne (New York: Carroll & Graf, 2005), 228.

35 See Escoffier, "Gay-for-Pay."

36 See C. R. Grudzen, M. N. Elliott, P. R. Kerndt, M. A. Schuster, R. H. Brook, and L. Gelberg, "Condon Use and High-Risk Sexual Acts in Adult Films: A Comparison of Heterosexual and Homosexual Films," *American Journal of Public Health* 99, no. S1 (2009): 1–5; Alexandre Padilla, "Self-Regulation in the Adult Film Industry: Why Are HIV Outbreaks the Exception, and Not the Norm?" (2008), https://papers.ssrn.com/sol3/papers.cfm?abstract_id=1285283; Jeffrey Escoffier, *Bigger Than Life: The History of Gay Porn Cinema from Beefcake to Hardcore* (Philadelphia: Running Press, 2009), 177–204.

37 See Mark De Walt, "The Eye of Kristen Bjorn," *Blueboy*, January 1998, 52–55.

38 Paul Cressey, *The Taxi-Dance Hall: A Sociological Study in Commercialized Recreation and City Life* (1932; New York: Greenwood, 1969).

39 See Cressey, *Taxi Dance Hall*.

40 See Robert J. Stoller, *Observing the Erotic Imagination* (New Haven, CT: Yale University Press, 1985), 3–43.

41 Jeffrey Escoffier, "Porn Star / Stripper / Escort: Economic and Sexual Dynamics in a Sex Work Career," in *Male Sex Work: A Business Doing Pleasure*, ed. Todd G. Morrison and B. W. Whitehead (New York: Haworth Press, 2007).

42 Escoffier, "Porn Star/Stripper/Escort."

43 See Chris Anderson, "Long Tail Economics," in *The Long Tail: Why the Future of Business Is Selling Less of More* (New York: Hyperion, 2008), 125–146.

44 Escoffier, "Porn Star / Stripper / Escort."

45 Stacey M. Jones, "Teachers and Tipping Points: Historical Origins of the Teacher Quality Crisis," in *Economic Evolution and Revolution in Historical Time*, ed. Paul W. Rhode, Joshua L. Rosenbloom, David F. Weiman (Stanford, CA: Stanford University Press, 2011), 336–356; Stephen Ellingson, Edward O. Lauman, Anthony Paik, and Jenna Mahay, "The Theory of Sexual Markets," in *The Sexual Organization of the City*, ed. Edward O Lauman, Stephen Ellingson, Jenna Mahay, Anthony Paik, and Yoosik Youm (Chicago: University of Chicago Press, 2004), 3–38.

Chapter 8   Porn Star / Stripper / Escor

This chapter was originally published in *Journal of Homosexuality* 53, nos. 1/2 (Summer 2007) and published simultaneously in Todd G. Morrison and Bruce W. Whitehead, eds., *Male Sex Work: A Business Doing Pleasure* (New York: Haworth Press, 2007). I would like to thank all those performers in the industry who have talked to me, both on the record and off, about their experience as sexual entertainers and the complicated relations between performing in porn movies, dancing on the live stage, and other forms of sex work. Also, I would like to thank Andrew Spieldenner, Aaron Tanner, and the journal's two anonymous readers, who read earlier drafts of this chapter, for their many extremely useful comments, and Todd Morrison for his invitation to contribute a paper to the volume.

1   See Amy Flowers, *The Fantasy Factory: An Insider's View of the Phone Sex Industry* (Philadelphia: University of Pennsylvania Press, 1998); Katherine Frank, *G-Strings and Sympathy: Strip Club Regulars and Male Desire* (Durham, NC: Duke University Press, 2002); Katherine Liepe-Levinson, *Strip Show: Performances of Gender and Desire* (New York: Routledge, 2002); Sylvia Plachy and James Ridgeway, *Red Light: Inside the Sex Industry* (New York: Powerhouse Books, 1996); Ron Weitzer, "Why We Need More Research on Sex Work," in *Sex for Sale: Prostitution, Pornography and the Sex Industry*, ed. Ron Weitzer (New York: Routledge, 2000).

2   See Fredrick S. Lane III, *Obscene Profits: The Entrepreneurs of Pornography in the Cyber Age* (New York: Routledge, 2001); B. Marvel, "Porn: As Profits Explode, Stigma Persists" (2002), www.DallasNews.com.

3   See Jeffrey Escoffier, *Bigger Than Life: The History of Gay Porn Cinema from Beefcake to Hardcore* (Philadelphia: Running Press, 2009).

4   See Weitzer, *Sex for Sale*.

5   See Brian McNair, *Striptease Culture: Sex, Media and the Democratisation of Desire* (London: Routledge, 2002).

6   See Edward O. Lauman, John H. Gagnon, Robert T. Michael, and Stuarts Michaels, *The Social Organization of Sexuality: Sexual Practices in the United States* (Chicago: University of Chicago Press, 1964).

7   Howard Becker, *Outsiders: Studies in the Sociology of Deviance* (New York: Free Press of Glencoe, 1963); Erving Goffman, *Stigma: Notes on the Management of Spoiled Identity* (Engelwood Cliffs, NJ: Prentice-Hall, 1963).

8   Edgar Morin, cited in Richard Dyer, *Stars* (London: British Film Institute, 1998).

9   Michael De Angelis, *Gay Fandom and Crossover Stardom: James Dean, Mel Gibson and Keanu Reeves* (Durham, NC: Duke University Press, 2001); Chris Rojek, *Celebrity* (London: Reaktion Books, 2004).

10   See Elizabeth Cowie, "Pornography and Fantasy: Psychoanalytic Perspective," in *Sex Exposed: Sexuality and the Pornography Debate*, ed. Lynne Segal and Mary McIntosh (New Brunswick, NJ: Rutgers University Press, 1993).

11   See Leo Braudy, *The World in a Frame: What We See in Films* (Garden City, NY: Anchor Books, 1977); Stanley Cavell, *The World Viewed: Reflections on the Ontology of Film*, enlarged ed. (Cambridge, MA: Harvard University Press, 1979); De Angelis, *Gay Fandom and Crossover Stardom*; Richard de Cordova, *Picture Personalities: The Emergence of the Star System in America* (Urbana: University of Illinois Press, 1990).

12   See Braudy, *World in a Frame*.

13   Jeffrey Escoffier, "Gay-for-Pay: Straight Men and the Making of Gay Pornography," *Qualitative Sociology* 26, no. 4 (2003): 531–555.

14   See Gary S. Becker, *Human Capital* (New York: National Bureau of Economic Research, 1964); Dyer, *Stars*.

15   J. A. Thomas, "Porn Stars," in *glbtq: An Encyclopedia of Gay, Lesbian, Bisexual, Transgender and Queer Culture* (2002), www.glbtq.com/arts/pornstars.html.

16   Roger Edmonson, *Boy in the Sand: All-American Sex Star* (Los Angeles: Alyson Books, 1998).

17   Roger Edmonson, *Clone: The Life and Legacy of Al Parker, Gay Superstar* (Los Angeles: Alyson Books, 2000).

18   See William Spencer, "Interview with Jeff Stryker," *Manshots*, September 1998.

19   David Groff, "Letter from New York: Fallen Idol," *Out Magazine*, June 1998, 43–50.

20 Jerry Douglas, "Comeback: Interview with Ken Ryker," *Manshots*, November 1998, 30–33, 80–81; Charles Isherwood, *Wonder Bread and Ecstasy: The Life and Death of Joey Stefano* (Los Angeles: Alyson Books, 1996).

21 H. Fenwick, "Changing Times for Gay Videomakers," *The Advocate*, February 1988, 36–37, 63–66.

22 J. Antalek, "Porn in the USA," *Q San Francisco*, October/November 1997, http://qsfmagazine.com/9711/index.html; Jeffrey Escoffier, "Scripting the Sex: Fantasy, Narrative and Sexual Scripts in Pornographic Films," in *The Sexual Self: The Construction of Sexual Scripts*, ed. Michael Kimmel (Nashville: Vanderbilt University Press, 2007).

23 Douglas, "Comeback"; Groff, "Letter from New York."

24 See Sharon Abbott, "Motivations for Pursing an Acting Career in Pornography," in Weitzer, *Sex for Sale*; Jenna Jameson with Neil Strauss, *How to Make Love Like a Porn Star: A Cautionary Tale* (New York: Regan Books, 2004).

25 "Rod Barry," in *Adam Gay Video 2003 Directory* (Los Angeles: Knight, 2002), 16.

26 Jerry Douglas, "Interview with Rod Barry," *Manshots*, June 10, 1998, 73.

27 See J. C. Adams, "Less Bang for the Buck," *HX*, no. 447 (March 31, 2000): 29–30; J. C. Adams, "Pay 4 Porn," *Badpuppy*, no. 5 (2003); Aaron Tanner, interview by the author, April 1, New York, 2002.

28 Rod Barry, interview by the author, Los Angeles, October 8, 2004.

29 Susan Faludi, "Waiting for Wood," in *Stiffed: The Betrayal of the American Man* (New York: William Morrow, 1999), 538; Escoffier, "Gay-for-Pay."

30 Jerry Douglas, "Jaguar Productions: Interview with Barry Knight and Russell Moore," *Manshots*, pt. 1: June 1996, 10–15; pt. 2: August 1996, 10–15.

31 Jerry Douglas, "Behind the Camera: John Travis," *Manshots*, March 10, 1990.

32 Jerry Douglas, "Behind the Camera: Matt Sterling," *Manshots*, September 1988.

33 Dino Phillips, "12 Questions," *Unzipped*, no. 188 (December 7, 1999): 12–13.

34 Escoffier, "Gay-for-Pay."

35 Rod Barry, interview by the author, Cherry Grove, Fire Island, New York, September 13, 2003.

36 Paul Cressey, *The Taxi-Dance Hall: A Sociological Study in Commercialized Recreation and City Life* (1932; New York: Greenwood, 1969).

37 H. A. Carson, *A Thousand and One Night Stands: The Life of Jon Vincent* (n.p.: 1st Books, 2001).

38 Robert J. Stoller, *Observing the Erotic Imagination* (New Haven, CT: Yale University Press, 1985).

39 Escoffier, "Scripting the Sex."

40 T. Hitman, "Atlas Shagged: Interview with Jon Galt," *Unzipped*, April 2005, 42.

41 Spencer, "Interview with Jeff Stryker," 33.

42 Bryan Holden, "An Interview with Travis Wade" (September 2000), www.radvideo.com.

43 Holden, "An Interview with Travis Wade."

44 Lily Burana, *Strip City: A Stripper's Farewell Journey across America* (New York: Hyperion, 2001); Joseph De Marco, "The World of Gay Strippers," *Gay and Lesbian Review*, March/April 2002, 12–14.

45 Holden, "Interview with Travis Wade."

46 Frank, *G-Strings and Sympathy*, xix.

47 Barry interview.

48 De Walt, "Eye of Kristen Bjorn," 55.

49 See Matt Adams, *Hustlers, Escorts, Porn Stars: The Insider's Guide to Male Prostitution in America* (Las Vegas: Insider's Guide, 1999); David F. Lukenbill, "Deviant Career Mobility: The Case of Male Prostitution," *Social Problems* 33, no. 4 (1986): 283–296.

50 Braudy, *World in a Frame*, 19.

51 Elizabeth Bernstein, "The Meaning of the Purchase: Desire, Demand and the Commerce of Sex," *Ethnography* 2, no. 3 (2001): 389–420.

52 Profile page for Rick Gonzales, http://www.male4malescorts.com/start.htm, accessed February 2006; website no longer active.

53 Profile page for Rick Gonzales.

54 See De Angelis, *Gay Fandom and Crossover Stardom*.

55 See Stacey M. Jones, "Teachers and Tipping Points: Historical Origins of the Teacher Quality Crisis," in *Economic Evolution and Revolution in Historical Time*, ed. Paul W. Rhode, Joshua L. Rosenbloom, and David F. Weiman (Stanford, CA: Stanford University Press, 2011), 336–356; Stephen Ellingson, Edward O. Lauman, Anthony Paik, and Jenna Mahay, "The Theory of Sexual Markets," in *The Sexual Organization of the City*, ed. Edward O Lauman, Stephen Ellingson, Jenna Mahay, Anthony Paik, and Yoosik Youm (Chicago: University of Chicago Press, 2004), 3–38.

56 See Ellingson et al., "The Theory of Sexual Markets."

57 Walter W. Powell and Laurel Smith-Doerr, "Networks and Economic Life," in *The Handbook of Economic Sociology*, ed. Neil J. Smelser and Richard Swedburg (Princeton, NJ: Princeton University Press, 1994), 368–402.

58 See Ellingson et al., "Theory of Sexual Markets."

Chapter 9   Trans Porn, Heterosexuality, and Sexual Identity

This chapter is based on a presentation given at Pornography and Anxiety: Psychoanalysis, Morality, and Culture, a series sponsored by the Psychoanalytic Psychotherapy Study Center and *Studies in Gender and Sexuality: An Interdisciplinary Journal* (New York, October 23, 2009). This is an updated and revised version of "Imagining the She/Male: Pornography and the Transsexualization of the Heterosexual Male," *Studies in Gender and Sexuality* 12, no. 4 (October–December 2011), Taylor and Francis Publishing Group. This article was originally titled "Imagine the She/Male: The Transsexualization of the Heterosexual Male" and was published in 2011. Since then the terms for gender, gender identity, gender expression, and sexual identity have evolved. In addition to the change over time, there was and is a significant discrepancy between the language used in the adult film industry and LGBTQ+ communities. In this version, I have attempted to adopt a more generic terminology that does not reflect disparaging and inaccurate conceptions. For other discussions, see the "GLAAD Glossary of Terms: Transgender" at https://www.glaad.org/reference/transgender as well as the discussion on "Transgender and Transsexual Dating" at http://www.tsgirlfriend.com. I would like to thank Tom Moore, Yasmin Lee, La Cherry Spice, Mr. Pam, and Rod Barry for their conversations with me about this genre of video pornography and Gilbert Cole for his invitation to present this work and the editors of *Studies in Gender and Society* for their comments and suggestions.

1 Thomas Hackett, "The Execution of Private Barry Winchell: The Real Story Behind the 'Don't Ask, Don't Tell' Murder," *Rolling Stone*, March 2, 2000; David France, "An Inconvenient Woman," *New York Times Magazine*, May 2, 2000.

2 See Madison Claire, "Man's Secret Love of Transsexual Women: Do New Trends Predict a Second Sexual Revolution?, pt. 1," Examiner.com, August 27, 2009, http://www.examiner.com/x-18935-Phoenix-Transsexual-Relationships-Examiner ~y2009m8d27-Mans-Secret-Love-of-Transsexual-Women-Do-new-trends-predict-a-second-Sexual-Revolution, accessed September 2009; as of printing date, website no longer exists.

3 See Claire "Man's Secret Love of Transsexual Women."

4 Jonathon Ames, ed., *Sexual Metamorphosis: An Anthology of Transsexual Memoirs* (New York: Vintage, 2005); David Valentine, *Imagining Transgender: An Ethnography of a Category* (Durham, NC: Duke University Press, 2007).

5 Jean Laplanche and Jean-Bertrand Pontalis, "Fantasy and the Origins of Sexuality," in *Formations of Fantasy*, ed. Victor Burgin, James Donald, and Cora Kaplan (London: Methuen, 1986), 5–34.

6 Jeffrey Escoffier, "Scripting the Sex: Fantasy, Narrative and Sexual Scripts in Pornographic Films," in *The Sexual Self: The Construction of Sexual Scripts*, ed. Michael Kimmel (Nashville: Vanderbilt University Press, 2007); Jeffrey Escoffier, *Bigger Than Life: The History of Gay Porn Cinema from Beefcake to Hardcore* (Philadelphia: Running Press, 2009), 336–337.

7 Robert J. Stoller, *Observing the Erotic Imagination* (New Haven, CT: Yale University Press, 1985), 3–69; Elizabeth Cowie, "Pornography and Fantasy: Psychoanalytic Perspectives," in *Sex Exposed: Sexuality and the Pornography Debate*, ed. Lynne Segal and Mary McIntosh (New Brunswick, NJ: Rutgers University Press, 1993).

8 Jeffrey Escoffier, "Gay-for-Pay: Straight Men and the Making of Gay Pornography," *Qualitative Sociology* 26, no. 4 (2003): 531–555; Roland Barthes, "The Reality Effect," in *The Rustle of Language*, trans. Richard Howard (New York: Hill & Wang, 1986).

9 Brett Kahr, *Who Been Sleeping in Your Head? The Secret World of Sexual Fantasies* (New York: Basic Books, 2008), 164–185.

10 Joanne Meyerowitz, *How Sex Changed: A History of Transsexuality in the United States* (Cambridge, MA: Harvard University Press, 2002), 168–207.

11 Meyerowitz, *How Sex Changed*, 170, emphasis added.

12 Meyerowitz, 201–202.

13 Meghan Chavalier, *Confessions of a Transsexual Porn Star* (Bloomington, IN: Author House, 2007); J. R. Ryan, "Transgendered Sex Workers," in *Encyclopedia of Prostitution and Sex Work*, ed. Melissa H. Ditmore (Westport, CT: Greenwood, 2006), 499–506.

14 Ryan, "Transgendered Sex Workers," 499–506.

15 See Laurence O'Toole, *Pornocopia: Porn, Sex, Technology and Desire* (London: Serpent's Tail, 1999).

16 JoAnn Cachapero, "Tranny Content Comes of Age," *X-Biz*, July 1, 2006, www.xbiz.com/articles/article_piece_print.php?id=80628.

17 Cachapero, "Tranny Content Comes of Age."

18 John H. Gagnon and William Simon, *Sexual Conduct: The Social Sources of Human Sexuality* (Chicago: Aldine, 1973); John H. Gagnon, "Scripts and the Coordination of Sexual Conduct," in *Proceedings of the Nebraska Symposium on Motivation*, ed. J. K. Cole and R. Dienstbier (Lincoln: University of Nebraska Press, 1974).

19   Gagnon and Simon, *Sexual Conduct*, 98–104; Gagnon, "Scripts and the Coordination of Sexual Conduct."

20   Linda Williams, *Hard Core: Power, Pleasure and the "Frenzy of the Visible"* (Berkeley: University of California Press, 1989), 271–275; Erving Goffman, *Gender Advertisements* (New York: Harper, 1976).

21   John H. Gagnon, "Gender Preference in Erotic Relations: The Kinsey Scale and Sexual Scripts," in *An Interpretation of Desire: Essays in the Study of Sexuality* (Chicago: University of Chicago Press, 2004), 99–129.

22   See Cowie, "Pornography and Fantasy," 133; Laplanche and Pontalis, "Fantasy and the Origins of Sexuality," 5–34.

23   Slavoj Žižek, "Courtly Love, or Woman as Thing," in *The Metastases of Enjoyment: Six Essays on Woman and Causality* (London: Verso, 1994), 104–108.

24   See Brian Pronger, *The Arena of Masculinity: Sports, Homosexuality, and the Meaning of Sex* (New York: St. Martin's, 1990).

25   Russ Kick, "She-Males: The Best of Both Worlds?," *Disinformation*, February 10, 2001, http://old.disinfo.com/archive/pages/dossier/id791/pg1/index.html.

26   Don Operario, J. Burton, K. Underhill, and J. Savelius, "Men Who Have Sex with Transgender Women: Challenges to Category-Based HIV Prevention," *AIDS and Behavior* 12, no. 1 (2007): 18–26.

27   Operario et al, "Men Who Have Sex with Transgender Women," 18–26.

28   Jonathan Ames, interview by Rachel Kramer Bussel, *Village Voice*, March 3, 2005.

29   Operario et al, "Men Who Have Sex with Transgender Women."

30   Operario et al, 18–26.

31   www.ecommercejournal.com, August 20, 2009, accessed September 2009. As of printing date, website is no longer active.

32   "How to Date a Pre-Op Transsexual Women," www.tsgirlfriend.com, accessed May 2008. As of printing date, website is no longer active.

33   Operario et al., "Men Who Have Sex with Transgender Women."

34   Operario et al, 18–26.

35   See Jeffrey Escoffier, "Porn Star / Stripper / Escort: Economic and Sexual Dynamics in a Sex Work Career," in *Male Sex Work: A Business Doing Pleasure*, ed. Todd G. Morrison and B. W. Whitehead (New York: Haworth Press, 2007); see also Escoffier, "Gay-for-Pay," 543–544.

36   "Kurt Lockwood," IMDb, https://www.imdb.com/name/nm1524001/.

37   Escoffier, "Gay-for-Pay," 543–544; Escoffier, *Bigger Than Life*, 305–311.

38   Google Answers, "Shemale Pornography, Relationships and Society," http://answers.google.com/answers/threadview/id/329452.html.

39   See Dear Cupid, "Relationship Advice," www.dearcupid.org/keyword/transexual%20porn, www.dearcupid.org/question/my-husband-looks-at-she-male-porn-.html.

40   Stoller, *Observing the Erotic Imagination*, 155; Sigmund Freud, "Fetish" (1927), reprinted in *Sexuality and the Psychology of Love*, ed. Phillip Rieff (New York: Touchstone, 1963), 204–209.

41   Freud, "Fetish," 206.

42   John Phillips, "Walking on the Wild Side: Shemale Internet Pornography," in *International Exposure: Perspectives on Modern European Pornography, 1800–2000*, ed. Lisa Z. Sigel (New Brunswick, NJ: Rutgers University Press, 2005), 267.

43   See Freud, "Fetish,"

44 Williams, *Hard Core*, 271, emphasis added.
45 Susan Stryker, *Transgender History* (Berkeley: Seal Press, 2008), 121–154.
46 See Meyerowitz, *How Sex Changed*; Susan Stryker, "(De)Subjugated Knowledges: An Introduction to Transgender Studies," in *The Transgender Studies Reader*, ed. S Stryker and S. Whittle (New York: Routledge, 2006).
47 See Leo Bersani, *Baudelaire and Freud* (Berkeley: University of California Press, 1977); Leo Bersani, *The Freudian Body: Psychoanalysis and Art* (New York: Columbia University Press, 1986); Toni Bentley, *The Surrender: An Erotic Memoir* (New York: Regan Books/HarperCollins, 2004), 3–6.
48 Bersani, *Baudelaire and Freud*, 77.
49 Williams, *Hard Core*, 272–273; see also Jeffrey Escoffier, "Pornography, Perversity and Sexual Revolution," in *Sexual Revolutions in the West*, ed. Gert Hekma and Alain Giami (Houndmills: Palgrave Macmillan, 2014).

Epilogue

1 Maureen O'Connor argued that Pornhub was "the Kinsey Report of our time" and that it "may have done more to expand the sexual dreamscape than Helen Gurley Brown, Masters and Johnson or Sigmund Freud." Maureen O'Connor, "Pornhub Is the Kinsey Report of Our Time," *New York*, June 12, 2017.
2 See Jean Laplanche and Jean-Bertrand Pontalis, "Fantasy and the Origins of Sexuality," in *Formations of Fantasy*, ed. Victor Burgin, James Donald, and Cora Kaplan (London: Methuen, 1986); Robert J. Stoller, *Perversion: The Erotic Form of Hatred* (New York: Dell, 1975); Robert J. Stoller, *Sexual Excitement: The Dynamics of Erotic Life* (New York: Simon & Schuster, 1979); Robert J. Stoller, *Observing the Erotic Imagination* (New Haven, CT: Yale University Press, 1985); Slavoj Žižek, *Looking Awry: An Introduction to Jacques Lacan through Popular Culture* (Cambridge, MA: MIT Press, 1991).
3 Stoller, *Perversion*, 114–134.
4 Michel Foucault, *The History of Sexuality: An Introduction*, vol. 1 (New York: Pantheon, 1978), 15–49.
5 Stoller, *Perversion*, 116.
6 Holliday offers a survey of the best (successful) porn made between 1970 and 1986: Jim Holliday, *Only the Best: Jim Holliday's Adult Video Almanac and Trivia Treasury* (Van Nuys, CA: Cal Vista Direct, 1986), 13–158. See Stoller's interview with Holliday: Robert J. Stoller, *Porn: Myths for the Twentieth Century* (New Haven, CT: Yale University Press, 1991), 160–180.
7 O'Connor, "Pornhub Is the Kinsey Report."
8 The "secret museum" was a gallery, not open to the public, established to house the erotic art found during the excavation of Pompeii and Herculaneum. Along with the "Private Case" at the British Library, it represented the early modern European attitude toward pornographic and erotic materials. Walter Kendrick, *The Secret Museum: Pornography in Modern Culture* (New York: Viking, 1987).
9 See Susanna Paasonen, *Carnal Resonance: Affect and Online Pornography* (Cambridge, MA: MIT Press, 2011).
10 See Jean Laplanche's discussion about "finding" or "re-finding" one's object in *Life and Death in Psychoanalysis* (Baltimore: Johns Hopkins University Press, 1976), 19–25.

11 See Paasonen, *Carnal Resonance*; and Margret Grebowicz, *Why Internet Porn Matters* (Stanford, CA: Stanford University Press, 2013).

12 This is what Stoller called "progression in pornography." See Robert J. Stoller, *Sweet Dreams, Erotic Plots* (London: Karnac 2009), 67–71.

13 Laura Kipnis, *Bound and Gagged: Pornography and the Politics of Fantasy in America* (New York: Grove Press, 1996), 167.

14 See Stoller's chapter on "Risk vs. Boredom" in *Perversion*, 114–134.

15 See Stoller, *Sweet Dreams*, 9–18.

16 See Linda Williams, *Hard Core: Power, Pleasure and the "Frenzy of the Visible"* (Berkeley: University of California Press, 1989), 272–275; Jeffrey Escoffier, "Pornography, Perversity and Sexual Revolution," in *Sexual Revolutions*, ed. Gert Hekma and Alain Giami (Houndmills: Palgrave Macmillan, 2014).

17 Laplanche discusses the "finding" or "re-finding" of one's object in *Life and Death*, 19–25.

18 Stoller devoted a chapter to "The Necessity of Perversion" in *Perversion*, 215–219. In his last book, he gives an account of how daydreams and sexual behavior may change over time. See Stoller, *Sweet Dreams*, especially the section called "Progression in Pornography," 67–71.

Index

Acconci, Vito, 57

Adam Gay Video Guide, 117, 149, 161

Adult Film Database, 127

Adult Video News (*AVN*), 90, 134, 140, 168; and the *AVN* Awards, 172, 177

AIDS: and condom use in gay porn, 106; and growth of popularity of gay video porn during the 1980s, 104, 128, 148, 183; and pre-AIDS gay culture, 10, 47, 50–51, 58, 63, 69, 75–77; and research on and expansion of knowledge vis-à-vis gay sexuality, 49, 63; and stigmatization of gay porn performers, 139

Altman, Dennis, 71

Alvarez, Robert, 41

Ames, Jonathan, 167

anal sex, 3, 11, 23, 25, 36–39, 42, 44, 107; and the AIDS crisis, 52; as central feature of gay porn, 45, 121; as culmination of gay porn narratives, 85, 89; and extreme versions of, 158; and industry differentiation of gay porn performers, 113, 153; and the "perverse dynamic," 184; in public settings in homo-realist porn, 61; and public sex in New York City, 65; and the "top" role in gay porn, 96, 117, 148, 154; in trans porn, 169–175, 179, 180; and women in porn, 131

Angel, Buck, 177

Anger, Kenneth, 34, 35, 41, 42, 66

arousal: and "gay-for-pay" porn, 107; and the gay porn viewer, 24, 32, 55; and male porn performers, 131, 154; and sexual scripts, 6, 108, 172; and the simulation of "reality" in gay porn films, 84–86, 96–98, 106; and trans porn, 173, 174, 180

ars erotica, 4, 51

Ashbee, Henry Spence, 52

Ashe, Danni, 138–139

auteur theory, 83, 89, 136

authenticity, 106, 107, 109, 116, 164

Back Row, The, 41, 42, 50, 59–62, 72, 93, 104, 148

Ballet Down the Highway, 70, 71

Baltrop, Alvin, 56–58

Barry, Rod, 100; and the construction of the gay-for-pay persona, 110, 114, 115, 118, 149; and description of live performance, 160; and expansion of sexual repertoire to prolong career, 158, 177; and the insufficiency of earnings from gay porn as primary income, 150, 154

Barthes, Roland, 53

Bataille, Georges, 43, 44, 52

bathhouses, 48, 50, 56, 58, 63, 64, 68, 70

Bazin, Andre, 4, 66

BDSM: and classification of trans porn, 175, 177; as market niche in pornography, 6, 172; and perversity, 26, 46, 179, 184

Becker, Howard, 146

About the Author

JEFFREY ESCOFFIER writes on the history of sexuality, pornography, and LGBTQ politics. He is the author of *American Homo: Community and Perversity* and *Bigger Than Life: Gay Porn Cinema from Beefcake to Hardcore* and the editor of *Sexual Revolution*, an anthology of the most influential writing on sex from the 1960s and 1970s. He is the coauthor with Rod Barry of the screenplay as well as the videographer of the "Behind the Scenes" feature of the hardcore video *Down the Drain* (All Worlds Video, 2005). He was one of the founders and the publisher of the pioneering LGBTQ journal *OUT/LOOK* from 1989 to 1992. He is currently a research associate and a faculty member at the Brooklyn Institute for Social Research.